Content-Area Reader

TEACHER'S GUIDE

The Ancient World
Prehistory to the Roman Empire

Senior Consultant
Dr. Judith Irvin
Florida State University

HOLT, RINEHART AND WINSTON
A Harcourt Classroom Education Company

Austin · New York · Orlando · Atlanta · San Francisco · Boston · Dallas · Toronto · London

Staff Credits

EDITORIAL

Manager of Editorial Operations
Bill Wahlgren
Executive Editor
Patricia McCambridge
Senior Editor and Project Editor
Eileen Joyce
Component Editors: Jane Archer Feinstein, Scott Hall, Carolyn Logan, Stephanie Wenger
Assistant Editor: Tracy DeMont
Copyediting: Michael Neibergall, *Copyediting Manager;* Mary Malone, *Copyediting Supervisor;*
Christine Altgelt, Joel Bourgeois, Elizabeth Dickson, Emily Force, Julie A. Hill, Julia Thomas
Hu, Jennifer Kirkland, Millicent Ondras, Dennis Scharnberg, *Copyeditors*
Project Administration: Marie Price, *Managing Editor;* Lori De La Garza, *Editorial Operations Coordinator;*
Heather Cheyne, Mark Holland, Marcus Johnson, Jennifer Renteria, Janet Riley, Kelly Tankersley, *Project
Administration;* Ruth Hooker, Casey Kelly, Joie Pickett, Margaret Sanchez, *Word Processing*
Writers: Darleen Ramos, Ed Combs
Editorial Permissions: Susan Lowrance, *Permissions Editor*

ART, DESIGN, AND PHOTO

Book Design
Richard Metzger, *Design Director*
Graphic Services
Kristen Darby, *Manager*
Design Implementation
The Format Group, LLC
Image Acquisitions
Joe London, *Director;* Jeannie Taylor, *Photo Research Supervisor;* Sarah Hudgens, *Photo
Researcher;* Michelle Rumpf, *Art Buyer Supervisor;* Gillian Brody, *Art Buyer*
Cover Design
Curtis Riker, *Director;* Sunday Patterson, *Designer*

PRODUCTION

Belinda Barbosa Lopez, *Senior Production Coordinator;* Beth Prevelige, *Prepress Manager;*
Carol Trammel, *Production Supervisor*

MANUFACTURING/INVENTORY

Shirley Cantrell, *Supervisor of Inventory and Manufacturing*
Wilonda Ieans, *Manufacturing Coordinator*
Mark McDonald, *Inventory Planner*

Cover Photo Credits: (mummy), Gerard Rollando/The Image Bank; (terra cotta army of Emperor Qin), Stock
Boston, © Michele Burgess; (Tholos, Sanctuary of Athena, Delphi), Greece-© Superstock

Contents

Selection Notes

CHAPTER 1

Before History Began: Prehistory

CHAPTER 2

Between Two Rivers: Ancient Mesopotamia

CHAPTER 3

Civilizations of the Nile: Ancient Egypt and Kush

CHAPTER 4
The People of the Book: The Ancient Hebrews

CHAPTER 5
Early Civilizations in Asia: Ancient India and China

CHAPTER 6
The Classical World: Ancient Greece and Rome

Selection Tests
CHAPTER 1
Before History Began: Prehistory

CHAPTER 2
Between Two Rivers: Ancient Mesopotamia

CHAPTER 3
Civilizations of the Nile: Ancient Egypt and Kush

CHAPTER 4
The People of the Book: The Ancient Hebrews

CHAPTER 5
Early Civilizations in Asia: Ancient India and China

CHAPTER 6
The Classical World: Ancient Greece and Rome

Content-Area Reading Strategies

Blackline Masters for Graphic Organizers

Using This Teacher's Guide

This Teacher's Guide is intended to

- *provide maximum versatility and flexibility*
- *serve as a ready resource for background information on each selection*
- *act as a catalyst for discussion, analysis, interpretation, activities, and further research*
- *provide reproducible blackline masters that can be used for either individual or collaborative work, including discussions and projects*
- *provide multiple options for evaluating students' progress*

The Selection Notes, Selection Tests, reading strategies essay, and blackline masters in this Teacher's Guide have been created to provide support for teaching the selections and features in the *Content-Area Reader* Pupil's Edition. In this Teacher's Guide, you will find instructional background and other resources that will help you to teach content-area reading skills effectively to all of your students.

Selection Notes

Selection Notes, arranged by chapter and selection, are included for every selection in the Pupil's Edition, providing teachers with the tools they need to help students get the most out of their content-area reading.

- **Before Reading** activities introduce students to important issues in the selection, provide further background for the teacher, offer instruction in both high-utility and content-area vocabulary, and present basic reading skills and reading strategies to implement those skills.
- **During Reading** activities provide extra information about selection features, such as the side-margin features and the art that accompanies the selection. In addition, teaching suggestions for Learners Having Difficulty, English-Language Learners, and Advanced Learners are offered to help teachers meet the needs of all students.
- **After Reading** activities provide answers to the **Reading Check** questions in the Pupil's Edition so that you can assess students' content comprehension. A **Reteaching** feature for students who had difficulty with the reading skill and strategy helps ensure that all students learn content-area reading skills. **Connecting to Language Arts** activities offer students in the language arts classroom a chance to create a personalized response to the selection, using such approaches as journal entry writing, ad or brochure copy writing, video presentations, and interviews involving role-playing. **Connecting Across the Curriculum** provides activities to extend students' interest by researching materials related to the selection topic and completing a project based on their investigations. **Rubrics for Cross-Curricular Activities** in the Pupil's Edition are provided at the end of each chapter.

Selection Tests

- A **Selection Test** for each title offers multiple-choice questions about the content and multiple-choice or matching questions to assess vocabulary comprehension. The vocabulary that is tested appears underscored in the selections in the Pupil's Edition.

Content-Area Reading Strategies for the Language Arts Classroom

In this section of the Teacher's Guide, Senior Consultant Dr. Judith Irvin provides an informative essay on content-area reading skills and offers eleven strategies for approaching content-area reading in the classroom. In order to successfully read expository text, students need to be aware of the basic text structures used in nonfiction literature. Students also need to have access to a variety of tools—strategies—for understanding expository text. Dr. Irvin's reading strategies are cross-referenced throughout the Selection Notes in the first section of the Teacher's Guide, and graphic organizers to support various reading strategies are provided in reproducible blackline masters in the final section of the Teacher's Guide.

Graphic Organizers

A selection of various graphic organizers in reproducible blackline masters form appears at the back of the Teacher's Guide. These graphic organizers can be used with the various reading strategies presented in the selection Teaching Notes.

CHAPTER 1

Before History Began
Prehistory 2 million B.C.–4,500 B.C.

The Permafrost Crumbles

from *Raising the Mammoth,* a Discovery Channel Web site
by DIRK HOOGSTRA
(student text page 3)

Reading Level: Average

Text Summary

This selection is an entry from the daily journal of Dirk Hoogstra, a Discovery Channel correspondent. Hoogstra writes about his experiences with an excavation team in Siberia who are preparing a frozen woolly mammoth for transportation to an ice cave. The team must keep a layer of permafrost around the mammoth to preserve its integrity. Once in the cave, the mammoth will be slowly defrosted, and scientists can begin studying the 23,000-year-old specimen.

BEFORE READING

Make the Connection

Ask students if any of them have ever discovered something while digging—an arrowhead, a piece of pottery, a spoon, some old keys, animal bones. Did they wonder how old the objects were? Did they wonder why the objects were there or who originally used them? Did they attempt to find out more about the pieces or add them to a collection? Tell students that scientists ask such questions when they make a discovery, such as the remains of the woolly mammoth described in this selection.

Build Background

■ More About the Topic

The woolly mammoth is an extinct mammal that some scientists believe roamed the earth during the Ice Age, two million years ago (Pleistocene epoch), long after the dinosaurs were extinct. Mammoths are usually recognized by their long, curving tusks and shaggy, thick fur. We know they lived at the same time as humans, because cave paintings in France have depicted herds of mammoths. Suited to cold weather, mammoths lived mainly in the Arctic tundra of Europe, Asia, and North America. Although quite large, they were herbivores. The last mammoths are believed to have died out 4,000 years ago (early Holocene epoch). There are several theories about their demise. Some scientists believe that warming conditions affected their food supply; others believe the mammoths were hunted to extinction.

Vocabulary Development

The following words are underscored and defined in the student text.
estimate: a rough or approximate calculation.
preserved: unspoiled; undamaged.
specimen: sample of something or one person or thing of a group.
ambitious: challenging, requiring much effort.
pungent: a strong, sharp sensation of smell.
Before assigning the reading, you may want to introduce students to any words that could cause pronunciation or definition problems.

─ *Vocabulary Tip* ─

Recognizing Multiple Meanings Before you introduce the vocabulary words, you may want to ask students what they think of when they hear the word *preserve.* Students may think of keeping food fresh using chemical preservatives. Some students may think of jam; others may think of land set aside as a safe place for animals. Explain that in this selection *preserved* means much the same thing as we mean when we talk about preserving food.

Although the following words are important to an understanding of the text selection, some of them may be unfamiliar to students. You may wish to present this list of words and definitions to your students. Ask students to predict what they think a selection containing these words will be about. [Students may suggest that the text will discuss searching and digging for something.]

intact: unbroken; whole.
expose: to show or display.
***extracted:** pulled out by force.
excavation team: professionals who carefully dig to uncover rare finds.
***site:** the location of something.
expedition: mission or exploration.

*Although students may be familiar with other meanings of these words, the words as used in the selection have a specific meaning that pertains to the content area.

Reading Informational Material

Reading Skill
Analyzing Chronological Order
Tell students that chronological order is the sequence in which events happen. A text arranged in chronological order tells what happened first, then what happened second, and so on.

▶ **Teaching Tip**
Web Site Account This excerpt is from a daily account the author wrote for a Web site. Remind students that because it highlights one day's activities, it does not present a full picture of the entire event. Point out that this excerpt focuses only on the author's perspective.

Reading Strategy
Understanding Text (Strategy 2)
To help students analyze the sequence of events in this selection, use Strategy 2 described in Content-Area Reading Strategies. Provide students with a Sequence or Chronological Order Chart (Graphic Organizer 10) to help them keep the events in order as they read.

DURING READING

Using the Side-Margin Feature
■ Bigger Than Big
Ask students what they know about mammoths. [Students might mention that mammoths had long tusks or that they had sloping backs.] Then, ask students if they have ever heard the word *mammoth* used to describe something. Have students think of ways to use *mammoth* as an adjective, and write their suggestions on the board. [Example: mammoth project; mammoth building; mammoth problem]

▶ **Teaching Tip**
Mathematical Figures Large numbers, such as 20,000 years or 26 tons, can be difficult for students to visualize. Making comparisons can provide students with a frame of reference. For example, students might note that the mammoth lived long after the dinosaurs died out, but both shared the land with humans. To think about how much a mammoth weighs, consider this: A standard pickup truck weighs between two and four tons.

Differentiating Instruction
■ Learners Having Difficulty
Use a pair/share approach by pairing learners having difficulty reading the selection with more able readers. Ask the students to make a two-column chart. In the first column, have them list what they know about mammoths before reading the selection. In the second column, have them write what they learn about the mammoth from reading the selection. Students can share the information in their charts with the class.

AFTER READING

✔ Reading Check

The following are sample answers to questions on student text page 7.

1. The workers are using the jackhammers to chop through the ice surrounding a mammoth. The mammoth has been frozen 23,000 years.

2. This mammoth will be kept frozen until scientists are ready to study it, and then it will be slowly defrosted.

3. The mammoth excavated in 1902 was dug up by melting the ice around it with hot water. Using this method, scientists washed away clues about the mammoth's environment.

4. The scientists think that they will find the rear legs, midsection (including the vertebrae and ribs), internal organs, skin, and hair in the ice.

5. The Dolgan nomads who discovered the mammoth removed the tusks. They were reattached to the mammoth before it was airlifted so that people could visualize how the animal is positioned in the ice.

Reteaching

If students are still struggling with the sequence of events, have them locate time-order signal words in the first two paragraphs (*now, over the weekend, at this point, the next step, then, finally*). Then, work with students to list in sequential order the events connected with the signal words. (You can write students' responses on the chalkboard or an overhead transparency.) Once students are familiar with this process, have them work in pairs to continue to the end of the selection. [First two paragraphs: 1. Over the weekend, the excavation team dug through the ice and cut a trench around the mammoth. 2. Next, they will drill under the mammoth. 3. Then, they will build an enclosure. 4. Finally, they will construct a harness to lift the beast.]

Connecting to Language Arts

▪ Writing

Diary The writer describes his experience of working with the remains of an extinct animal. He tells the reader how he feels, what he sees, and what he is thinking. Ask each student to pretend he or she is the one who discovered the frozen mammoth and to write a diary entry describing the experience. Have them include details that show how they feel about the discovery. Some students may want to illustrate their diary entries or read them aloud.

▪ Speaking and Listening

Radio News Have students write a brief radio announcement about the unearthing of the woolly mammoth in Siberia. Students should make sure they answer the *5W-How?* questions (*Who? What? When? Where? Why?* and *How?*). Have students

tape their announcements and play them to the class.

Connecting Across the Curriculum: Science

Digging In the Dirt Have students investigate what an archaeologist does. What is an archaeologist's educational background? Does an archaeologist specialize in one area or participate in a variety of different kinds of digs? How do archaeologists determine if a find is significant? Do they live in harsh conditions? What is their salary range? Students may use library resources or the Internet. After students have completed their research, they may want to pool their findings or work independently to present the results of their investigations. They might create one of the following products:

- a newspaper advertisement in the "Help Wanted" section seeking archaeologists willing to work in Siberia
- a videotaped interview of an archaeologist
- a brochure for a college that includes photographs or illustrations of important sites and descriptions of the archaeologists

Further Resources

▪ **Books**

On the Track of the Ice Age Mammals by Anthony Sutcliffe

Frozen Fauna of the Mammoth Steppe by Dale R. Guthrie

Wild and Woolly Mammoth by Aliki

▪ **Video**

Raising the Mammoth, a Discovery Channel film (#156588) of the recovery of the Jarkov Mammoth

▪ **Other resources**

Find out more about woolly mammoths at the Web sites of the Santa Barbara Museum of Natural History, the Waco Mammoth Site, and the Mammoth Site Museum in Hot Springs, SD.

(Assessment)

Turn to page 123 for a multiple-choice test on the selection.

Test Answers

1. c **2.** b **3.** a **4.** d **5.** b
6. d **7.** b **8.** c **9.** a **10.** d

Summer in the Pits—Going for the Goo

from Discovery.com
by MARK WHEELER
(student text page 8)

Reading Level: Above average

Special Considerations

The Rancho La Brea Tar Pits are famous for their well-preserved fossils, some of which are thought to be at least 40,000 years old. Although it is not explicitly mentioned in the article, the subject of evolution could arise in discussion. If so, point out to students that there are differing opinions on the validity of evolutionary theory.

Text Summary

"Summer in the Pits" is an article about the Rancho La Brea Tar Pits in California. Jerry Smith, a senior excavator, explains how paleontologists and volunteers conduct the digging in tar pits and what they find. Trained volunteers work at Pit 91 during the summer months, when the asphalt is the most viscous. With picks and shovels, they excavate big bones as well as microfossils. Based on the findings from the excavation, Smith theorizes that the animals who were trapped in the tar became targets for their predators.

BEFORE READING

Make the Connection

Ask students to describe what happens to their shoes when they walk in mud or clay. Then, ask what problems they would encounter if, while being chased, they stepped in tar!

Build Background

▪ More About the Topic

To form a fossil, the hard part of a plant or animal must immediately be protected from decay. At the Rancho La Brea Tar Pits, animal bones and plants were first covered with asphalt and then buried under water-borne sediment. This process preserved the integrity of the original organic material. With such richly preserved fossils, paleontologists can study climatic changes and make educated guesses about why some animals in the region became extinct.

Vocabulary Development

The following words are underscored and defined in the student text.

extract: to pull out using great force or effort.
legacy: something handed down from the past.
excavation: act of digging or uncovering by digging; something uncovered.
intact: whole or entire, with no part damaged or removed.
protruding: sticking out from the surroundings.
Before assigning the reading, you may want to introduce students to any words that could cause pronunciation or definition problems.

─ Vocabulary Tip ─

Using Affixes Before you introduce the vocabulary words, remind students that they can determine the meaning of an unfamiliar word if they know the meaning of one of its word parts. For example, *–ion* is a suffix that means "act or condition of." Ask students to identify other prefixes or suffixes from the list. [extract: *ex–* "out"; intact: *in–* "not"]

CONTENT-AREA VOCABULARY

Although the following words are important to an understanding of the text selection, some of them may be unfamiliar to students. You may wish to present this list of words and definitions to your students. Ask students what they predict they will read about in a selection using these words. [Students may suggest the words involve a discovery and recovery of animal relics from the distant past.]

predator: an animal that feeds on other animals.
captives: prisoners.
entombed: buried.
microfossils: extremely small fossils.
hapless: unlucky.
unveiled*: revealed.

*Although students may be familiar with other meanings of this word, the word as used in the selection has a specific meaning that pertains to the content area.

Reading Informational Material

Reading Skill
Analyzing Text Structure: Chronological Order
Tell students that the selection describes the steps in a process; therefore, the events in the text are arranged in chronological order (the order in which they happen). You may want to remind students that narrative texts are also frequently arranged in chronological order. Ordinarily, in narrative texts, the writer tells what has happened; in process texts, the writer tells what someone is currently doing or should do.

▶ **Teaching Tip**
Multiple Text Structures Explain to students that texts can have more than one type of structure. In this selection, for instance, the writer uses the process structure to explain the steps involved in excavating Pit 91. However, he also uses the comparison–contrast structure to compare the excavations of 1908 with those of today and the narrative structure to tell the story of the La Brea Tar Pits from prehistoric times to their possible future.

Reading Strategy
Constructing Concept Maps (Strategy 4)
To help students analyze the process described in this selection, use Strategy 4 described in Content-Area Reading Strategies. Have students complete a Sequence or Chronological Order Chart (Graphic Organizer 10) to help them organize the major points in the selection.

DURING READING

Using the Side-Margin Feature
■ Tiger, Tiger
Ask students to visualize a saber-toothed tiger and to tell what they see. [Students might mention its long teeth.] Tell students that the saber-toothed tiger is one of the most common fossils found at the Rancho La Brea Tar Pits. Paleontologists have discovered that saber-toothed tigers cared for each other, lived in packs, and hunted together, just as

today's lions do. Saber-toothed tigers were more social than modern tigers, which prefer to hunt alone.

Differentiating Instruction
■ English-Language Learners
This selection is divided by subheadings into five sections. Divide students into five groups. Have each group read a different section two or three times and prepare an oral summary of the section. Students may use a sheet of paper with key words to aid in presenting their summaries to the class. For example, for the section titled "Fossil display," students might write the words *skeletons*, *bones*, *museum*, and *predators*.

AFTER READING

Reading Check

The following are sample answers to questions on student text page 13.

1. The tar pits are actually made of asphalt that comes from petroleum deep in the earth.

2. Animals stuck in the Rancho La Brea Tar Pits either starved to death or were killed by predators.

3. Just a few inches of tar could trap a mammoth. When Jerry Smith stepped into the tar, he didn't sink, but it took a couple of people to pull him out.

4. People work during the summer months due to budget constraints and the fact that the tar is most viscous in the summer.

5. Today's excavators save everything because even the microfossils can provide clues about the past.

Reteaching
If students are having difficulty analyzing the structure of the text, have them identify the signal words that indicate the steps in the process of excavating the fossilized remains. To give students a frame of reference, tell them that the selection starts by giving background information about the La Brea Tar Pits and previous digs, then explains how excavation is done today, and finally discusses

the future of the tar pits. Provide students with a list of sequence signal words used in the selection *(once, by the end of the day, later, eventually)* and discuss how these words indicate time order. Have students work in pairs to identify signal words in the selection and plot the events these words indicate on the Sequence or Chronological Order Chart (Graphic Organizer 10).

Connecting to Language Arts
▪ Speaking and Listening

Oral Report Have each student research and prepare an oral report on one of the animals whose bones have been discovered in the Rancho La Brea Tar Pits—dire wolf, saber-toothed tiger, mammoth, mastodon, ground sloth, short-faced bear, horse, lion, or coyote. Encourage students to use visual aids such as drawings, transparencies, or time lines in their presentations.

Connecting Across the Curriculum: Science

Earth Prints Have students find out more about prehistoric times by investigating specific eras—Precambrian, Paleozoic, Mesozoic, and Cenozoic. Divide the class into four groups and have each group research the climate and life forms of one of these eras. Each group can make an illustrated time line and present their findings to the class. Then, have the groups put their time lines together to create a complete display.

Further Resources
Books

Dry Bones and Other Fossils by Gary E. Parker, et al

Eyewitness: Fossil by Paul D. Taylor and Colin Keates

If You Are a Hunter of Fossils by Byrd Baylor and Peter Parnall

Make Your Own Dinosaur Out of Chicken Bones: Foolproof Instructions for Budding Paleontologists by Christopher McGowan, et al

Other resources

Find out more about the excavations and view photos of fossils at the Web site of the Page Museum at the La Brea Tar Pits (located in Los Angeles, CA).

Assessment

Turn to page 124 for a multiple-choice test on the selection.

Test Answers

1. c 2. d 3. b 4. c 5. b
6. b 7. d 8. a 9. b 10. a

Mary Leakey, 1913–1996

from *Newsweek* magazine
by SHARON BEGLEY
(student text page 14)

Reading Level: Average

Special Considerations

Remind students that science is the body of knowledge gained from the observation and study of the natural world. Since scientists were not present to observe and record the origins of humankind, the beliefs or theories about human origins are based on *interpretations* of scientific observations and cannot be proved as fact. Explain to students that when writers write about deeply held beliefs or convictions, they often state their beliefs as facts. This selection is written from the evolutionary point of view. Challenge students to identify words and phrases that indicate the author's stance. You might also ask students how they think proponents of other theories of origin might interpret Leakey's discoveries. Remind students in their discussion to be respectful of beliefs that may differ from their own.

Text Summary

"Mary Leakey, 1913–1996" is an obituary of the archaeologist Mary Leakey. She is best known for her discovery of footprints on the Laetoli plain in Tanzania, a find that changed theories about how the human brain developed. Leakey also discovered what appeared to be a piece of the skull of a Proconsul, persuading many scientists to believe Darwin's theory that Africa was the cradle of humankind.

BEFORE READING

Make the Connection

Have each student brainstorm a list of life goals he or she would like to achieve. Ask students what they would like to be remembered for. [For example, one student may wish to be known for discovering a cure for Alzheimer's disease; another might like to be remembered as a great father.] Have students discuss why some people are remembered more than others.

Build Background
■ More About Mary Leakey

Mary Douglas Nicol was born February 6, 1913, in London. Her father, a painter, showed her the Dordogne cave paintings in France, which piqued her interest in archaeology. As a child, she was fascinated with digging and with drawing prehistoric tools. Later, Mary became an illustrator and met archaeologist Louis Leakey while illustrating a book for him. They married and moved to Africa in 1936. Excavating sites with her husband, Mary became an experienced archaeologist in her own right. Although she was not formally educated, she received several medals and honorary doctorates from various universities, including Yale. Her autobiography, *Disclosing the Past*, was published in 1984 after she retired. She had three sons, Jonathan, Richard, and Phillip.

Vocabulary Development

The following words are underscored and defined in the student text. Ask students to identify the verbs [*encased, ambled, transcends*] and the nouns [*impression, notion*]. Have students identify word parts that provide clues to a word's function. [Words that end in *–ed* and *–s* are usually verbs. Words that end in *–ion* are usually nouns.]

impression: a visible mark made on a surface by pressing something hard into something softer.

encased: enclosed; closed on all sides.

ambled: walked at an easy pace.

transcends: goes beyond; is not limited.

notion: belief.

Before assigning the reading, you may want to introduce students to any words that could cause pronunciation or definition problems.

Vocabulary Tip

Using Multiple Meanings Before you introduce the vocabulary words, ask students to write a sentence using the word *impression*. Students may think of an effect or feeling left by something, as in "She made a good impression." Explain that in this selection, the meaning is more concrete; when you *press* something into something else, you leave an impression. Have students brainstorm a list of related words. [*impress, impressive, impressionable, impressionist, impressionistic*]

CONTENT-AREA VOCABULARY

Although the following words are important to an understanding of the text selection, some of them may be unfamiliar to students. You may wish to present this list of words and the definitions to your students. Have students predict what they think a selection containing these words will be about. [Students may suggest that the words indicate the selection will involve discoveries about the distant past.]

prehistoric: the period before history was recorded.
chiseled: cut out.
eons: ages; an extremely long time.
anthropologist: one who studies humans, especially their customs, culture, and physical characteristics.
*find: a discovery; something significant or worthy of study that is found.

*Although students may be familiar with other meanings of this word, the word as used in the selection has a specific meaning that pertains to the content area.

Reading Informational Material

Reading Skill
Analyzing Text Structure: Cause and Effect
Explain to students that one event can cause another event to happen. The first event is the cause and the second the effect. Analyzing causes and effects can help readers see the relationships among events in a text.

▶ **Teaching Tip**
Obituary Tell students that an obituary announces a person's death and highlights the significant events in his or her life. As obituaries are usually printed in magazines or newspapers, they are normally short.

Explain that an obituary is not a biography, which is a more complete telling of someone's life.

Reading Strategy
Using Graphic Organizers (Strategy 3)
To help students locate the cause-and-effect relationships in this selection, use Strategy 3 described in Content-Area Reading Strategies. Provide students with a Cause-and-Effect Organizer (Graphic Organizer 2) to help them analyze the causes and effects in the selection.

▶ **Teaching Tip**
Cause and Effect Remind students that an event can be both a cause and an effect. For example, in this selection, early hominids standing up on two feet is a cause. The effect is that their hands were freed for toolmaking. That their hands were freed for toolmaking then becomes a cause, and its effect is that brain capacity expanded.

DURING READING

Differentiating Instruction
▪ Learners Having Difficulty
Have students work in pairs to read the selection. Students should construct a two-column chart, labeling the left-hand column *What Happened?* and the right-hand column *What Was the Result?* First, have students read the first two paragraphs and answer these questions on their chart. Then, have students read the third paragraph, beginning with "Without Leakey . . ." Students should then fill in the chart again. Finally, have students read the last paragraph and answer the questions in the chart.

AFTER READING

✔ Reading Check

The following are sample answers to questions on student text page 16.

1. Mary Leakey will be most remembered for her find of hominid footprints on the Laetoli plain. Leakey also discovered a piece of the skull of a Proconsul, teeth and part of the jaw of *Australopithecus boisei*, and the remains of *Homo habilis*.

2. Leakey was trained as an artist. After she married Louis Leakey, an archaeologist, she moved to Africa and began making her own archaeological discoveries.

3. The action identified by Leakey as "intensely human" was the hominid's pausing and turning before continuing on with the others.

4. Leakey's discovery of the Proconsul skull supported Darwin's theory that Africa was the cradle of humankind.

5. Jonathan found the fossil fragments of *Homo habilis*, "handy man."

Reteaching

If students are still struggling with identifying the cause-and-effect relationships in the selection, write the first event (cause) in a Cause-and-Effect Organizer (Graphic Organizer 2) and make and distribute copies to the class. [Mary Leakey found a human footprint in the volcanic ash.] Work with students to complete the cause-and-effect chain. Ask students to look at the selection and determine what happened as a result of this find. [It overturned current thinking: Standing up was the biggest event in evolution, not the development of a big brain.] Then have students look at the effect of this theory. [Humans' hands were free to make tools. Toolmaking was challenging, thus the brain grew bigger.] Allow students to work with a partner to complete the rest of the chain.

Connecting to Language Arts

▪ Writing

Eulogy Tell students that a eulogy is a formal speech praising someone, usually someone who has recently died, whereas an obituary is a written announcement of someone's death. Ask each student to choose a person, such as a historical figure, writer, scientist, musician, athlete, or friend who has made an impression on him or her and to write a eulogy for that person. Students may need to do some research before writing their eulogies. Ask volunteers to read their eulogies aloud.

Connecting Across the Curriculum: Geography

Journey to Tanzania Assign students to find out more about Tanzania, the African country where Mary Leakey found hominid footprints. Have students pinpoint its location on a map. Then, have students research its physical land features, bodies of water, climate, official language, form of government, the peoples and their cultures. After students have completed their research, they may work independently or with a partner to present the results of their investigation. Students may write a report or create one of the following:

- a trivia game about Tanzania
- a map that shows major cities, land features, bodies of water, and the Olduvai Gorge
- a replica of Tanzania's flag and the words to the national anthem
- a crossword puzzle about Tanzania
- a chart that illustrates Tanzania's currency, cash crops, and major industries

Further Resources

▪ Books

Disclosing the Past by Mary Leakey

Olduvai Gorge: My Search for Early Man by Mary Leakey

Ancestral Passions: The Leakey Family and the Quest for Humankind's Beginnings by Virginia Morell

▪ Other resources

The PBS Web site contains an "Online Focus" feature on Mary Leakey in the "Online Newshour" section of the site. The Scientific American Web site also contains an article about Leakey.

Assessment

Turn to page 125 for a multiple-choice test on the selection.

Test Answers

1. b 2. c 3. a 4. d 5. d
6. c 7. a 8. b 9. a 10. d

Swimming into the Ice Age

from *Muse*
by DAVE GETZ
(*student text page 17*)

Reading Level: Average

Text Summary

After six years of keeping secret an underwater Mediterranean cave he has discovered, professional diver Henri Cosquer comes forward when he learns about the deaths of three divers in the cave. With a team of divers and more powerful lights, Cosquer discovers what he believes to be prehistoric art on the walls of the cave—images of animals, human hands, and geometric shapes. To determine whether the art is indeed original and not a hoax, the French Ministry of Culture sends a diver/archaeologist and his team to investigate. The animal drawings are found to be 18,500 years old, and the drawings of hands and geometric designs are found to be 27,500 years old. Scientists can only speculate as to the purpose of the paintings.

BEFORE READING

Make the Connection

Ask students if any of them have ever been in a cave or have swum underwater. Have any of them been scuba diving? Encourage students to share their experiences. Then, have them imagine what it would be like to swim through an underwater passage and discover a cave. Would it be scary? Exciting? Ask students what they would do if they discovered a cave. Would they keep it a secret or share their discovery? Have them explain their answers.

Build Background

▪ More About the Topic

Under the Sea The Cosquer Cave is unusual because of its entrance. The only way in is through a tunnel that runs 120 feet beneath the surface of the Mediterranean Sea. Although the cave is filled with air, digging an entrance to the cave would expose it to different climatic conditions, which could ruin the fragile prehistoric art. Additionally, creating an entrance might cause more water to enter the cave,

thus covering some of the art with water. Because entering the cave is extremely dangerous, the French government is keeping the cave closed to the public. However, exploration of the cave continues by researchers who have now identified 142 images. Some remarkable images include rectangular shapes with handles, similar to suitcases.

Vocabulary Development

The following words are underscored and defined in the student text. Point out that the prefix *e–* in *emerged* and *ex–* in *extinct* are both forms of the same prefix, meaning "out." Have students brainstorm a list of other words using forms of this prefix.

emerged: came out.

transparent: clear; easily seen through.

geometric: based on simple shapes such as a line, circle, or square.

extinct: no longer alive and having no descendants.

depiction: picture; representation.

Before assigning the reading, you may want to introduce students to any words that could cause pronunciation or definition problems.

┌─ *Vocabulary Tip* ─────────────

Using Prefixes Before you introduce the vocabulary words, have students use a dictionary to define the prefixes *trans–* and *geo–* ["across" and "the earth"]. Have students brainstorm a list of familiar words that begin with these two prefixes. [*transmitter, transform, transatlantic, geometry, geography, geology*] Remind students that knowing the definitions of prefixes can help them determine meanings of unfamiliar words.

└──────────────────────────────

(**CONTENT-AREA VOCABULARY**)

Although the following words are important to an understanding of the text selection, some of them may be unfamiliar to students. You may wish to present this list of words and definitions to students.

scuba: acronym for *s*elf-*c*ontained *u*nderwater *b*reathing *a*pparatus; equipment used to breathe underwater.

encrusted: covered with a hard coating.

hoax: a fraud or a fake.

*lifeline: a rope divers use for signaling and for finding their way in dark places.

*charcoal: the carbon formed when wood or organic material is burned.

ritual: formal or ceremonial practices.

*Although students may be familiar with other meanings of this word, the word as used in the selection has a specific meaning that pertains to the content area.

Reading Informational Material

Reading Skill

Analyzing Text Structure: Problems and Solutions

Explain to students that problem/solution is a text structure that identifies one or more problems and that offers one or more solutions. Students should identify problems and try to predict the solution to each as they read.

▶ **Teaching Tip**

Magazine Article This magazine article poses many questions that the author then answers. Have students identify these questions as they read, and ask them to predict the outcome before they read the answers.

Reading Strategy

Using Graphic Organizers (Strategy 3)

To help students identify the problems and solutions presented in the selection, use Strategy 3 described in Content-Area Reading Strategies. Provide students with a Problem and Solution Chart (Graphic Organizer 9) to help them chart the problems and solutions in their reading.

DURING READING

Using the Side-Margin Feature

■ Hold Your Breath

Ask students what happens to writing on a piece of paper if left outside for a month. Students might mention that the writing fades or that the paper disintegrates. Explain to students that just as the outdoor elements can ruin the writing on paper, other elements can have equally damaging effects.

The breath of over a million visitors at the Lascaux Cave damaged the fragile artwork. The solution was to build a replica. Have students discuss whether they agree or disagree with closing the real cave to the public. Is the solution a good one?

Differentiating Instruction

■ Learners Having Difficulty

Point out to students that sometimes a drawing or illustration can help them visualize what is happening in a selection. Have pairs of students work to illustrate how the archaeologists were able to get into the underwater cave. Students may use the detail of the *Archaeonaute,* page 21, to help them with their drawings.

AFTER READING

✓ Reading Check

The following are sample answers to questions on student text page 23.

1. The air seeped in through tiny cracks in the ceiling of the cave, which was above water. Cosquer saw a handprint and assumed a living person had made it recently. After investigating further, Cosquer found that the walls were covered with paintings.

2. Researchers knew the paintings were old because they were below layers of calcite that formed over thousands of years. They were also able to carbon date the charcoal they found. The two time periods in which people worked in the cave were 18,500 years ago and 27,500 years ago.

3. The prehistoric painters walked into it. During the Ice Age, the oceans were lower, and the cave was on land, not under water.

4. Scientists do not think the painters lived in the cave because there are no bones from the animals that they would have killed and cooked. Clottes believes the paintings were made for religious or magic ceremonies.

5. Some animals that were alive when the animal paintings on the walls of the cave were made are now extinct—auks, megaloceros, aurochs, and a

type of bison. The Mediterranean region used to be cold. However, there are still reindeer, red deer, and horses, and people still kill one another.

Reteaching

If students are still struggling with the problem/solution structure in the selection, have each of them divide a sheet of paper into three columns. They should label the columns *Cosquer, Clottes*, and *Courtin*. Make a similar chart on the chalkboard or an overhead transparency. Divide each column in half, then label the top half *Problem* and the bottom half *Solution*. Have student volunteers identify the problem each person had and how he solved it. [Cosquer's problem: He wanted to prove the cave art he had discovered was authentic. Solution: He turned his photographs over to the French Ministry of Culture. Clottes's problem: He needed to authenticate the photos, but he was not a diver. Solution: He sent Jean Courtin, a diver and archaeologist, to investigate the cave. Courtin's Problem: The assignment was dangerous—people had already drowned. Solution: He ran lifelines, electrical lines, and phone lines from a submersible ship to the cave.]

Connecting to Language Arts

▪ Writing

Editorial The Cosquer Cave is closed to the public to protect it and to protect people who would try to enter. Have students discuss this issue for a few minutes and decide if they are for or against closing the cave to the public. Then, have each student write a letter to the director of security for Historic Monuments within the French Ministry of Culture, expressing his or her position on this matter. Students should justify their positions with reasons or evidence.

▪ Speaking and Listening

Animal Protection The article mentions a few animals that are now extinct. Some died due to natural selection, while others, like the auks, were killed off. Today, the United States federal government has a program that identifies endangered species in order to protect them. Have students research an endangered animal from your area. Then, have students present their findings to the class in short oral reports, poems, or drawings.

Connecting Across the Curriculum: Science

A Cave Is Formed Encourage students to find out how a cave is formed. What are stalagmites and stalactites? What are other common formations and structures found inside caves? In addition, have students research what kind of life exists in caves and what role caves played in human history. Have students present their findings to the class. Encourage students to use visual aids such as a diorama or poster to help explain the formation process.

Further Resources

Books

The Cave Beneath the Sea: Paleolithic Images at Cosquer by Jean Clottes and Jean Courtin, translated by Marilyn Garner

Other resources

Students can take a virtual tour of the Cosquer Cave at the Web site of the French Ministry of Culture.

Assessment

Turn to page 126 for a multiple-choice test on the selection.

Test Answers

1. a   2. b   3. d   4. c   5. c
6. d   7. a   8. b   9. b   10. d

What the Art May Tell

from *Painters of the Caves*
by PATRICIA LAUBER
(student text page 24)

CONTENT-AREA CONNECTIONS

VISUAL ART •
HISTORY •

Reading Level: Easy

Special Considerations

This selection includes several controversial ideas, including the supernatural abilities of shamans in modern tribes, possible magical beliefs of prehistoric people, and numerous speculations about early humankind. (For example, early humans lacked a written language and were ignorant of agricultural and farming methods.) Point out to students that we can only speculate about the beliefs and daily life of early people, since few facts are known. Such speculation is usually based on our beliefs or presuppositions. You might challenge students to identify the underlying beliefs on which the theories in the selection are based. What other possible explanations for the cave art can students generate? How might theories about the art differ given different underlying assumptions about early humans?

Text Summary

This selection presents four ideas on the meaning and purpose of cave art—to perform hunting magic, to represent spirit animals that shamans worked with, to serve as places for ceremonies, and to serve as memory aids. At the end of the Ice Age, with the development of agriculture, the patterns of human life changed, and the cave paintings were gradually forgotten.

BEFORE READING

Make the Connection

Have students brainstorm a list of questions they have when they think of cave art. For example, students might ask *Who created the paintings?* or *Why did they paint animals?* Then, have students read the first paragraph. Write the question *What do cave paintings mean?* on the board. Before reading the selection, have students make predictions about the answer.

Build Background

■ More About the Author

Patricia Lauber (1924–   ) is the author of more than ninety nonfiction books. From alligators to planets, volcanoes to cattle ranching, Lauber likes to explain how things work. She also writes children's stories, including the "Clarence" series of books about her dog. She won the Newbery Honor Medal for *Volcano: The Eruption and Healing of Mt. St. Helens. Painters of the Caves* won her the 1998 Best Book of the Year award from the *School Library Journal.*

Vocabulary Development

The following words are underscored and defined in the student text.

scaffolds: raised platforms or frameworks to support people working high on a wall or a building.

spiritual: relating to the spirit or soul; supernatural.

appealed: made a plea to; requested something of.

impression: impact; effect; feeling.

glaciers: huge masses of ice that flow very slowly down a mountain or over land.

Before assigning the reading, you may want to introduce students to any words that could cause pronunciation or definition problems.

Vocabulary Tip

Using Roots Before you introduce the vocabulary words, you may want to ask students what the word *glacier* makes them think of. [ice, cold, Alaska, mountains] Tell students that *glacier* comes from the French word for ice, *glace,* which in turn comes from the Latin word for ice, *glacies.* The word was first used in 1744 to describe any large body of ice that moves across a land surface. Today glaciers cover the polar regions and some mountain valleys at higher elevations. During the ice ages, glaciers covered large parts of the globe.

Although the following words are important to an understanding of the text selection, some of them may be unfamiliar to students. You may wish to present this list of words and definitions to students. Ask students to predict what they think a selection containing these words will be about. After reading the selection, have students write a short paragraph using all the words.

trance: a dreamlike state sometimes brought on by religious enthusiasm.

shaman: holy man or woman; medicine man or woman.

ceremonies: formal practices, often of a religious or spiritual nature.

game*: animals hunted for food.

*Although students may be familiar with other meanings of this word, the word as used in the selection has a specific meaning that pertains to the content area.

Reading Informational Material

Reading Skill
Making Predictions

Tell students that making predictions as they read the excerpt will help them to focus their reading and to remember the information in the selection.

Reading Strategy
Making Predictions (Strategy 7)

To help students maintain their reading focus and increase their comprehension, use Strategy 7 described in Content-Area Reading Strategies. Before reading, have students list words about the topic of the selection and group them into categories. Have students use these categories to develop a concept map, or provide them with a Cluster Diagram (Graphic Organizer 3) to complete with their word categories. After students read the selection, have them add new information from their reading to their concept maps.

DURING READING

Reading Informational Material

▶ **Teaching Tip**
Signal Words As students read, have them look for signal words that indicate the start of a new idea.

When they begin reading the new paragraph at the top of page 25, they will read *Another idea* . . . Have students go back and identify the first reason for cave paintings (immediately following the question, *What did it mean?*) In the second complete paragraph on page 26, they will read *A third idea* . . .

Differentiating Instruction
▪ English-Language Learners

Have students list words from the selection that they do not know. Then, have them work in a group to prepare a final list of words. Students should look the words up in the dictionary, prepare their own definitions, and provide an illustration if possible.

AFTER READING

✔ Reading Check

The following are sample answers to questions on student text page 28.

1. People did not live in the caves, which were dark, damp, and slippery. Caves were not comfortable places to live or to paint.

2. The four ideas the author presents to explain why cave art may have been created are to generate hunting magic, to express people's belief in spirits, to create ceremonial places, and to aid memory.

3. A shaman is a person with spiritual powers. In a cave society, the shaman was a healer, a priest, and a link with the spirit world.

4. Cave paintings were not created for us. Since there are no written records of their purpose, we can only guess at the meaning of the art.

5. The era of cave paintings came to an end when the climate warmed at the end of the Ice Age. As people began raising crops and animals and building cities, cave paintings were forgotten.

Reteaching

If students are still having difficulty making predictions, provide them with a brief reading selection on which to practice (an excerpt from another book or history text on a related topic, for instance). Give students a general idea of the topic of the selection and ask them to write predictions about the selection based on this information. Then, provide students with additional information. Have students brainstorm to generate questions about the text they will be reading based on their predictions and the additional information.

Connecting to Language Arts

▪ Writing

Story Telling According to the selection, one reason cave paintings may have been created was to assist memory. Have students choose one of the paintings in the book and create a replica on a separate sheet of paper. Underneath the illustration, have students write a paragraph that tells a story about the illustration. Students can write about a historical event that might have occurred, a myth that explains a natural phenomenon, rules that people were to follow, or guidelines for hunting. Students may wish to publish their work in a small book for the class.

Connecting Across the Curriculum: Social Sciences

People of the Ice Assign students to work in pairs or small groups to find out about the so-called "moderns," the Cro-Magnons, believed to have painted the cave art. Students should research current theories about the Cro-Magnons. What did they hunt? Were they gatherers? What did they use for tools and weapons? What were their dwellings like? What kind of clothing did they wear? After students have completed their research, have them present their findings in an oral or written report. Students could also create cave paintings (on butcher paper) based on their findings and display them in the classroom.

Further Resources

Books

Painters of the Caves by Patricia Lauber

Dawn of Art: The Chauvet Cave: The Oldest Known Paintings in the World by Jean Marie Chauvet, et al.

Other resources

Students can find out more about the Chauvet Cave at the Web site of the French Ministry of Culture.

Assessment

Turn to page 127 for a multiple-choice test on the selection.

Test Answers

1. d 2. c 3. b 4. a 5. c
6. d 7. b 8. a 9. d 10. a

A Bundle of Bog Bodies

from *Bodies from the Bog*
by JAMES M. DEEM
(student text page 29)

Reading Level: Average

Special Considerations

The description of some of the bodies may seem gruesome to some students. You may want to discuss possible reasons why some corpses in ancient societies would not have received a proper burial.

Text Summary

This excerpt from the book *Bodies from the Bog* investigates bodies that have been discovered preserved in the bogs of northern Europe. The selection provides a chronological review of bog body discoveries, including that of the Grauballe Man. Based on the condition of the bog bodies and their clothing, scientists have been able to speculate about the reasons for their deaths.

BEFORE READING

Make the Connection

Write the following words on the board: *bogs* (or *swamps*), *death, mummies, murder.* Allow students to think for a few minutes; then have them freewrite a short paragraph using the selected words. Ask volunteers to share their stories. Tell students the selection they are about to read is about the discovery of ancient bodies found in the bogs of northern Europe.

Build Background

▪ More About the Topic

Documentation of bog mummies dates back to the 1600s; however, no one knows for sure how many bog bodies have been uncovered. Because many of the bodies died a violent death, it is believed that they were human sacrifices—offerings to the gods. Additionally, ornaments, vessels, weapons, and wagons were deposited into the bogs. Wonderfully preserved by the bogs, the mummies provide clues about the past. Today, peat cutting from bogs is prohibited in many European countries, thus minimizing the possibility of future discoveries of bog mummies.

Vocabulary Development

The following words are underscored and defined in the student text. You may wish to have students look up the suffix *–ly* in a dictionary and then discuss with them its meaning in the words *mortally* and *grisly.*

ground: crushed into a fine powder.
mortally: fatally; causing death.
customary: usual.
grisly: horrifying; frightening.
deposited: put into.

Before assigning the reading, you may want to introduce students to any words that could cause pronunciation or definition problems.

⌐ *Vocabulary Tip* ¬

Using Context Clues Before you introduce the vocabulary words, remind students that they can sometimes determine the meaning of a word by using context clues in a sentence or paragraph. Read aloud the paragraph containing the vocabulary word *customary* (beginning on student text page 31). Ask students what context clues hint at the word's meaning. [A bog body was found in 1946, another in 1947, and a third in 1948. The curator sent all to the National Museum. Since a body had been found each year, the note stating that this is the "customary annual bog body" helps you guess that *customary* means usual.]

(CONTENT-AREA VOCABULARY)

Although the following words are important to an understanding of the text selection, some of them may be unfamiliar to students. Present this list of words and definitions to your students. Ask students to predict what they think a selection containing these words and the vocabulary words will be about. [The selection may concern the discovery of something in a swamp.]

bog: wet lowlands; swamp; spongy ground.

discovery: something that has been uncovered or made famous.

peat: a decayed plant that is used as fuel, usually found in bogs.

*deposited: dropped into.

*pegged: pinned down securely with pointed pieces of wood.

*Although students may be familiar with other meanings of these words, the words as used in the selection have a specific meaning that pertains to the content area.

Reading Informational Material

Reading Skill
Analyzing Chronological Order
Explain to students that chronological order is the order in which events happen. Point out that the selection uses dates to tell the story in chronological order.

Reading Strategy
Understanding Text (Strategy 2)
To help your students understand the sequence of events in this selection, use Strategy 2 described in Content-Area Reading Strategies. Provide students with a Sequence or Chronological Organizer Chart (Graphic Organizer 10) to help them track the sequence of events as they read.

DURING READING

Using the Side-Margin Feature
■ You Think *That's* Old . . .
Have students create a time line of the Neolithic Age, the Bronze Age, and the Iron Age. Have them list the bog bodies in the appropriate eras. Using dictionaries, encyclopedias, or the Internet, have students find out why the ages were named Stone, Bronze, and Iron.

Text Features
▶ **Teaching Tip**
Details Point out to students that dates and other numerical figures in a selection can be overwhelming. When looking for sequential order, they should write the dates on their organizers. (The other figures are supporting details.)

Differentiating Instruction
■ Learners Having Difficulties
Divide students into three groups—paper bog bodies, 1940s, and 1950s. Each group will summarize the main idea for their topic. Have the first group answer the following questions: What are paper bog bodies? Why are they called that? What significant dates apply? The 1940s and 1950s groups should answer the following questions: How many bog bodies were discovered? Where were the discoveries made? What was unusual about the discoveries?

AFTER READING

✔ Reading Check

The following are sample answers to questions on student text page 34.

1. The earlier bog bodies were reburied, dried and ground up, or sold. They no longer exist because of this treatment.

2. A "paper" bog body is one that is mentioned in newspaper articles or other written accounts but was never authenticated or scientifically studied.

3. The man found in Osterby wore his hair in a Swabian knot. This revealed that he lived about 2,000 years ago when people wore their hair this way.

4. The cord around the Tollund Man was evidence that he probably was hanged.

5. The Zweeloo Woman had very short bones from her elbows to her wrists and from her knees to her ankles. Based on this, we can guess that she probably had difficulty walking.

Reteaching

If students are still struggling with the chronology of the selection, work with them to create a time line of the events using the following dates: 1600, 1800, 1946, 1947, 1948, 1950, 1951, and 1952. Have student volunteers tell what happened during those dates while you write their responses on the chalkboard or a transparency. Remind students that two events are described for each of the years 1946 and 1948.

Connecting to Language Arts

▪ Writing

Police Report The writer of the selection describes the bodies of several ancient people. Using the facts presented in the selection, have students choose one body to describe in a police report. They may create details about the circumstances that led to the victim's death, but students must include facts about the body from the selection to support their theories.

▪ Speaking and Listening

Important Breaking News Have students write a brief television news announcement about the discovery of one of the bog bodies. Students should explain where the body was found, what condition it was in, and any theories scientists have about the cause of death. Have students videotape their breaking news and play the tape to the class.

Connecting Across the Curriculum: Environmental Science

What's a Wetland? Encourage students to find out more about wetlands. What is a bog? How are bogs formed? What are the differences between bogs, fens, and marshes? What kinds of animal and plant life are found in wetlands? After students have completed their research, they may want to pool their findings or work independently to present the results of their investigations to the class in an oral or multimedia presentation.

Further Resources

Books

Bodies from the Bog by James M. Deem

Other resources

For photos of and more information about the bog bodies, visit the Web site of the Archaeological Institute of America.

Assessment

Turn to page 128 for a multiple-choice test on the selection.

Test Answers

1. d   2. c   3. a   4. b   5. d
6. c   7. d   8. d   9. a   10. b

The following criteria can help you evaluate each student's success in completing the activities prompted by the Cross-Curricular Activities feature in the student textbook.

Art/Social Science
Caving in to Art
- The student uses a limited number of colors: black, red, brown, and yellow.
- The student renders images in a style that mimics the simple and abstract appearance of prehistoric cave paintings, demonstrating the student's understanding of the basic characteristics of cave art.
- The student's choice of subject matter and execution of the work shows imagination and creativity.

Music/Dance/Drama
Performing an Ancient Story
(Since this activity requires the involvement of more than one student, you may wish to evaluate each student on his or her specific and individual contribution to the piece and then give the partners or group an overall rating.)
- The student conducts research to find an event or story from prehistory that would make an interesting performance piece.
- The student chooses an effective means of telling the story he or she has chosen, using drama, music, dance, or a combination of performance art forms.
- The student's performance effectively conveys a story line or event, leaving the audience with a clear picture of what happened.
- The performance is relatively free of performance errors. If used, props, costumes, music, sound effects, and other enhancements contribute to the overall effectiveness of the performance piece.

Health/Science
They Were What They Ate
(Since this activity requires the involvement of more than one student, you may wish to evaluate each student on his or her specific and individual contribution to the piece and then give the partners or group an overall rating.)
- The student conducts research to find exactly what early hunter-gatherers ate, how their diet affected their health, and what changes took place in the human diet once agriculture developed.
- The student reports his or her findings to the class.

Science/Speech
Start Cloning Around
- The student conducts research on the Siberian woolly mammoth study and on current scientific views of cloning.
- The student chooses a "pro" or "con" position and debates the scientific possibilities of successfully cloning a woolly mammoth.
- The student addresses whether he or she thinks it would be wise to clone a woolly mammoth, what we could learn from the cloning, and what could go wrong.

Language Arts/Art
Reading the Past
- The student creates a list of the most important objects an archaeologist one thousand years in the future would find in the remains of the student's backpack, locker, or room.
- The student writes a brief report on these contents from the archaeologist's point of view. The report may include drawings.
- The student addresses what would most puzzle the archaeologist and what inferences that person would make about the student's way of life and what he or she valued most.

Between Two Rivers
Ancient Mesopotamia 5000 B.C.–500 B.C.

Hammurabi's Babylonia

CONTENT-AREA CONNECTION
HISTORY •

from *The Babylonians*
by ELAINE LANDAU
(student text page 39)

Reading Level: Average

Special Considerations

Because the penalties described in Hammurabi's code may seem severe to some students, you might lead a discussion about how legal penalties indicate what the society considers important. For example, the legendary practice of hanging horse thieves in the Old West would show the importance of the horse to survival on the frontier in the nineteenth century, but would seem barbaric and extreme to us today.

Text Summary

This title in the *Cradle of Civilization* series examines the history of the Babylonian empire and the evolution of its society, including the legal code of Hammurabi. Although some of Hammurabi's laws may seem harsh by present-day standards, his code was an important step toward creating a society in which everyone's rights were recognized to some degree.

BEFORE READING

Make the Connection

Ask students to state reasons for having laws. [fairness, safety, protection] Then, have students brainstorm rules they could set up for classroom behavior. Have students consider the consequences of breaking those rules.

Build Background

■ More About the Topic

While the influence of Hammurabi's code is accepted worldwide, not everyone knows the code was literally carved in stone. (At that time most cuneiform writing was done in clay.) Vincent Scheil, a French archaeologist, found stone tablets bearing pieces of the code during an archaeological dig in 1901 at Susa, the ancient capital of Elam (part of modern Iran). The tablets had apparently been taken from Babylon as spoils of war by Elamite invaders.

Vocabulary Development

The following words are underscored and defined in the student text.

thrived: grew, flourished, or prospered.
artisans: persons trained to work at a trade requiring skill with the hands.
code: a body of laws, principles, or rules.
accusations: charges of wrongdoing.
prescribed: authorized; established.

Before assigning the reading, you may want to introduce students to any words that could cause pronunciation or definition problems.

> ### *Vocabulary Tip*
> **Discovering Multiple Meanings** Before you introduce the content-area vocabulary words, you may want to ask for student input on the meaning of the word *code.* Students may think of *code* as referring to area code, ZIP code, Morse code, or a secret code. Explain that in this selection *code* has a specific legal meaning.

Although the following words are important to an understanding of the text selection, some of them may be unfamiliar to students. You will want to introduce the words to students before they begin reading. Ask students what they predict they will read about in a selection using these words and the ones in the vocabulary-development list. [laws or a legal system]

code*: a body of laws, principles, or rules.
legal: of or pertaining to the law.
statute: a law.
justice: fair treatment under the law.
disputes: disagreements.
penalties*: punishment fixed by law.

*Although students may be familiar with other meanings of these words, the words as used in the selection have a specific meaning that pertains to the content area.

Reading Informational Material

Reading Skill
Finding the Main Idea

Explain to students that the main idea is an overall topic being developed in an article or in part of an article.

▶ **Teaching Tip**
Reading an Excerpt This selection is from a book. Remind students that because of its length, a book does not have one main idea. Point out to students that this selection has two main sections [the prosperity of Hammurabi's kingdom and Hammurabi's code] and that each section has its own main idea.

Reading Strategy
Anticipating Information (Strategy 9)

To help students find the main idea of a major part of this selection, use Strategy 9 described in Content-Area Reading Strategies. You may wish to provide students with an Anticipation Guide (Graphic Organizer 1) to help them organize their thoughts on the main idea as they move through the reading process.

DURING READING

Correcting Misconceptions
Students may hear of doctors today buying expensive malpractice insurance and being sued by any patient who feels his or her treatment is inadequate. However, students may not be aware that the roots of these practices lie in early civilizations, such as Babylonia, which held surgeons liable for their treatments.

Using the Side-Margin Feature
■ Death Pits

Ask students what they know about burial customs in other cultures. Students might mention the Hindu funeral pyres, the Egyptian mummies and pyramids, or other cultures' practice of burying items useful for the afterlife.

▶ **Teaching Tip**
Noting Text Features Point out to students that text structure features, like bullets, may help them recognize the organization of the text. For example, students might note that the development of one main idea—that Hammurabi attempted to develop fair laws—is exemplified by the actual bulleted list of laws.

Viewing the Art
■ Hammurabi's Stone Tablets

You may wish to refer students to page 43 and the picture of the stone pillars on which Hammurabi's original laws were carved. You may want to discuss the implications of the expression "carved in stone."

Differentiating Instruction
■ Learners Having Difficulty

Use a pair/share approach by pairing a learner who might experience difficulty reading the selection with a more able reader. Ask the students to take turns reading a small section aloud. Before switching readers, partners should discuss the section. Focus of the discussion should be on clarification. Model the process for the whole class before pairing the students.

AFTER READING

✔ Reading Check

The following are sample answers to questions on student text page 44.

1. Babylonia prospered under Hammurabi. He maintained an irrigation system, ensuring fertile fields for crops. Surplus grain meant increased trade for raw materials such as wood, metals, and livestock. Scientists made advances in astronomy.

2. Babylon's location on the Euphrates River helped make it a trading center.

3. Babylonian slaves could hold jobs in their time off, accumulate money, own property, enter into business agreements, and buy their freedom. Married women could have their own property and money.

4. The code included about 280 sections. Hammurabi trusted that the reasoning behind the original code would be applied to situations not specifically covered.

Reteaching

If students are still struggling with the concept of main idea, write a statement of main idea in the center of a Cluster Diagram (Graphic Organizer 3 and Reading Strategy 3) and make and distribute copies to the class. [For example: **Main Idea:** Babylonia thrived under Hammurabi's rule.] Have students fill in the next level with supporting statements. [Scientists and mathematicians made advances in astronomy, algebra, and geometry. Writers and artists created great poetry, statues, and carvings. Agriculture and trade flourished.] Students may want to go to a deeper level by adding examples that develop the supporting statements. [Under "trade," students could add bubbles for "exported crops, cloth," and "imported wood, livestock, precious metals, and gems."]

Connecting to Language Arts
▪ Writing

Talk Show Have students select two examples of Hammurabi's code and compare them to laws today for the same crime. Ask how the punishment might have changed. What might have caused the change? Have students write the script for a talk show. Then, have them stage the show with a selected host to discuss this topic.

Connecting Across the Curriculum: Social Sciences

The Street Where I Live Assign students to find out what a typical street in the capital city of Babylonia looked like. What materials were used to construct the public buildings? How were the homes of the people different from those of the upper classes or of the slaves? How were the palaces decorated? After students have completed their research, they may want to pool their findings or work independently to present the results of their investigations. They might create one of the following:

- a "help wanted" ad seeking artisans for building and decorating projects
- an illustrated street map with small sketches of typical buildings
- a floor plan for a dream house in Babylonia
- a diorama of the city center

Further Resources
Online Resource
The Washington State University site has information on Mesopotamia, The Code of Hammurabi, and Cuneiform.

Assessment

Turn to page 129 for a multiple-choice test on the selection.

Test Answers
1. a 2. b 3. d 4. c 5. a
6. d 7. a 8. c 9. b 10. c

Writing and Alphabets

from *Alphabetical Order: How the Alphabet Began*
by TIPHAINE SAMOYAULT
(student text page 45)

Reading Level: Average

Special Considerations

Using animal livers to search for signs from the gods may strike modern readers as barbaric, so you might lead a discussion on the changing attitudes humans have about animals. For example, people once thought that cats were evil beings who consorted with witches. Today, we consider cats to be friendly house pets.

Text Summary

This excerpt from *Alphabetical Order: How the Alphabet Began* discusses some of the earliest known forms of writing. In most civilizations, writing started out with connections to religion and magic but soon came to be used for business and daily life. Cuneiform, the oldest known writing system, was developed by the Sumerians in order to keep track of business and trade.

BEFORE READING

Make the Connection

Ask students to state reasons that an alphabet might be considered an important invention. [Students might say the alphabet is important because it allows people to communicate with each other in writing or because it makes keeping track of business transactions easier.] Then, ask students to think of the various ways that an alphabet makes modern society possible. For example, having an alphabet makes independent learning, such as a game or computer program, easier by making written instructions possible.

Build Background

▪ More About the Topic

As a system of writing, cuneiform could be adapted for use by other cultures with different languages. As a result, cuneiform was the most widespread form of writing in the ancient Middle East for about three thousand years. Cuneiform remained in wide use until the Phoenicians developed a more efficient writing system. By 500 B.C., hardly anyone used cuneiform. In fact, cuneiform disappeared so completely that the ancient Greeks hardly knew it had existed.

Vocabulary Development

The following words are underscored and defined in the student's text.

literally: based on exactly what is said.
distinctive: clear; marking a difference from others.
inspiration: a bright idea or impulse.
triangular: shaped like a triangle, a three-sided figure.

Before assigning the reading, you may want to introduce students to any words that could cause pronunciation or definition problems.

Vocabulary Tip

Using Related Words Help students compile a list of words that are related to those in the vocabulary-development list. [*literal; distinct; inspire; triangle*] Have students working in small groups compose sentences using the vocabulary words and the words from the compiled list. Have the class as a whole work to determine parts of speech of the key words. You may want to tell students that some suffixes change the part of speech of a word. You can explain that these suffixes are called *derivational suffixes,* and the *–ly* suffix, for example, changes the word to an adverb meaning "in such a manner." For example, *slowly* means "in a slow manner," *literally* means "in a literal manner," and *eventually* means "in an eventual manner."

Although the following words are important to an under-standing of the text selection, some of them may be unfamiliar to students. You will want to introduce the words to students before they begin reading. Ask students what they predict they will read about in a selection using these words. [about early means of written communication].

hieroglyphics: pictures or symbols representing words or syllables in ancient written languages.

ideograms: two or more pictures or symbols used to represent a single thing or idea.

pictograms: pictures or symbols used to represent things or ideas in place of specific words or phrases.

Reading Informational Materials

Reading Skill
Summarizing
Remind students that a summary is a short restatement of the important ideas and details of a work.

Reading Strategy
Constructing Concept Maps (Strategy 4)
To help students identify the important ideas and details of the selection, use Strategy 4 described in Content-Area Reading Strategies. Some students may be more comfortable using a Cluster Diagram (Graphic Organizer 3) to guide them in organizing their ideas.

▶ **Teaching Tip**
Finding Main Points Students who generate long lists of every detail or idea in a selection some-times are overwhelmed at the notion of narrowing their lists to two or three main points. You might suggest that they try comparing two details at a time and strike the least important from their lists. Then they would compare the next two items on their lists, eliminating one. By cutting their lists in half this way, students may feel less intimidated.

DURING READING

Differentiating Instruction
■ Learners Having Difficulty
Students having difficulty summarizing the selection may benefit from working in small groups to narrow their focus. Tell students that each paragraph in the

selection also contains a main idea—often stated in the first or last sentence of the paragraph. Ask them to find the main idea of the second para-graph on student text page 46. [the first sentence] For further practice, ask them to locate the main idea in paragraphs three and four.

▶ **Teaching Tip**
Selecting Details Students sometimes have diffi-culty determining whether a detail is important enough to be mentioned in a summary. You might want to briefly discuss with these students the main idea of the selection. Then, instruct students to ask of each point or detail in the selection "Is this neces-sary to my understanding the writer's main idea?"

AFTER READING

✓ Reading Check

The following are sample answers to questions on student page 48.

1. Writing was developed before alphabets. Early writing connected meaning with natural or manmade markings.

2. The priests looked for any distinctive mark that could be seen as a message from a god. These may have been the inspiration for writing.

3. Writing was first used by priests to convey messages from the gods.

4. The Mesopotamians needed to trade corn, vegetables, meat, leather, and clay for wood, stone, and metals, and other items their region lacked. Writing helped traders keep track of trade items.

5. Cuneiform spread throughout the Middle East because it did not represent a particular language but stood for objects familiar in many places.

Reteaching
Students who are struggling to summarize infor-mation may find that a Sequence or Chronological Order Chart (Graphic Organizer 10) works better for them. When students decide which steps to include in a Sequence or Chronological Order

Chart, they are also deciding which ideas and details are most important. Students can then recount the important ideas in their summary.

Connecting to Language Arts

▪ Writing

International Symbols Have students research international symbols used for various things, such as road signs. What do these symbols have in common with an ideogram? [International symbols can be understood by different cultures as words in their language. For example, a red circle with a slash means "not allowed."] What advantages do such symbols have? [They enable people who speak different languages to understand the same signs.] Then, working in groups, have students make a catalog of at least twenty international symbols or write a story using only symbols.

▪ Speaking and Listening

Got Cuneiform? Discuss with students the advantages that cuneiform writing offered to ancient Sumerians. [Cuneiform helped Sumerians track their business transactions. Cuneiform symbols could be used by other cultures to write their language.] Then have students work in small groups to write a radio or television script for a public service announcement publicizing the importance of cuneiform literacy to ancient Sumerians. The groups can then deliver their scripts to the class.

Connecting Across the Curriculum: Art

Take a Letter Have students work alone or in groups to invent a writing system. Students can create a new alphabet by assigning a different symbol to each letter of the English alphabet, or they can make up a writing system consisting of 25–30 symbols, each standing for a single word. Students should create a key showing what each symbol in their writing system stands for. Students can use their invented writing systems in one of the following ways:

- Design a magazine cover with the headlines written in the invented alphabet
- Write a note in the invented alphabet
- Inscribe a name or a short phrase in the invented alphabet on a slab of air-drying clay

Students can then use each other's keys to decipher the invented alphabet messages.

Further Resources

Graphics

historical atlas with a map of Mesopotamia during Sumerian times

Online Resources

Washington State University has a site with information on cuneiform.

The University of Pennsylvania Museum of Archaeology and Anthropology has links to other sites.

Assessment

Turn to page 130 for a multiple-choice test on the selection.

Test Answers

1. c   **2.** a   **3.** d   **4.** b   **5.** a
6. d   **7.** c   **8.** a   **9.** d   **10.** b

Enheduana of Sumer

from *Outrageous Women of Ancient Times*
by VICKI LEÓN
(student text page 49)

Reading Level: Average

Special Considerations

A possible sensitive issue in this selection and in the sidebar titled "Ringing in the New Year" is the mention of animal sacrifice. You may wish to lead students in a brief discussion of the Sumerian belief system. Sumerians believed that human beings were made when the gods mixed clay with the flesh and blood of a sacrificed god. The gods protected only those mortals who respected and served them. Everyone else was at the mercy of demons. Being in favor with the gods was so important that Sumerians were willing to go as far as to sacrifice animals to show their loyalty.

Text Summary

This excerpt from *Outrageous Women of Ancient Times* recounts the life of Enheduana, the earliest author in literary history whose name we know today. Enheduana was the daughter of the Akkadian king Sargon. While still a teenager, she was named high priestess to Nanna, the moon-god of Sumer. In her spare time, Enheduana wrote poems and hymns to the kingdom's temples and to the goddess Inanna. These writings were inscribed on clay tablets. Unlike previous writers, Enheduana's name was included on the tablets so people would know that she was the author.

BEFORE READING

Make the Connection

Ask students to state reasons that an author's name might appear on the cover of a book. [Students might respond that a writing credit might soothe the author's ego or encourage people to seek other work by that author.] Then, ask students how they would feel if books they wrote were about to be published. Would they want their names on the covers? How would they feel if their books were published without their names and then became bestsellers? Mention that readers may need to know the author's name to check on his or her credibility. Encourage them to think critically about the sources of information they read.

Build Background

▪ Building Prerequisite Skills

Before presenting this strategy to your class, create a brief exercise to prepare students for grouping words by category. Begin by selecting two or three distinct categories [food, transportation, animals]. Then select three to five words that clearly belong in one category [vegetables, grains, meat]. Model the exercise by putting one word in each of the food subgroups [carrots, wheat, beef]. You can then choose to have students complete the task as a class, as individuals, or in small groups.

Vocabulary Development

The following words are underscored and defined in the student text.

crescent: a shape like the moon when it is in a quarter phase.

sacred: holy.

sacrifices: something precious, such as animal or human lives, offered to a god or goddess.

supreme: greatest or highest in power or authority.

composing: creating or producing, usually a musical or literary work.

Before assigning the reading, you may want to introduce students to any words that could cause pronunciation or definition problems.

─ *Vocabulary Tip* ─

Finding Roots The word *supreme* comes from the Latin root *supremus* meaning "upper" and is derived from *super.* This is the same root that gives us the prefixes *super–* and *supra–,* meaning "above" or "over." Knowing this prefix can help you guess the meaning of words such as *superior, supervise, superhuman,* and *supraliminal.*

Although the following words are important to an understanding of the text selection, some of them may be unfamiliar to students. Present these words to students. Encourage students to discuss other meanings they know for these words.

stylus*: a stick or reed with a pointed end that was used to press cuneiform marks into wet clay.

tablets*: slabs of material used to write on.

account*: a story or retelling.

verse: a portion of a poem.

proverb: a brief saying that often reveals a truth about life.

*Although students may be familiar with other meanings of these words, the words as used in the selection have a specific meaning that pertains to the content area.

Reading Informational Materials

Reading Skill
Making Predictions

Explain to students that making predictions before reading a new selection can help them connect to what they already know about a subject and increase their understanding of the text. Predictions can be based on keywords in the text.

Reading Strategy
Making Predictions (Strategy 7)

To help students make predictions about a selection, use Strategy 7 described in the Content-Area Reading Strategies. Students may also benefit by using a Cluster Diagram (Graphic Organizer 3) to help them organize their thoughts prior to making predictions about the content of a new reading selection.

DURING READING

Using the Side-Margin Feature
- Life in River City

Lead students in a brief discussion of what day-to-day life must have been like for men and women in each of the three classes of Mesopotamian society. As an extension activity, you may wish to have students write a short diary entry from the perspective of a citizen of Mesopotamia.

Differentiating Instruction
- English-Language Learners

Since the Making Predictions exercise focuses on grouping words together, you may wish to have English-language learners team up with students who speak English more proficiently to make predictions about the text. You may also choose to allow English-language learners to use a translating dictionary to come up with English words to add to their word list.

AFTER READING

✓ Reading Check

The following are sample answers to questions on student text page 53.

1. Books were clay tablets that had the shape of little pillows. The tablets were written on with a pointed stylus while the clay was wet.

2. Enheduana and her family lived in Akkad in Sumer. Her father was the King of the city-states Akkad and Kish.

3. Enheduana was appointed high priestess to the moon-god, Nanna. Her duties included offering prayers, carrying out rituals, making sacrifices to the gods, and reenacting the marriage of a goddess and human each new year. Enheduana lost her job when her nephew became king and appointed his daughter as high priestess.

4. Archaeologists found the same poem written on fifty tablets for distribution.

5. Enheduana described an unsuccessful revolt against her father.

Reteaching

If students are still struggling with categorizing and classifying the words they generate, create a class word game using words from the Concept Maps and Cluster Diagrams. Working in groups, students print the lists on cards, one word per card. The game is to match a word to its category. As students become more adept at classifying and categorizing, more words can be added to the game.

▶ Teaching Tip

Knowing Alternative Spellings If your students are doing further research on Enheduana, you might let them know that there are alternative spellings of her name. In addition to *Enheduana*, spellings include *Enheduanna* (with two *n*'s) and *En hedu'anna*.

Connecting to Language Arts

▪ Writing

Invitation to a Celebration Have students work individually or in small groups to write the copy for an invitation to an annual Mesopotamian New Year's celebration featuring Enheduana as the high priestess. Students may use information gathered from the selection and the "Ringing in the New Year" sidebar to compose the invitations, or you may assign them additional research. As an extension activity, you may choose to have students design the invitation on paper or with a computer graphics program.

▪ Speaking and Listening

Improvised Interview Have students work in groups to compile notes for an interview of Enheduana by a radio or television reporter. Students should compile notes for both the interviewer and Enheduana. They should have the interviewer ask specific questions that can be answered based on information in the selection. Have students use their notes to stage the interview.

Connecting Across the Curriculum: Architecture

Ziggurats Assign students to research the design and construction of ziggurats in Mesopotamia. What did they look like? What construction materials were used? How was the interior space of the temple on top designed? What other buildings might have been near them? After students have completed their research, they may present their findings in small groups or individually. They might create one of the following:

- architectural drawings, such as floor plans or drawings of the exterior
- an advertisement for a ziggurat construction company
- a three-dimensional model or cross section of a ziggurat
- a newspaper report about the construction of a ziggurat

Further Resources

Graphics

maps of Mesopotamia during Enheduana's time

illustrations of typical Mesopotamian cities

Assessment

Turn to page 131 for a multiple-choice test on the selection.

Test Answers

1. d **2.** b **3.** a **4.** d **5.** c
6. c **7.** a **8.** b **9.** d **10.** c

The Patient and Persistent Babylonians

from *Greek and Roman Science*
by DON NARDO
(*student text page 54*)

Reading Level: Above average

Text Summary

This excerpt from *The Patient and Persistent Babylonians* compares and contrasts Babylonian development in mathematics and astronomy with that of the Egyptians. In the area of mathematics, the excerpt explains the Babylonian's system of counting and their understanding of square and cube roots. In astronomy, Babylonians developed a system of tracking the movement of heavenly bodies, compiled detailed records of those movements, and were the first to name planets after deities.

BEFORE READING

Make the Connection

Ask students to name the nine planets in our solar system. [Mars, Earth, Venus, Mercury, Jupiter, Saturn, Uranus, Neptune, Pluto] Write the names of the planets on the chalkboard and ask students what the names have in common. [except for Earth, all of the planets are named after Greek or Roman gods] Tell students they will be learning more about the practice of naming planets for deities.

Build Background

■ More About the Topic

With the exception of Earth, all of the planets in our solar system were named after Greek or Roman gods. Planets named after Roman gods are Mars, god of war; Venus, goddess of love; Mercury, messenger of the gods; Jupiter, god of thunder and sky; Saturn, god of agriculture; Neptune, god of the seas; and Pluto, god of the underworld. Uranus was the Greek god who personified the heavens. Many of the Roman gods and goddesses had Greek counterparts. For example, the Roman goddess Venus was the counterpart of the Greek goddess Aphrodite, and the Roman god Jupiter was comparable to the Greek god Zeus.

■ Building Prerequisite Skills

You can prepare students for comparing and contrasting by leading them in a discussion of the similarities and differences between dogs and cats. Draw a Venn Diagram on the chalkboard with one circle labeled "Dogs" and the other "Cats." Then, ask students what dogs and cats have in common. [They are mammals, they have four legs; they have fur; they have sharp teeth.] Write these in the area where the two circles overlap. Ask them how dogs and cats differ. [Dogs bark while cats meow; dogs are eager to please while cats are independent.] Write these qualities in the appropriate circles. Explain to students that they have just completed a comparison-contrast diagram, a useful tool for detailing similarities and differences between two or more things.

Vocabulary Development

The following words are underscored and defined in the student text.

divisible: capable of being divided.

remnants: traces; fragments.

predecessors: ancestors or people who came before.

archives: documents or records that are kept as evidence.

rudimentary: beginning; elementary.

Before assigning the reading, you may want to introduce students to any words that could cause pronunciation or definition problems.

┌─ *Vocabulary Tip* ──────────────

Using Affixes Prefixes and suffixes often provide good clues to the meanings of words. In the word *divisible*, the suffix *–ible* means "able." So "*divisible* by 2, 3, and 4" means "able to be divided by 2, 3, and 4." The suffix is sometimes spelled *–able*, but with either spelling, one can easily guess the meaning of words such as *visible, preventable,* or *reasonable.*

└──────────────────────────

Although the following words are important to an understanding of the text selection, some of them may be unfamiliar to students. Present these words to students, and have students brainstorm connections between these words. [All relate to mathematics or science. *Decimal* and *sexagesimal* relate to counting systems.] Ask students what word from the vocabulary-development list fits this theme. [divisible] Ask students to explain how the prefixes *dec*– and *sex*– relate to the meanings of *decimal* and *sexagesimal*. [*Dec*–means "ten"; *sexageni* means "sixty."]

decimal*: based on the number ten.

sexagesimal: based on the number sixty.

order of magnitude: a mathematical term for increasing quantity; for example, in the number 43, the 4 stands for 40, which has a higher magnitude than the 3.

square and cube roots: mathematical terms in which *square* refers to a number multiplied by itself once (3 x 3) and *cube* refers to a number multiplied by itself three times (3 x 3 x 3). *Root* refers to the opposite calculation, so 3 is the square root of 9, and the cube root of 27.

astronomy: the scientific study of stars, planets, and other heavenly bodies.

*Although students may be familiar with other meanings of this word, the word as used in the selection has a specific meaning that pertains to the content area.

Reading Informational Materials

Reading Skill
Analyzing Text Structure: Comparison and Contrast
Explain to students that comparison and contrast refer to detailing the similarities and differences between at least two things. *Comparison* relates to similarities, while *contrast* relates to differences.

▶ **Teaching Tip**
Understanding Comparison and Contrast You might want to tell your students that more than two ideas or items may be used in a piece of writing that compares and contrasts.

Reading Strategy
Understanding Text (Strategy 2)
To help students identify the comparison and contrast pattern in this selection, use Strategy 2 in the Content-Area Reading Strategies. Provide students with a Venn Diagram (Graphic Organizer 11) to help them visualize the similarities and differences detailed in the selection.

DURING READING

Using the Side-Margin Feature
▪ Is There a Doctor in the House?
Ask students what impressions they have of the medical practices of ancient civilizations and distant historical eras. Students might respond with comments indicating that ancient cultures had a less scientific understanding of medicine than we do today. Students may also refer to outdated treatments, such as using magical potions or bleeding with leeches.

Differentiating Instruction
▪ Learners Having Difficulty
Some students may have difficulty identifying similarities and differences between more than two things. You may want to have these students focus on just two categories. For example, this selection compares and contrasts Babylonian mathematics and astronomy with Egyptian, Greek, Roman, and modern mathematics and astronomy. You may wish to instruct learners having difficulty to compare and contrast astronomy in two civilizations, for example, Babylonia and Egypt.

▶ **Teaching Tip**
Examining Text Structure Consider telling your students that informational writing may include a variety of structures, or methods of organization, such as comparison and contrast or problem and solution. However, usually one type of structure dominates. For example, most of this selection uses a comparison-contrast structure, but in the last paragraph the author focuses on description rather than comparison and contrast.

AFTER READING

✓ Reading Check

The following are sample answers to questions on student text page 57.

1. According to the author, the Egyptians were more advanced in medicine. The Babylonians were more advanced in math and astronomy.

2. The Babylonians used a decimal system for numbers one to fifty-nine. For quantities of sixty or higher, they used a sexagesimal system based on the number sixty.

3. The Babylonians observed the stars from ziggurats. They kept their records for many centuries.

4. The Babylonian name for the planet Venus was Ishtar, for the goddess of love and beauty. The Greeks copied the Babylonians, but named the planet Aphrodite after their own goddess of love. When the Romans adopted the Greek deities and changed the names, the planet became Venus.

5. Nabu-rimanni was the first person to calculate the length of a year most accurately. His year was too long by twenty-six minutes and fifty-five seconds.

Reteaching

If students are still struggling to identify the comparison-contrast structure of this selection, you may wish to have them identify the structure of a single paragraph. Begin by reading aloud—or having a student read aloud—the first paragraph in the selection. Then, ask students to identify the signal or transition words or phrases in the paragraph [*but, like the, but only*]. Write students' responses on the chalkboard. Ask students to identify the structure that uses these words or phrases [comparison-contrast]. Repeat this process with other paragraphs, or have students analyze paragraphs individually, in pairs, or in small groups.

Connecting to Language Arts

▪ Writing

Renaming the Planets Divide students into eight groups and assign each group one of the eight planets named after Roman or Greek deities. Within each group, have members nominate real or mythical personalities they feel deserve to have planets named after them. Then, have the group prepare a brief written testimonial defending their choice. One member of each group should present the testimonial to the class, with students using "thumbs up" to vote for the new name and "thumbs down" to support the traditional name.

Connecting Across the Curriculum: Math/Art

In Caesar We Trust Have students research the Roman numerical system. You can guide their research with questions such as these: Does the Roman system of counting seem easier or more difficult than the Babylonian system? How does each of the Roman letters relate to our decimal system? How did the Romans combine letters to make different numbers? After students have finished their investigation, they may choose to work independently or with a partner to present the results of their research. Students may choose one of the following activities:

- design paper money or coins in a variety of Roman-numeral denominations with a Roman emperor or god on one side
- draw a poster illustrating the Roman numerical system and showing how it relates to our decimal system
- create a series of flash cards with Roman numerals on one side and the corresponding decimal numerals on the other
- design a menu for an Italian restaurant with the prices and other numbers in Roman and decimal numerals

Further Resources

Graphics

map of the solar system showing all nine planets

Videos

Several videos, such as the National Geographic Society series, are available that tell about the planets and take the reader on a tour of the solar system.

Assessment

Turn to page 132 for a multiple-choice test on the selection.

Test Answers

1. b 2. a 3. c 4. b 5. d
6. a 7. c 8. b 9. a 10. c

from **The Monster Humbaba**

from *Gilgamesh: Man's First Story*
by BERNARDA BRYSON
(student text page 58)

Reading Level: Average

Special Considerations

Possible sensitive issues in this selection include depictions of violent incidents and grotesque monsters. You might lead students in a discussion of how violence depicted in today's entertainment media, such as television, movies, and video games, compares with ancient depictions. What are the arguments for and against depicting violence? [Some students may say people are so accustomed to seeing violence in the media and in life that they are no longer moved by it. Others may say that exposure to violence affects people harmfully.]

Text Summary

This excerpt from *Gilgamesh: Man's First Story* details the slaying of a monster called Humbaba by Gilgamesh and Enkidu. The selection begins with Gilgamesh and Enkidu trekking to the mountain where Humbaba lives. As they sleep, Gilgamesh and Enkidu have dreams that foreshadow the coming battle. During a pitched battle with Humbaba, Gilgamesh gravely wounds Humbaba and begins to pity the suffering monster. Enkidu, however, realizes that Humbaba's suffering is a trick and finishes off the monster.

BEFORE READING

Make the Connection

Ask students what they know about epics and myths. What epics or myths have they heard about [possibly *The Iliad* or *The Odyssey*]? Can they think of any television shows, movies, or modern books that have elements of epics and myths [*Star Trek, Star Wars, Indiana Jones and the Raiders of the Lost Ark, Hercules*]?

Build Background

▪ **More About the Topic**

The real Gilgamesh ruled a city-state called Uruk. The mythological Gilgamesh, part human, part god, was a great warrior and leader who knew everything there was to know on earth. However, he was a harsh king. The god Anu, hoping to temper Gilgamesh's rule, created Enkidu. Gilgamesh defeated Enkidu in battle, after which Enkidu became Gilgamesh's friend. Together, they defeated the monster Humbaba, earning Gilgamesh a marriage proposal from the goddess Ishtar. When Gilgamesh declined, Ishtar sent a bull to destroy him. After helping Gilgamesh defeat the bull, Enkidu fell ill and died. Gilgamesh visited Utnapishtim, who had survived a great flood, and asked him the secret of escaping death. Utnapishtim gave Gilgamesh a plant that restored youth, but it was stolen by a snake. The epic ends with Enkidu's spirit visiting Gilgamesh and telling him about the underworld.

▪ **Building Prerequisite Skills**

Establishing Chronological Order Lead students in a brief discussion of the various steps they could take to prepare for a test. Write the most common activities that students suggest on the chalkboard. Then, ask students which of these activities usually occurs first, which occurs second, which occurs third, and so forth. As you lead students through this process, write the appropriate number next to the item on the chalkboard.

Vocabulary Development

The following words are underscored and defined in the student text.

paralyzed: unable to move or feel.

flail: to move or beat wildly about.

poised: balanced.

ignited: caught fire.

reverberated: echoed back or resounded.

Before assigning the reading, you may want to introduce students to any words that could cause pronunciation or definition problems.

CONTENT-AREA VOCABULARY

Although the following words are important to an understanding of the text selection, some of them may be unfamiliar to students. Present these words to students. Encourage students to discuss other meanings they know for these words. [Students may notice that the words all relate to things that grow or have grown.]

meal*: a coarsely ground grain.
timbers: trees.
ancient: very old.
boughs: limbs of trees.
masts: poles that hold up the sails on ships.

*Although students may be familiar with other meanings of this word, the word as used in the selection has a specific meaning that pertains to the content area.

Reading Informational Materials

Reading Skill
Identifying Text Structure: Chronological Order
Explain to students that *chronological order* refers to the order that events occur in over time.

Reading Strategy
Using Graphic Organizers (Strategy 3)
To help students identify chronological order in the selection, use Strategy 3 in the Content-Area Reading Strategies. Have students use the Sequence or Chronological Order Chart (Graphic Organizer 10) to help organize their thoughts and identify the sequence of events in the story.

▶ **Teaching Tip**
Identifying Chronological Order Students can sometimes get bogged down in details when trying to identify chronological order, which can result in a graphic organizer that goes on for pages. Tell your students that before writing an event in their Sequence/Chronological Order organizer, they should ask themselves if the event is an important step toward the outcome of the selection.

DURING READING

Using the Side-Margin Feature
■ A Gutsy Monster
Ask students what the monsters they see in popular entertainment have in common with Humbaba. Students might mention that most monsters are quite ugly and interested in little except murder and mayhem. What purpose do they think monsters serve in storytelling? [Their power creates suspense.] Why are monsters often depicted as repulsive? [The more despicable the monster, the more heroic its opponent appears.]

Differentiating Instruction
■ Advanced Students
Skilled readers are not likely to have difficulty identifying the sequence of events, especially in a selection that is strictly chronological. To make this assignment more challenging, have advanced readers team up with less-skilled readers. The students can take turns identifying the next event, or the advanced reader can ask questions to help guide the student having difficulty.

AFTER READING

✔ Reading Check

The following are sample answers to questions on student text page 62.

1. Gilgamesh pours meal upon the earth to gain the good will of the gods and to persuade them to reveal their purpose in his and Enkidu's dreams.

2. In the first dream, Gilgamesh sees the mountain collapse. Enkidu says it means that Humbaba is the mountain and will fall. In the second dream, Gilgamesh sees the mountain fall on him and he is rescued. He isn't sure if this means Enkidu or someone else will rescue him.

3. Humbaba's face is creased and grooved like rock. He probably represents a volcano.

4. Gilgamesh withdraws the sword because he feels pity for the monster. The danger is that now the monster can kill Gilgamesh.

Reteaching

Students who are still having problems identifying chronological order in the selection might benefit from focusing their attention on a single paragraph. Direct their attention to the first paragraph in the selection. Ask students to identify what happens in the first sentence of that paragraph [Gilgamesh and Enkidu walk toward a mountain]. Then have them enter that action in their Sequence/Chronological Order organizer. Then, guide them through the paragraph by having them repeat that process for each sentence. Tell students that they can do the same thing for the entire selection by identifying what happens in each paragraph rather than in each sentence. Breaking a longer selection into paragraph-sized chunks can help prevent students from feeling overwhelmed.

Connecting to Language Arts
▪ Writing
A Humorous Epic Like most epics, the story of Gilgamesh involves dangerous journeys, battles with monsters, soaring triumphs, and devastating tragedies. Have students think about an everyday occurrence in their lives, such as doing their homework or walking home from a friend's house. What could happen during these activities to make them worthy of an epic? Have students work independently or in groups to compose a humorous epic based on an everyday occurrence in their lives.

▪ Speaking and Listening
Gilgamesh on Broadway Lead a discussion of the selection, having students use their organizers to provide a chronology of the events. Then, have students divide the events into scenes. Once the class has established three or four scenes, divide the students into groups to create scenes for a short play. Each group can then present its scene for the class.

Connecting Across the Curriculum: Art/Music
Drawing on History Have students research the clothing, weaponry, architecture, and art of the ancient Babylonians. How did they dress? What kinds of weapons did they use? What did their homes look like? After students have completed their research, they can present the results of their investigations individually or in groups. They might choose one of the following projects:
- draw a comic book based on the selection
- design costumes for an epic movie about Gilgamesh
- draw a cover for a book about the myth of Gilgamesh
- design a stamp commemorating the defeat of Humbaba
- write the lyrics for a song celebrating Gilgamesh's victory

Further Resources
Online Resources
Washington State University has a Web site with information on Gilgamesh as well as the story.

> ## Assessment
>
> Turn to page 133 for a multiple-choice test on the selection.
>
> *Test Answers*
> 1. d   2. a   3. b   4. a   5. c
> 6. b   7. c   8. a   9. c   10. d

from Education: The Sumerian School

from *The Sumerians: Their History, Culture, and Character*
by SAMUEL NOAH KRAMER
(student text page 63)

Reading Level: Average

Text Summary

This excerpt from *The Sumerians: Their History, Culture, and Character* was translated from Sumerian tablet and recounts a conversation between a Sumerian father and his son. The exchange begins with the father asking his son where he spends his time. The father warns his son that he will not be successful if he wastes time hanging out in the public square and urges him instead to go to school, "seek out the first generations," and "inquire of them."

BEFORE READING

Make the Connection

Ask students to recall conversations with their parents or guardians about the importance of attending school. What reasons did their parents or guardians present while having this conversation? How did students feel? What was their response to this advice?

Build Background

■ Building Prerequisite Skills

To help students understand the value of previewing, tell them to think about the last time they were browsing for movies at their local video store. What drew their attention to a particular video? The title? The illustration on the front of the video case? The blurb on the back? The names of the stars or director? All of these bits of information provide a preview of what the video is about. In the same way, previewing text can help the reader get the most out of a selection.

Vocabulary Development

The following words are underscored and defined in the student text.

recite: to answer questions orally or to read aloud publicly.

monitor: a student appointed to assist a teacher; a person who warns or instructs.

Before assigning the reading, you may want to introduce students to any words that could cause pronunciation or definition problems.

┌─ *Vocabulary Tip* ─────────────

Using Prefixes The word *recite* uses the Latin root *citare*, meaning "rouse" or "set in motion." This is the same root that gives us the word *cite*, meaning "to quote as proof or as an example." By adding the prefix *re–*, meaning "again," to the word *cite*, we get *recite*, meaning "to quote again." Knowing this prefix can help students guess the meaning of such words as *recite*, *repeat*, and *readjust*.

└──────────────────────────────────

CONTENT-AREA VOCABULARY

Although the following words are important to an understanding of the text selection, some of them may be unfamiliar to students. Present these words to students. Encourage students to discuss other meanings they know for *tablet*.

tablet*: a slab of clay on which ancient Sumerians wrote cuneiform.
inquire: ask.

*Although students may be familiar with other meanings of this word, the word as used in the selection has a specific meaning that pertains to the content area.

Reading Skill

Finding the Main Idea

Explain to students that the main idea is the most important point, or central message, in a piece of writing.

▶ **Teaching Tip**

Previewing Students may have trouble understanding how previewing titles, photos, and vocabulary can help them identify the main idea. Tell students that since editors use the main idea to select titles and photos, paying close attention to these clues can lead to important conclusions about the main idea of the selection.

Reading Strategy

Previewing Text (Strategy 1)

To help students find the main idea of the selection, use Strategy 1 in the Content-Area Reading Strategies. You may find it helpful to provide students with a PACA (Graphic Organizer 8) to help them organize their thoughts on the main idea as they move through the reading process.

DURING READING

Differentiating Instruction

▪ Learners Having Difficulty

In this dialogue between a father and a son, the reader must use context clues to figure out which of the two is speaking. If your students are having difficulty identifying the speaker, you may want to have the selection read aloud in class. One student could read the father's comments and a second student could read the words spoken by the son.

AFTER READING

✓ Reading Check

The following are sample answers to questions on student text page 64.

1. The father instructs the son to go to school, recite his assignment, and write on his tablet.

2. The father tells the son that he must go to school to learn what the generations before him learned.

Reteaching

If students are still struggling with the concept of main idea, consider approaching the problem from the opposite direction. Write a statement of the main idea in the center of a Cluster Diagram (Graphic Organizer 3). [For example: **Main Idea:** The father believes that attending school will ensure success.] Distribute copies and have students reread the selection. Whenever they find a statement that supports the father's main argument, they should pause and fill in the next level of the cluster diagram. [The father urges his son to go to school; the father is concerned about his son's "idle" ways; the father encourages his son to curry favor with his monitor; the father tells the son that school will be a benefit.] Discuss with students how the main idea of a piece of writing is usually backed up by supporting statements throughout the reading.

Reading Informational Materials

▶ **Teaching Tip**

Discovering Main Idea When using a prereading strategy to guess the main idea of a selection, it is crucial that students revisit their predictions and determine whether they were correct. The key benefit of predicting the main idea *before* reading is that it helps ensure that students will be on the lookout for the main idea *while* reading.

Connecting to Language Arts

▪ Writing

Dear Diary The surviving portion of the cuneiform tablet containing this father-son discussion does not indicate how the son felt about what his father said. Ask students to put themselves in the son's place and consider the thoughts he may have had during this discussion. Then, have students write a diary entry from the son's point of view.

▪ Speaking and Listening

School for Girls With very few exceptions, Sumerian schools were for boys only. Have students prepare a speech urging that all girls be allowed to attend Sumerian schools. How would educating girls benefit not only the girls, but society as a whole? Should Sumerian boys and girls go to the same school, or should they attend separate schools? Students may then deliver their speeches to the class and the class can evaluate their effectiveness.

Connecting Across the Curriculum: Education

School, Sweet School Have students research the Sumerian educational system. What subjects were important? Who were the teachers? What was the school building like? How were students treated? How does the Sumerian educational system compare with that of schools today? After students complete their research, they can work together or independently to present the results. Students may choose one of the following activities:

- write an editorial arguing for or against change in the Sumerian educational system
- write and design a brochure touting the school system to the parents of prospective students
- draw a mural for a Sumerian school administration building depicting the important aspects of the educational system
- design a magazine cover for a special report on Sumerian education
- create a diorama depicting a typical day in a Sumerian classroom

Further Resources

Online Resources

The Social Studies School Service has information on teacher background materials on Sumer.

Assessment

Turn to page 134 for a multiple-choice test on the selection.

Test Answers

1. a **2.** b **3.** d **4.** c **5.** b

Rubrics for *Cross-Curricular Activities* (*student text page 65*)

The following criteria can help you evaluate each student's success in completing the activities prompted by the Cross-Curricular Activities feature in the student textbook.

Language Arts/Art
Heroes and Villains
(Since this activity may require the involvement of more than one student, you may wish to evaluate each student on his or her specific and individual contribution to the piece and then give the partners an overall rating.)

- The student creates a list of real-life villains or villainous characters in books, movies, or video games.
- The student uses the list to create a Venn diagram to show similarities or differences between today's villains and the monster Humbaba.
- The student writes in order to compare and contrast today's villain with Humbaba. The student may include illustrations of both villains.
- The student's writing clearly reveals how the villains are alike or different from one another.

Science/History
Who's on First?
- The student re-reads the selection.
- The student conducts research in order to date when significant scientific and mathematical discoveries were likely made by ancient Babylonians.
- The student creates a time line to reveal the results of the research.
- The student may also research when these significant Babylonian discoveries were made or adopted in ancient Greece, Egypt, China, India, or Europe.
- The time line clearly shows when important discoveries were made. If more than one civilization is included on time line, each civilization's dates are color-coded for readability.

History/Drama
Listen Up!
(Since this activity may require the involvement of more than one student, you may wish to evaluate each student on his or her specific and individual contribution to the activity and then give the partners an overall rating.)

- The student reviews what each knows about ancient Mesopotamian society.
- The students role-play the parts of the father and son from *The Sumerians* excerpt, adding their own dialogue to create an original performance.

History/Art
Coming Soon!
- The student sketches out ideas for a movie about King Hammurabi.
- The student chooses art and words to create a movie poster for the film, focusing on a key scene or character from the film.
- The student chooses words or phrases that convey the mood of the film and that create interest in the film.

Civilizations of the Nile
Ancient Egypt and Kush 5000 B.C.–500 B.C.

The Wonders of the Pyramids

from *Cricket*

by GERALDINE WOODS
(*student text page 69*)

CONTENT-AREA CONNECTIONS
SCIENCE ●
HISTORY ●

Reading Level: Advanced

Text Summary

"The Wonders of the Pyramids" explains how the pyramids of Egypt were constructed. Equipped with only a lever, an inclined plane, and a wedge, workers built some of the largest monuments for Egypt's pharaohs. Lacking today's construction machinery, the Egyptians were quite resourceful. They used water to level the area and quarried limestone and granite to build the enormous blocks. Architects incorporated secret burial chambers as well as false chambers to trick grave robbers.

BEFORE READING

Make the Connection

Ask students to name some of the largest human-made structures in the world. [The Great Pyramid, the Empire State Building, Stonehenge, the Eiffel Tower, and so on] Write their responses on the chalkboard. Then, ask which structures were built without modern machinery. [The Great Pyramid, Stonehenge] Ask students to provide theories on how the pyramids were built, and write their suggestions on the chalkboard. Then, ask them to think about why the pyramids were built.

Build Background

■ More About the Topic

In the late twentieth century, a team led by archaeologist Mark Lehner attempted to re-create the construction of a small pyramid at Gîza. As a

result, the team calculated that it would take from twenty to forty years for five thousand workers to replicate the Great Pyramid. This number includes workers in the local quarry, cutters, and builders. It does not include those workers in the granite quarries of Aswan. Now, hoping to find out about the daily lives and origins of the workers, Lehner is excavating the nearby bakeries.

┌ *Vocabulary Tip* ─

Looking at Word Parts Before you introduce the vocabulary words, remind students that they can determine the meaning of an unfamiliar word if they know the meaning of one of its parts. For example, *–or* is a suffix that often refers to a person who does what the base word specifies. A *surveyor* is one who surveys. Ask students to identify other suffixes that refer to a person by the role he or she undertakes. [*–er, –ist*] Then, have them list words that end in these suffixes: *–or, –er,* and *–ist*. [*actor, creator, teacher, painter, lawyer, pianist, machinist*]

Vocabulary Development

The following words are underscored and defined in the student text.

remains: ruins, especially of ancient times.

exposed: made visible or uncovered.

site: the place where something is located.

excavated: dug out; hollowed out.

surveyor: a person who takes measurements and applies mathematical principles to determine boundaries, areas, and elevations.

Before assigning the reading, you may want to introduce students to any words that could cause pronunciation or definition problems.

Although the following words are important to an understanding of the text selection, some of them may be unfamiliar to students. Present this list of words and the definitions to your students and have students brainstorm connections between the words. [Most of the words concern construction.] Ask students what denotations the words *pyramid, pharaoh,* and *work gang* have.

pyramid: a structure or shape with a square bottom and four triangular sides that meet at a common point.

structure: something that has been built.

pharaoh: a ruler or king in ancient Egypt.

chamber*: a room.

granite: a hard igneous rock, usually a pink or gray color.

work gang: a work crew or team.

chisel: a hand tool with a blade used to carve or cut wood or stone when struck by a hammer.

*Although students may be familiar with other meanings of this word, the word as used in the selection has a specific meaning that pertains to the content area.

Reading Informational Material

Reading Skill
Identifying Text Structure: Sequence
Point out to students that an article explaining how something is built will follow a sequential order. The author should explain the steps in order and describe what materials should be used in the process.

▶ **Teaching Tip**
Previewing the Selection Have students preview the selection to see if they can identify signal words that indicate order. Suggest that they mark these words or phrases with a self-adhesive note.

Reading Strategy
Activating and Using Prior Knowledge (Strategy 8)
To help students understand the main concept of this selection, use Strategy 8 described in Content-Area Reading Strategies. You may wish to provide students with a KWLS chart (Graphic Organizer 7)

to help them organize what they know about pyramids and to keep them thinking during the reading process.

DURING READING

Using the Side-Margin Feature
- Pyramid Security System
Lead students in a discussion about the ethics of tomb robbing. Students may think that entering a tomb or grave for any reason is unacceptable. Others may say that jewels and treasures should not be buried for eternity, but they will probably agree that stealing is wrong. Ask students whether they think valuables today should be buried with their owner. Why or why not?

▶ **Teaching Tip**
Topic Sentence Point out to students that a question can serve as a topic sentence for a paragraph. For example, the first paragraph on page 71 begins with a question. The answer is developed in the paragraph, which explains how Egyptians were able to work without modern instruments. Encourage students to use this technique occasionally in their own writing.

Differentiating Instruction
- English-Language Learners
Divide students into groups of three to skim through the selection with each student focusing on a specific aspect of the topic. One student will read to find out why the pyramids were built. The second student will find out what materials were used and how the stones were cut and transported. The third will read to learn about chambers and underground rooms. Have each group member summarize, in two to three sentences, his or her findings.

AFTER READING

✓ Reading Check

The following are sample answers to questions on student text page 74.

1. Archaeologists have discovered over eighty pyramids in Egypt. The oldest pyramid is about 5,500 years old.

2. The pyramids were built for kings and nobles. The wedge, the lever, and the inclined plane were used to build the pyramids.

3. The Egyptians knew that free-flowing water makes a level surface. The builders made interconnected trenches in the desert's rock floor and flooded them with water. Then they marked the water level in the trenches, drained them, and cut the surface of the rock down to the watermarks.

4. False tunnels and empty rooms were built to make things harder for tomb robbers. A pyramid contains a chamber for the pharaoh's coffin, a room for his treasures, and in some pyramids, a room for the pharaoh's wife.

5. Pyramids were built around a core of limestone. The interior chambers were made of granite. The granite was quarried about five hundred miles upriver.

Reteaching

If students are still struggling with the concept of sequence, help them create a flow chart titled "Building a Pyramid." Have them make two columns at the top, labeling them "Materials/Tools" and "Steps." Ask them to draw six boxes at the bottom of the flow chart. Have students work in pairs to list the materials and steps. [For example: "Materials: limestone, granite, and so on. Tools: lever, chisel, mallet, and so forth. Steps: Level area, cut stones, transport stones, smooth blocks, and so on."] Once students have listed the steps, have them number the steps in sequential order; then, fill in the flow chart. Tell students to add more boxes if necessary. Some may want to add boxes to develop their flow charts further, explaining each step. [Under "cut stones," students could add the following: "Draw marks on stone to outline block. Chip cracks into stone, and insert wooden wedge. Soak area with water."]

Connecting to Language Arts
- Writing

I've Been Working on the Pyramids All the Livelong Day Tell students to imagine they are involved in building the pyramids. Have students research a worker's life in ancient Egypt, and tell them they will use the information to write a letter to a friend or family member about their work experience. What do they do—dig trenches, cut stones, transport them? Are they designing booby traps inside? What do they like and dislike about their work? What do they miss about home?

Connecting Across the Curriculum: Social Sciences

Live Like an Egyptian Assign students to find out about the people of ancient Egypt. How did ordinary Egyptians live? What kinds of jobs were available? What were their homes like? What did they eat? What kind of clothing did they wear? Did children go to school? Then, have students find out about life in modern Egypt, using similar questions. After students have completed their research, have them focus on one aspect of daily life to develop a pictorial presentation about the two lifestyles. Students may draw the pictures or find them in acceptable sources. Students can put their pictures in a single scrapbook to share with other classes.

Further Resources
Books
The Complete Pyramids: Solving the Ancient Mysteries by Mark Lehner

The Great Wonder: The Building of the Great Pyramid by Annabelle Howard and Stephen Wells

Online
PBS (Public Broadcasting Stations) includes a virtual tour of a pyramid on its Nova Online page. Look for "Pyramids: The Inside Story."

Assessment

Turn to page 135 for a multiple-choice test on the selection.

Test Answers
1. d 2. c 3. b 4. a 5. d
6. c 7. b 8. a 9. d 10. b

What Was Inside a Pyramid?

from *Who Built the Pyramids?*
by JANE CHISHOLM AND STRUAN REID
(*student text page 75*)

Reading Level: Easy

Text Summary

The highly pictorial selection "What Was Inside a Pyramid" shows the basic steps used to create a mummy. According to ancient Egyptian beliefs, preserving the body was necessary for a person to continue living in the afterlife.

BEFORE READING

Make the Connection

Ask students what they know about burial customs in ancient Egypt. Most students will mention mummies. Allow them to discuss what they know about mummies, based on Hollywood movies and books they have read. How are mummies often portrayed in movies? How did these stereotypes get started? Do students know of another culture that mummified the dead? [Incan] Have students discuss other burial practices they may know about.

Build Background

▪ More About the Topic

The first Egyptian mummies were probably made by accident when the dry desert air and sand may have preserved some of the bodies placed in shallow graves. Later, the mummification process was done intentionally, preserving the pharaohs and other people of nobility. It took seventy days to make a mummy, a process that began with embalming. The brain was removed by pulling pieces through the nose with hooked instruments, often disfiguring the face. An incision on the left side of the abdomen was made to remove the lungs, liver, stomach, and intestines. These organs were preserved in canopic jars that were buried with the mummy. However, the Egyptians did not remove the heart, as they believed it was the core of one's essence and intelligence. Linen was used to wrap the body and to fill any cavities, such as the eye sockets. Fingers and toes were sometimes wrapped individually. While embalmers were busy at their tasks, craftsworkers and artists made and decorated coffins. When the mummy and the tomb and its contents were ready, the funeral began. Before the mummy was sealed in the coffin, a priest performed the most important ceremonial rite, called The Opening of the Mouth. The priest had to touch the mouth with religious instruments so that the mummy could eat and talk in the next world.

Vocabulary Tip

Using Definitions or Restatement Before you introduce the vocabulary words, remind students that they may be able to determine the meaning of an unfamiliar word if they look for a restatement or definition of the unknown word in the sentences that surround it. Have students look under the heading **"What is a mummy?"** to find the word *embalmed*. Ask students to find familiar words that restate or define what *embalmed* means. [*preserved, doesn't decay*] Then, have them find restatements in the selection for the rest of the content vocabulary words.

CONTENT-AREA VOCABULARY

Although the following words are important to an understanding of the text selection, some of them may be unfamiliar to students. Present this list of words and the definitions to your students, and have them brainstorm connections between the words. [All the words relate to the burial customs of the ancient Egyptians.]

canopic jar: an urn or vase used to hold the organs of the mummified dead. The lids of the jars usually had representations of human heads or the Four Sons of Horus, guardians of the internal organs.
natron: an especially absorbent kind of salt used to dry out the body for mummification.
amulets: charms or ornaments worn to keep away evil spirits.

sarcophagus: a limestone coffin, often with decorative drawings and carvings.

hieroglyphics: ancient writing that used pictures or symbols to represent letters, words, or sounds.

bitumen: natural asphalt, a tarlike material.

Have students work in small groups to find the etymologies of these words in a dictionary.

(Reading Informational Material)

Reading Skill
Identifying Text Structure: Sequence
Tell students that an article describing a process will follow a sequential order. The author will list the steps in the order in which they happen and will describe the materials used.

Reading Strategy
Visualizing Information (Strategy 5)
To help students visualize the mummification process, use Strategy 5 described in Content-Area Reading Strategies. Provide students with a Sequence or Chronological Order Chart (Graphic Organizer 10) to help them list the steps in the process as they read the selection.

DURING READING

(Reading Informational Material)

▶ Teaching Tip
Using Visuals Point out to students that pictures are included in a text to facilitate reading. Ask them to evaluate the graphics in this selection and tell you which ones are the most helpful. Have them explain their answers.

Differentiating Instruction
■ Advanced Learners
Working in pairs, ask advanced learners to select a process used in ancient Egypt, such as building a pyramid, sailing on the Nile, baking bread, riding a camel, or writing with hieroglyphs. Once they have researched the process, allow the pairs to choose the most practical method to illustrate the steps of the process. [drawings, posters, models and so on] Display the projects in the classroom.

AFTER READING

(✓ Reading Check)

The following are sample answers to questions on student text page 78.

1. A mummy is a body that is embalmed or preserved so that it does not decay. Egyptians mummified bodies so that the person could continue living in the next world.

2. The first step in making a mummy involves taking out the internal organs and placing them in canopic jars. Amulets, or lucky charms, were placed between the layers of bandages.

3. The Egyptians used a salt called natron to cover the body to dry it out.

4. The priest who said prayers for the mummy wore the mask of the god Anubis, the god of the dead.

Reteaching
If students are still struggling with the concept of sequence, have them identify words that tell them when and in what order things happened. [*first, then, next, finally*] Then, point out that each step is numbered 1–4. Use the Sequence or Chronological Order Chart (Graphic Organizer 10) made into a transparency for the overhead projector. Have students provide the four steps for you to write on the transparency. Tell students to begin each step with a verb. [1. Take out internal organs. 2. Dry out body with natron and so on.] Once students have listed the four basic steps, have them develop the steps further. [For example, under "Dry out body with natron," students could add the following: "Wait several days for body to dry. Stuff insides with linen, sawdust, natron, and herbs."]

Connecting to Language Arts
▪ Writing

Plan for Eternity Tell students that they work for an advertising agency and have been asked to design a Yellow Pages ad for a company that mummifies bodies. Have students look at the Yellow Pages before they create their own ads. Point out the persuasive language used in advertisements. Have students decide what makes their service desirable. Will they emphasize the lovely canopic jars or the decorative sarcophagus? Each students should create a name for the business and illustrate his or her ad.

▪ Speaking and Listening

Starring the Mummy Have students work in small groups to create and perform for the class a skit featuring a mummy. Each group member should have either an acting or a behind-the-scenes role in the production. Students need to set the scene by including some background, such as who the ruler was or if there was a warning over the tomb.

Connecting Across the Curriculum: Art

Making a Mummy Case Students will need the following materials to make their mummy case:
- a 24 oz. or 36 oz. empty shampoo bottle or water bottle
- a used or new tennis ball or newspaper and tape
- strips of newspaper
- glue
- paint

First, students will cut a hole in the tennis ball to put it on top of the bottle (as the head). If students do not have tennis balls, they can crumple newspaper together to form a ball and tape it securely on top of the bottle. Students will then papier-mâché (or mummify!) the plastic bottle and head. (If students have not had past experience making papier-mâché, they may want to ask an art teacher for pointers.) Once the projects are dry, students will spray paint all outer cases gold. When the spray paint is dry, students will hand paint their cases. Some may want to bring plastic beads or sequins for decorations. [Provide books of photos for students to use as models. Students could do some research on the different styles of painting.] Once students have finished decorating, have them find out how to spell their names in hieroglyphs and write their names on the bottom of the cases. If time allows, students can also decorate a shoe box as their sarcophagus. Have them begin by painting the shoe box all one color. When it is dry, they can begin decorating it. Exhibit the art in the classroom.

Further Resources
Books
- *Mummies Made in Egypt* by Aliki
- *Pharaohs and Pyramids* by Tony Allan and Philippa Wingate

PBS's Nova Online Adventure hosts the page "Mummies of the World." Check out Akhet Egyptology for a "clickable mummy." This Scottish site explores numerous pages with excellent photographs.

Assessment

Turn to page 136 for a multiple-choice test on the selection.

Test Answers
1. c **2.** a **3.** b **4.** d **5.** c

from The Finding of the Tomb

from *The Tomb of Tutankhamen*
by HOWARD CARTER AND A. C. MACE
(student text page 79)

Reading Level: Advanced

Special Considerations

This firsthand account describes the excitement archaeologist Howard Carter feels upon discovering King Tut's tomb. Disturbing a burial chamber and removing the coffin may seem unethical to some students. You might lead a discussion about why archaeologists think it is historically important to open these ancient tombs and place the contents in safekeeping.

Text Summary

"The Finding of the Tomb" excerpt provides the sights, sounds, and emotions that Howard Carter experienced as he discovered the treasures of King Tutankhamen's tomb. On November 26, 1922, Carter's excavating team finally found the entrance to a burial chamber filled with gold, artifacts, and King Tut's coffin.

BEFORE READING

Make the Connection

Ask students if they have heard the name King Tut. What do they know about him? Have they seen any of his treasures in a museum or on a television program? Are they familiar with Tut's famous death mask? Have students look at the photograph of King Tut's death mask on student text page 81. Tell them that this golden mask was placed over the head of King Tut's mummy. Tell students Tut was a boy-king who assumed power at about age nine. Ask students what they would do if they became their country's ruler at such a young age.

Build Background
■ More About the Style

Howard Carter relied on his journals to co-author the book from which the selection is excerpted. Diaries or journals are a form of private writing. In addition to writing about events, the writer expresses his or her thoughts and feelings. Diaries

are written from the first-person point of view, using the personal pronoun *I*. Thus, "The Finding of the Tomb" is subjective writing, revealing Carter's feelings about the discovery of the tomb.

⎡ *Vocabulary Tip* ⎤

Using Context Clues Before you introduce the vocabulary words, remind students that they should use context clues in a sentence to determine the meaning of an unfamiliar word. For example, the sentence with the vocabulary word *replica* contains context clues, such as *second doorway, exact,* and *first*. Using those clues, students can determine that *replica* must mean "something that looks similar to or exactly the same as the original." What context clues can they use in the sentence with the vocabulary word *encumbered*? [*slowly, debris removed, at last, door clear*]

Vocabulary Development

The following words are underscored and defined in the student text.

plundering: robbing or looting.

replica: an exact or close copy.

vicinity: a surrounding area.

encumbered: blocked or obstructed.

verdict: a decision or judgment.

Before assigning the reading, you may want to introduce students to any words that could cause pronunciation or definition problems.

CONTENT-AREA VOCABULARY

Although the following words are important to an understanding of the text selection, some of them may be unfamiliar to students.

rubble: broken rocks and remains from buildings.

seals*: the marks, stamps, or official designs of someone important.

decisive: crucial or critical; determining.

precaution: a test carried out in anticipation of danger.

*Although students may be familiar with other mean-
ings of this word, the word as used in the selection has
a specific meaning that pertains to the content area.

Reading Informational Material

Reading Skill
Identifying Text Structure: Description

Explain to students that when writers want to
express themselves in a journal or diary, they focus
on their own experiences and thoughts. The
writer's use of sensory details may record his or her
first reactions and can make the reader feel a part
of the experience.

▶ Teaching Tip
Formal Style It is important to emphasize to students that this selection was written during the
1920s, a period when many people spoke formally
and conservatively. To modern readers this formality
may seem stilted or pompous and the vocabulary
unfamiliar.

Reading Strategy
Constructing Concept Maps (Strategy 4)

To help students understand the importance of
Carter's discovery and to identify sensory details,
use Strategy 4 described in Content-Area Reading
Strategies. Have each student make a Concept
Map, or offer students a Cluster Diagram (Graphic
Organizer 3) to help them organize sensory details
for what Carter saw, smelled, heard, and touched.

DURING READING

Using the Side-Margin Feature
- The Mummy's Curse

Ask students what they know about mummy
curses from some of the movies they have seen.
Then, share with students some interesting facts
about King Tut's "curse": Within seven years after
the tomb was opened, eleven people who were
involved with this discovery had died prematurely.
Lord Carnarvon and two of his relatives were

among those who died. Of the more than twenty
people who actually opened the tomb, six had died
by 1934. If the curse were real, one would expect
that Howard Carter, who discovered the tomb, and
Dr. D. E. Derry, the man who performed the
autopsy on Tut's mummy, would surely have been
cursed. Carter, however, died of natural causes
almost seventeen years after his discovery; Dr.
Derry died in 1969.

▶ Teaching Tip
Suspense Point out to students that finding King
Tut's tomb is important to the narrator. He is constantly encountering obstacles digging through the
debris and getting through the sealed doorways. By
conveying his own excitement and describing how
he gained access into the tomb, Carter creates
suspense, even though most readers know the
outcome.

Viewing the Art
- Art from the Tomb

Egyptian tomb art depicted scenes from every part
of the deceased's life—with one difference. The
world and people in it were shown as perfect. Life
in the next world, the ancient Egyptians believed,
was constructed from the images on the tomb's
walls. Naturally, imperfections were left out for the
future comfort of the deceased.

Differentiating Instruction
- Learners Having Difficulty

It may help students having difficulty with this
selection to write a journal entry about an event or
moment of excitement in their own life. Cue them
to include sensory details that make the reader feel
the writer's excitement, to build suspense by showing the difficult aspects of the event, and to
describe their own thoughts and reactions at the
time.

AFTER READING

✔ Reading Check

The following are sample answers to questions on student text page 81.

1. Evidence of plundering included broken vases, pottery, and other items from lower levels. In addition, water skins that were used in plastering the doors were signs of opening and reclosing of the plaster seals.

2. A cache contains artifacts only, whereas a tomb contains the body and many items for the person to use in the afterlife. Carter thought it was a cache because the arrangement of the stairs and the entrance was very similar to those of another cache nearby.

3. Archaeological work is slow because the delicate objects that are found in the rubble must be removed carefully.

4. At first, Carter sees nothing as his eyes adjust. Then, he sees "strange animals, statues, and gold." Carter's answer to Lord Carnarvon's question was, "Yes, wonderful things."

Reteaching

If students are still struggling with the concept of description, help them create a Cloze Concept Map. Write "King Tut's Tomb" in the center. Get students started by filling in the next level of boxes with sensory details, action details, and dialogue. Have students add appropriate examples. [**Sensory details:** broken jars, painted pottery, signs of opening on the plaster, trembling hands, darkness, foul gases, hot air escaping, candle flicker, mist, strange animals, glint of gold. **Action details:** cleared passage, found seal impressions, removed debris, opened second doorway, applied candle test. **Dialogue:** "Yes, wonderful things."] Allow students to work in small groups to complete their organizers. Tell students they can add more boxes if necessary as some students may want to develop their organizers more fully.

Connecting to Language Arts
- Writing

Alas, Poor Tut Have students research the life of Tutankhamen. Who were his parents? Why did he become a pharaoh at such a young age? Whom did he marry? What did he accomplish during his reign? How did he die? After students have completed their research, have them write an obituary for King Tutankhamen. Students may want to draw his death mask to accompany their article.

Connecting Across the Curriculum: Social Sciences

Valley of the Kings Assign students to find out about the role of pharaohs in ancient Egypt. What type of government did Egypt have? How much power did the pharaohs have over their people? Were they cruel or benevolent rulers? Who were some of the most influential pharaohs? Why is King Tutankhamen so famous? After students have completed their research, they may work alone or in small groups to create one of the following:

- a time line listing some of the well-known pharaohs and their accomplishments
- a "help-wanted" ad describing the job of a pharaoh and including such information as working hours, skills, workplace, benefits, and so on.
- a series of comic strips depicting major accomplishments of three pharaohs

Further Resources
Books
- *Tutankhamen's Gift* by Robert Sabuda
- *The Curse of King Tut (The Mystery Library)* by Patricia D. Netzley
- *Pharaohs of Ancient Egypt* by Elizabeth Payne, J. Thomas

Assessment

Turn to page 137 for a multiple-choice test on the selection.

Test Answers
1. c 2. b 3. a 4. d 5. a
6. d 7. c 8. b 9. a 10. d

Multitudes of Gods

from *The Ancient Egyptians*
by ELSA MARSTON
(student text page 82)

Reading Level: Average

Text Summary

"Multitudes of Gods" provides a brief look at some of the deities of ancient Egypt and includes some of their names, characteristics, and roles. The excerpt explains the importance of the Nile and its relationship to the many deities. In an attempt to keep the gods and goddesses happy, priests cared for the deities daily, people honored the deities in their festivals, and families made personal shrines.

BEFORE READING

Make the Connection

Write the word *Egypt* on the chalkboard or on an overhead transparency. Have students brainstorm a list of words they associate with the word *Egypt*. [Students will probably say *pyramids, mummies,* or *camels.*] Then, ask students if they know anything about Egyptian mythology. Some may refer to the half-human/half-animal drawings found in Egyptian art. Have students name some of the natural forces over which a god or goddess may have dominion. [sun, moon, earth, wind, water, fire, life, and death] Ask students to consider why certain cultures have many different gods and goddesses.

Build Background

■ More About the Topic

Life for the ancient Egyptians was intertwined with the forces of nature. People depended on the Nile to flood annually, providing water for their crops and maintaining life in the desert. Daily routines were marked by the rising and setting sun, which Egyptians believed the gods controlled. Like other early cultures, the Egyptians used myths to explain the world around them. However, the gods were not the only revered entities. When Ra became a king on earth, his action initiated the idea that the pharaoh was both ruler and god, hence the commitment to build large tombs for the pharaoh's voyage in the afterlife.

Vocabulary Development

The following words are underscored and defined in the student text.

deities: gods or goddesses.
dynasties: periods during which a certain family rules.
contradictory: opposing or opposite.
chaos: confusion and disorder.
famine: a great shortage of food that can occur over a large area for a long time.

Before assigning the reading, you may want to introduce students to any words that could cause pronunciation or definition problems.

┌─ *Vocabulary Tip* ─

Using Synonyms Remind students that many words have synonyms, words with a similar meaning. Yet, the words will have subtle differences between them. For example, possible synonyms for *famine* are *hunger* and *starvation. Hunger* refers to a strong desire, usually for food. *Famine* refers to a drastic and wide-ranging shortage of food. *Starvation* soon follows famine, as people suffer and die from a lack of food. Which of these three words refers to the mildest condition? [hunger]

(**CONTENT-AREA VOCABULARY**)

Although the following words are important to an understanding of the text selection, some of them may be unfamiliar to students. Present this list of words and the definitions to students. Have students brainstorm the connection between the words. [All of them can be used to describe. Although the words could be depicted symbolically or in a general way, one cannot draw a picture of any one of them that would be immediately understood.]

cosmic: having to do with the universe.
abstract*: having a theoretical quality; not existing in the real world.
symbolizing: one thing representing another thing.

contented: happy; satisfied.

*Although students may be familiar with other meanings of this word, the word as used in the selection has a specific meaning that pertains to the content area.

Reading Informational Material

Reading Skill
Listing Supporting Details
Explain to students that listing supporting details is one way to organize main points in expository writing. Students could use a concept map to show the descriptive qualities of listing.

▶ **Teaching Tip**
Speculating This selection is an excerpt from a book. Remind students that a book will elaborate on general ideas, providing more specific information than a short article. Ask students what information that is excluded here might appear in another part of the book. [other aspects of life for ancient Egyptians]

Reading Strategy
Constructing Concept Maps (Strategy 4)
To help students find the most important points of the text, use Strategy 4 described in Content-Area Reading Strategies. Have students draw a concept map, or provide them with a Cluster Diagram (Graphic Organizer 3) to help them organize the ideas listed in the selection.

DURING READING

Using the Side-Margin Feature
- Keep an Eye Out

Ask students to brainstorm a list of other symbolic animals, objects, or colors with which they are familiar. Students might mention that a dove and an olive branch are symbols of peace; a lion is often associated with royalty; water may represent purity or cleansing; and black can symbolize death or mystery.

▶ **Teaching Tip**
Supporting Details Point out to students that examples described in a paragraph must support the topic sentence. Have students find signal words on student text page 83 for the second and third paragraphs. [Paragraph 2: *For instance,* Paragraph 3:

for example] Have students discuss the examples provided and explain how they support the paragraphs' topic sentences.

Differentiating Instruction
- Advanced Learners

Now that they have been introduced to the Egyptian deities, have students extend their knowledge about deities from other cultures. Before students begin their new research, have them list the various qualities, powers, and responsibilities of specific Egyptian deities. Then, have each participating student choose a specific culture, such as Greek, Roman, Babylonian, and so forth, and research that culture's deities. Ask students to work together to compile a series of graphics to compare the similarities and differences among the major deities from each culture. Students may want to use a series of Venn diagrams, concept maps, or column charts. Students may wish to decorate the organizers with symbols associated with specific deities and display the charts in the classroom.

AFTER READING

✔ Reading Check

The following are sample answers to questions on student text page 85.

1. Ra, the sun god, was the most important god because the sun was seen as the source of all life.

2. Osiris was green or black, symbolizing the fertility of the soil.

3. Anubis, the protector of the dead, was shown with the head of a jackal probably because jackals were often seen around graveyards. Horus, the sky god, had the head of a falcon probably because many falcons were seen in the sky.

4. The Egyptians depended on the Nile's floods to grow their food, but sometimes the floods didn't come. Other times, the floods were destructive. Because of this uncertainty, people felt the need to make sure the gods were happy.

5. The gods had homes and families. Their statues were also cared for like humans, going through daily routines such as getting up, bathing, dressing, and eating.

Reteaching

If students are still struggling with the concept of listing, have them create a four-column organizer to list details about the deities. Have them put the names of the Egyptian gods and goddesses in the first column and write in the second column what the deity symbolized. In the third column, students should write what the deity looked like if description is provided in the text. The last column is reserved for students to create a drawing of the god or goddess. Allow students to work with a partner as they create their charts.

Connecting to Language Arts

- Writing

Book of Deities and Poems Have each student choose one of the gods or goddesses and research his or her story, or mythology. Students will create a drawing of their chosen deity and write his or her autobiography using the first-person point of view. For example, a student who chooses Ra might write "I am Ra, god of the sun. I create life and all living creatures," and so on. Once students have completed their work, make it into a booklet for the classroom or the school library.

Connecting Across the Curriculum: Geography

River of Life Assign students to learn about the role of the Nile River, in both ancient Egypt and today. The world's longest river, the Nile is the lifeline to the Egyptians. Have students research the river's source. Why does it flood annually? Has it been dammed? If so, where and when? What were the consequences of damming the river? What kinds of ships navigate the Nile, in both ancient times and now? What role does the river play in Egypt's religion? After students have completed their research, they may work with a partner or independently to create one of the following:

- a time line in the shape of a river, with descriptions or images of some important events associated with it

- a Venn diagram that compares and contrasts the importance of the Nile in ancient times with its role in modern times
- a poem that expresses the importance of the Nile
- a collage of images from ancient and modern Egypt river transportation
- models of ancient Egyptian ships

Further Resources
Books

- *Gods and Pharaohs from Egyptian Mythology* (The World Mythology Series) by Geraldine Harris
- *A Dictionary of Egyptian Gods and Goddesses* by George Hart
- *Egyptian Gods: Color & Story Album* (Troubador Color and Story Albums) by Kim Ostrow and Jenny Williams

Museums

The Web site maintained by the Carnegie Museum of Natural History features the Online Exhibit "Life in Ancient Egypt." The exhibit consists of six units including "Daily Life" and "Gods and Religion."

Assessment

Turn to page 138 for a multiple-choice test on the selection.

Test Answers
1. b 2. c 3. d 4. a 5. b
6. a 7. d 8. b 9. c 10. a

The Other Half of History: Women in Ancient Egypt

by FIONA MACDONALD
(student text page 86)

Reading Level: Average

Text Summary

Although women in ancient Egypt were forbidden to become divine rulers, many royal women found themselves in positions of power. "Three Famous Women Rulers" examines the situations that allowed Hatshepsut, Nefertiti, and Cleopatra to become influential rulers of Egypt.

BEFORE READING

Make the Connection

Ask students to brainstorm what they know about women in politics. What qualities would they expect to find in a ruler? Who are some famous women rulers—past or present? [Margaret Thatcher, Golda Meir, Indira Gandhi, Queen Elizabeth II, Mary McAleese] What particular contributions have they made? What do you think made these women successful?

Build Background

▪ More About the Style

A biography is the story of a person's life written by another person. Before writing a biography, the author must conduct extensive research by interviewing people and reading firsthand accounts, such as letters, journals, or historical documents. Most biographers include only factual information. Others will add details that are probable but not documented. When researching people who lived so long ago, the writer may find information sketchy. Biographers must then rely on historical data and the opinions of scholars. Point out to students that in the selection, the word *probably* occurs three times. Students may want to look for more signs of conjecture in the piece.

Vocabulary Development

The following words are underscored and defined in the student text.

exercising: using; putting into play.

regent: a person who rules when the ruler is too young, too sick, or otherwise unable to rule.

expeditions: groups of people making journeys with a definite purpose.

supervised: oversaw or managed others' work.

prosperity: success; good fortune.

Before assigning the reading, you may want to introduce students to any words that could cause pronunciation or definition problems.

┌─ *Vocabulary Tip* ─────────────

Using Word Origins Before you introduce the vocabulary words, remind students that knowing some roots will help them expand their vocabulary quickly. For example, the root for *regent* is *rêg*– from which *rex*, meaning "king or monarch," derives. The verb *regere* means "to rule." From these roots, we get the English words *regal*, *regalia*, *region*, *regiment*, and *regicide*. Have students write an approximate definition for these words, and then use a dictionary to confirm the meanings.

└────────────────────────────

⸨ **CONTENT-AREA VOCABULARY** ⸩

Although the following words are important to an understanding of the text selection, some of them may be unfamiliar to students. Present this list of words and the definitions to students, and have students look up the alternative meaning of the word *divine*. How are the two meanings related? [Both meanings suggest something special.]

divine*: godlike or spiritual.
pharaoh: king of ancient Egypt.
society: group of people who share common traits; a community.
scribes: people hired to write documents.

*Although students may be familiar with other meanings of this word, the word as used in the selection has a specific meaning that pertains to the content area.

Reading Skill

Using Text Features

Explain to students that when they read informational writing, they should preview the graphic aids beforehand. By skimming the pages and looking at illustrations, subheads, vocabulary, and footnotes, they can formulate an idea of what the text is about.

▶ **Teaching Tip**

Previewing Text Have students skim the selection and read the subheads. Have them formulate some questions about the selection from the subheads. As they read, ask them to be aware of the main ideas and supporting details the writer presents.

Reading Strategy

Previewing Text (Strategy 1)

You may wish to use Strategy 1 described in Content-Area Reading Strategies to help students set a purpose for reading. Provide students with a KWLS (Graphic Organizer 7) to help them organize their thoughts on the main idea as they move through the reading process.

DURING READING

Reading Informational Material

▶ **Teaching Tip**

Analyzing Subheads Point out to students that the selection is divided into sections. Ask students to summarize the main idea of each section after they read. Which subheads apply to Hatshepsut? [Keeping control, Successful ruler] to Nefertiti? [Power and influence] to Cleopatra? [Defeat and death] To what do the other heads refer? [the roles of Egyptian women] How do the sections help students understand the main idea? Is it easier to read a selection that has heads and subheads?

Viewing the Art

The Bust of Nefertiti

Only the head and shoulders, and sometimes the upper chest, are the subject of a bust, a portrait sculpture. This bust of Nefertiti has come to symbolize Egypt and is often reproduced in advertising, jewelry, and clothing. The original statue is housed in the Egyptian Museum and Papyrus Collection in Berlin, Germany. It was found during the excavation of a sculptor's studio in Amarna, the city built by Nefertiti's husband, Akhenaten. Because the worship Akhenaten promoted fell into deep disfavor, this unfinished painted bust was left behind when the city was abandoned. She wears an unusual crown not seen in portraits of other Egyptian queens.

Differentiating Instruction

▪ **Learners Having Difficulty**

To help students summarize the main idea for each section, have them create *5W-How?* charts—one for each of the women mentioned and one for women in general. Have students work in pairs to complete their charts.

AFTER READING

✔ Reading Check

The following are sample answers to questions on student text page 90.

1. Hatshepsut was often portrayed as a man conducting religious ceremonies and was referred to as a king.

2. Hatshepsut's army won many battles; she conducted successful trading expeditions.

3. Nefertiti is shown wearing a special crown; she stands at the pharaoh's side as an equal; she is shown fighting foreign enemies.

4. Mark Antony gave Cleopatra the right to rule Egypt on behalf of Rome. Mark Antony's enemies in Rome disapproved and declared war. Antony and Cleopatra committed suicide rather than be captured by Roman soldiers.

5. Priestesses took care of the goddesses' statues, made offerings, and supervised temple servants and estates. Women sang, danced, and played instruments in temple ceremonies.

Reteaching

If students are still struggling with the concept of text features, have a general discussion about the women featured in the selection. Using a transparency of a Cloze Concept Map, write *Women Rulers* at the top. Supply students with the name of one of the three women, and have them write the names of the other two women [Hatshepsut, Nefertiti, and Cleopatra] in the next level. Ask students why Hatshepsut was mentioned first. [She lived 1473–1458 B.C., so she lived before the others.] Then, have students fill in the next level, using the subheads as a starting point. For example, under *Hatshepsut*, students will write *Keeping Control*. Students should add details, such as "regent for young brother," "had herself crowned pharaoh," and "co-ruled with brother."

Connecting to Language Arts

- Writing

Historical Interview Tell students that they are going to have a chance to be part of the past by role-playing a famous person or by interviewing one. Have participating students act either as interviewers or as subjects. Allow the subjects to choose which of the three famous Egyptian women they would like to role-play and the interviewers to determine which woman they want to interview. Have each interviewer compile a list of questions to ask, and give the subjects appropriate lists for research purposes. Questions might include the following: Where were you born? Who were your parents? What person influenced your life most? What was the most important event or experience in your life? What accomplishments have changed your life or the lives of others? Subjects should thoroughly research the questions to be able to answer them for the interview. Once students are prepared, have them conduct the interviews, taking notes for a newspaper profile of the celebrity. Compile profiles on a student Web page or post them in the classroom.

Connecting Across the Curriculum: Social Sciences

Great Egyptian Queens Assign students to find out more about one of the women mentioned in the selection. What other information can they obtain about the woman's family? What important contributions did she make? Who were her enemies? What was her claim to fame? After students

have completed their research, they may work with a partner or independently to complete one of the following assignments:

- a family tree
- an illustration of the woman, complete with her name in hieroglyphs
- a poem that captures the ruler's accomplishments

Further Resources
Books

- *Hatshepsut, His Majesty, Herself* by Catherine M. Andronik
- *Queen Nefertiti* by the staff of Bellerophon Books
- *Cleopatra VII: Daughter of the Nile, Egypt, 57 B.C. (The Royal Diaries)* by Kristiana Gregory

Assessment

Turn to page 139 for a multiple-choice test on the selection.

Test Answers

1. d   2. c   3. a   4. a   5. b
6. c   7. b   8. a   9. b   10. d

from Kush–The Nubian Kingdom

from *Egypt, Kush, Aksum: Northeast Africa*
by KENNY MANN
(student text page 91)

Reading Level: Advanced

Text Summary

The excerpt from "Kush—The Nubian Kingdom" examines the ancient civilization of Nubia, or Kush, as it was once called. Kush's remote location has helped it to remain veiled in mystery. Even though the ancient Greeks and Romans had visited the region, Europeans knew very little about Nubia, perhaps largely because of racial bias. The Nubian civilization, which was once a rival of Egypt's, survived for a thousand years after Egypt ceased to play a major role in world advancement.

BEFORE READING

Make the Connection

Have students participate in a five-minute freewrite about an imaginary country hidden in Africa. What kinds of animals would they find there? What would the people be like? What treasures might be hidden there? As students read the selection, have them note any similarities to what they have written.

Build Background

■ More About the Topic

The area around the Aswan High Dam is not the only archaeological site that has provided important information about ancient Nubia. Recent digs, including an expedition to Jebel Barkal, have led to some amazing discoveries. Jebel Barkal, a mountain that resembles a crown adorned with a cobra, is believed to house a royal temple once used for crowning rulers. Here, archaeologists have found fascinating carved stones depicting stars in a blue sky and flying vultures. At a temple in Kerma, another team has uncovered amazing paintings that show an Egyptian influence, but mixed with a unique exotic element. Statues, pottery, and ceramic figurines predate Egyptian finds. Given these recent discoveries, archaeologists have formed a new opinion about ancient Nubia—it was a distinct and impressive civilization that developed independently from cultures in surrounding countries.

Vocabulary Development

The following words are underscored and defined in the student text.

inaccessible: not able to be accessed or known.
eminent: prominent; important.
bias: discrimination; prejudice.
gleaned: gathered.
dire: horrible, feared.

Before assigning the reading, you may want to introduce students to any words that could cause pronunciation or definition problems.

Vocabulary Tip

Using Prefixes Before you introduce the vocabulary words, remind students that knowing common prefixes is an easy way to learn new words. Knowing that the prefix *in–* means "not," one can guess at the meaning of the words *inaccessible* and *inexhaustible* in this selection. Encourage students to use their knowledge of prefixes and context clues to guess the meanings of unfamiliar words. They should verify meanings by looking up the words in a dictionary.

CONTENT-AREA VOCABULARY

Although the following words are important to an understanding of the text selection, some of them may be unfamiliar to students. Present this list of words and the definitions to your students, and discuss with students that words have different connotations. Have students label each word as positive, negative, or neutral.

inexhaustible: plentiful; abundant; never-ending.
exotic: unfamiliar or strange; fascinating.
extraordinary: amazing; uncommon.

accurate: precise; correct.
sophisticated: cultured; worldly.
wretched: miserable; disgusting.

Reading Informational Material

Reading Skill
Summarizing

Explain to students that summarizing is a way of retelling the most important events in a selection. Important details and events are included in a summary, but minor details are not.

▶ **Teaching Tip**
Organizing Information Have students fold a sheet of paper lengthwise. As they read, have them list important events on one side and important details on the other.

Reading Strategy
Constructing Concept Maps (Strategy 4)

To help students recognize the relationship between main points and supporting points, use Strategy 4 described in Content-Area Reading Strategies. Have students construct a concept map, or provide them with a Cluster Diagram (Graphic Organizer 3) to help them focus on and organize important points and supporting material from the text.

DURING READING

Reading Informational Material

▶ **Teaching Tip**
Transition Words Point out to students that knowing transition words can help them follow the organization of a selection. For example, the words *however* and *but* indicate a shift of topic to develop differences. *Also* and *like* show similarities. Have students find transition words in this selection and discuss what the words indicate.

Differentiating Instruction
▪ Advanced Learners

Students may be interested in putting the history of the ancient Nubians into a time context with which they are more familiar. Have students work in groups of four to create a time line of develop-

ments in the ancient world. Have each participant choose a major ancient culture, such as that of China, Greece, Babylon, or Egypt, and research the time of its primary contributions. Then students should research Kush or Nubia and add dates of achievements from that culture to the time line. Have students display their time lines in the classroom.

AFTER READING

✔ Reading Check

The following are sample answers to questions on student text page 94.

1. The construction of the Aswan High Dam led archaeologists to discover and preserve information about ancient Nubia. The author proposes that the low level of European interest in Nubia existed because the kingdom was far from Europe—its exact location uncertain—and it was a black African kingdom.

2. The ancient Greeks and Romans considered Nubia one of the greatest civilizations of the world. Herodotus described the Nubians as tall and handsome, living to be very old on a diet of meat and milk. Their temples were carved from a single stone, and their queen rode in a wheeled palace pulled by elephants.

3. Egyptians and other people sometimes ventured into Nubian lands to trade or to wage war. Some of the precious items from ancient Nubia included gold, ebony, ivory, cattle, ostrich feathers, panther skins, frankincense, and plant oils.

4. A letter from a Nubian queen to Alexander the Great offers evidence of an ancient racial bias.

Reteaching

If students are still struggling with the concept of summarizing, have them work in groups to discuss the selection. Students may use their reading notes to help them in their discussions. As recorder, one person will write down important ideas. All students in the group will help determine what the recorder should write. For each major event described in the selection, students should write a complete sentence. If there are two parts to the event, they may put both into one sentence, using such words and phrases as *then, after,* and *because.* When each group has finished, have the class create a summary together, based on their notes. First, allow groups to present their ideas by writing them on the chalkboard or on an overhead transparency. Then, eliminate repetitive information or minor details. Remind students that the final summary should be a short paragraph.

Connecting to Language Arts
- Writing

All Aboard the Time-Travel Express The selection describes what some travelers thought of ancient Nubia. Have students look at the travel section of Sunday newspapers, paying close attention to the articles and ads. Using details from the selection and additional research, have students write a travel brochure for a time-travel experience in ancient Nubia. They may add drawings or pictures to increase the appeal of the brochure.

Connecting Across the Curriculum: Social Sciences

The Kingdom of Kush Assign students to learn about Kush. Is there a difference between Kush and Nubia, or are they the same? When did the Kushites rule Egypt? Who were their rulers? What happened to their kingdom? Why is there confusion about the Kushite capital? After students have completed their research, they may work independently or with a partner to complete one of the following assignments:
- a map showing the boundaries of ancient Egypt, the kingdom of Kush and important Kushite cities
- a collage illustrating the unique treasures of Kush
- a model of Meroë, Kush's capital city, after 750 B.C.

- a time line showing the historical connections between Egypt and Nubia/Kush.
- a retelling of an important Nubian event through song, dance, story, or poem

Further Resources
Books

Nubian Kingdoms by Edna Russman
The Egypt Game by Zilpha K. Snyder

Assessment

Turn to page 140 for a multiple-choice test on the selection.

Test Answers
1. a 2. b 3. c 4. b 5. d
6. a 7. b 8. d 9. c 10. d

from Astronomy and Timekeeping

from *Science in Ancient Egypt*
by GERALDINE WOODS
(student text page 95)

Reading Level: Average

Text Summary

This selection provides an overview of how the ancient Egyptians measured time. As did other ancient cultures, Egyptians used natural occurrences to calculate months and years. Using the moon's cycle, they marked time in intervals of twenty-nine or thirty days, or months. Later, they discovered a more accurate way to reckon time—they used a solar calendar that was based on the constellations and the star Sirius, whose cycle is $365\frac{1}{4}$ days. This helped them predict the annual flooding of the Nile. Egyptian astronomers decided that a month would have three ten-day weeks and there would be twelve months, but that left them five days short of a year. The legend of Thoth states that the god won the extra days from the moon and gave them as holidays.

BEFORE READING

Make the Connection

Ask students to state reasons for needing to know the time. [to keep appointments, to know when it is time to go to school or soccer practice, to know when summer vacation is] Then, ask students if they know how the time system we use today developed. Who decided we would have twelve months in a year or seven days in a week? What is the basis for these calculations? Allow students to work with a partner and share their ideas with the class. Write students' ideas on the chalkboard.

Build Background

■ More About the Topic

Look up at the night sky, toward the constellation Canis Major, and you will see Sirius, the Dog Star, the brightest star in the sky. One reason Sirius is so bright is that it is a binary star, traveling with Sirius B, or "the Pup." Another reason Sirius is top dog is that it is only 8.6 light-years away. The Egyptians

called it Sothis and noted it for its heliacal rising (a celestial object making its first rise in the sky near sunrise). The heliacal rise of Sirius occurs in July and August, when temperatures and the Nile River both begin to rise. Hence, the Egyptian new year began in July. For the Romans, the heliacal rising of the Dog Star announced the scorching "dog days" of summer.

Vocabulary Development

The following words are underscored and defined in the student text.

fashioned: made or turned into.

constellations: groups of stars that have been given definite names.

reckoned: figured; calculated.

methodical: using a strict, orderly system or method.

prominent: easily seen; obvious.

Before assigning the reading, you may want to introduce students to any words that could cause pronunciation or definition problems.

> ## Vocabulary Tip
>
> **Using Multiple Meanings** Before you introduce the vocabulary words, remind students that words can have multiple meanings. *Fashion* has different meanings in different content areas. In this selection, it refers to something that is made or changed. For example, a person can *fashion* a tool from a piece of wood. In general usage, fashion means "the form or shape of something" or "the current style of clothing, speech, or conduct."

CONTENT-AREA VOCABULARY

Although the following words are important to an understanding of the text selection, some of them may be unfamiliar to students. Present this list of words and the definitions to students and have students brainstorm the connection between the words. [All the words can be used in a discussion of astronomy.] You may want to have students use a dictionary to find the meanings of the prefixes *astro–* [star] and *circum–* [surrounding].

astronomy: the study of the stars and planets.

cycles*: orbits; repeated periods of time required for a star or planet to complete a full revolution around another celestial body.

constellations: groups of stars that form an outline that is named after an animal, object, or mythological figure it resembles.

circumpolar: referring to a movement around the South or North Pole.

*Although students may be familiar with other meanings of this word, the word as used in the selection has a specific meaning that pertains to the content area.

Reading Informational Material

Reading Skill
Identifying Text Structure: Problem and Solution
Point out to students that some articles are written to explain a discovery. People often make a discovery when they are searching for a solution to a problem. In this article, students will learn about timekeeping. As students read, have them find the problem the Egyptians had. [how to predict when the Nile would flood] What solutions did they implement? [the lunar calendar, the solar calendar]

Reading Strategy
Building Background Information (Strategy 6)
To help students make predictions about how the ancient Egyptians solved the problem of timekeeping, use Strategy 6 described in Content-Area Reading Strategies. Provide students with a Problem-and-Solution Chart (Graphic Organizer 9) to help them organize their thoughts on the solutions as they move through the reading process.

DURING READING

▶ **Teaching Tip**
Using Topic Sentences to Preview Paragraphs
Point out to students that a topic sentence can provide key words or phrases that preview the paragraph. For example, on student text page 96, the last paragraph states that the heavenly bodies were divided into three categories. The paragraph then lists and explains each category—"the Unwearied," "the Imperishables," and "the Indestructibles." Ask students to name the three Egyptian seasons. [flooding of the Nile, planting season, and dry season] Encourage students to use this technique in their own writing.

Viewing the Art
Egyptian Water Clock
Called a clepsydra, this water clock was decorated in three sections, which corresponded to the three seasons of the Egyptian year. Water leaked out through a hole near the base of the bowl. As the water escaped, it revealed hour marks on the inside. While clepsydras were probably invented by the Babylonians, Egypt made use of them starting in about the 14th century B.C. Later, the shape of the clock was changed to a cylinder to produce a more constant flow of water and more precise hours. The Romans and Greeks, as well as some North American Indians and African peoples, used clepsydras to measure time.

Differentiating Instruction
▪ Learners Having Difficulty
This selection presents information in a chronological order. Have students work in small groups to plot the events on time lines, beginning with "all primitive people" and ending with the legend of Thoth. Students may wish to illustrate the important events on their time lines. Exhibit completed time lines in the classroom.

AFTER READING

✔ Reading Check

The following are sample answers to questions on student text page 98.

1. The Egyptians believed that Thoth gave them five extra days each year. The five days were created when Thoth played a dice game with the moon and won some of its light.

2. When the Egyptians used the moon's cycle to track time, the year was only 354 days long. Within a few years, the calendar did not match the season. To solve the problem, the Egyptians switched to a solar calendar.

3. The Egyptians were able to predict the flooding of the Nile. This was important because they needed to prepare for the flood—move their houses and livestock to higher ground and get the land ready for the crops.

4. Sirius's cycle is $365\frac{1}{4}$ days, the exact amount of time it takes the earth to revolve once around the sun. Therefore, the calendar followed the seasons correctly.

5. The Egyptians had three seasons—the flooding of the Nile, the planting season, and the dry season.

Reteaching

If students are still struggling with the concept of problem and solution, have them adapt a Problem and Solution Chart (Graphic Organizer 9). Write *General Problem: Creating a calendar to predict the flooding of the Nile* in the problem box. Have students fill in solutions in the right-hand boxes. [marking the days on a stick, using the moon's cycle to count months, using the constellations to track time, using Sirius to create a calendar] Then, have students go a step further, attaching more boxes to the solution boxes and filling them with the details for each solution. [For example, under *"using the constellations to track time,"* students could write "three categories of celestial bodies— the planets, the circumpolar stars, and the stars that gave the names to their weeks."]

Connecting to Language Arts
- Writing

Happy Holiday The ancient Egyptians enjoyed five holidays to make up for the days that were "lost" when the astronomers created their calendar. Have students look up the word *intercalate*. What do we intercalate every four years into our modern calendar? [extra day] The ancients had a wonderful legend about Thoth and a dice game. Now it is up to the students to create their own legend or story about Leap Day. Students should brainstorm ways to celebrate this holiday and give it a new name. Have them create a poster to invite people to their new festival. Remind them to include where and when the festival will be held.

Connecting Across the Curriculum: Science

Positively Lunar Assign students to learn more about the moon. What do they know about the lunar cycle and phases of the moon? What does it mean if the moon is at perigee or at apogee? What is the difference between a waxing and a waning moon? What do we know about the moon today that the Egyptians did not know? Students may even find other legends and folklore about the moon from other cultures. How many lunar landings have there been? After students have completed their research, they may work individually or with a partner to create one of the following assignments:

- a visual of the lunar cycle or the phases of the moon
- a song or poem about the moon
- a crossword puzzle featuring words associated with the moon
- a drawing of the moon, locating its major features

Further Resources
Books
- *Science in Ancient Egypt* by Geraldine Woods
- *Exploring the Night Sky: The Equinox Astronomy Guide for Beginners* by Terrence Dickinson

Assessment

Turn to page 141 for a multiple-choice test on the selection.

Test Answers

1. b 2. a 3. d 4. c 5. b
6. a 7. d 8. c 9. b 10. a

Rubrics for *Cross-Curricular Activities*   (*student text page 99*)

The following criteria can help you evaluate each student's success in completing the activities prompted by the Cross-Curricular Activities feature in the student textbook.

Health/Science
Healthy in Life and Death

- The student conducts research to find information about the physical health, exercise, and diet of the ancient Egyptians.
- The student conducts research to find information on common illnesses and a variety of treatments used by the ancient Egyptians.
- The student reports his or her findings to the class. The report is informative and clearly delivered, leaving the audience with a clearer understanding of the topic.

History/Art
Frieze It

(Since this activity may require the involvement of more than one student, you may wish to evaluate each student on his or her specific and individual contribution to the activity and then give the group an overall rating.)

- The students work to research important events in Nubia's history and make a list of possibilities to record on a frieze.
- The students sketch drafts of a frieze and present them to the class with explanations of the events depicted on the frieze.

Language Arts/Music
Ballad of the Boy King

- The student conducts research to discover details about the life of King Tutankhamen.
- The student creates song lyrics, a poem, or a ballad about Tutankhamen. The student may include fictional details about the boy king, if he or she desires.

History/Drama
Queen of the Silver Screen

(Since this activity may require the involvement of more than one student, you may wish to evaluate each student on his or her specific and individual contribution to this activity and then give the group an overall rating.)

- Students conduct research about Queen Hatshepsut.
- Students work together to create a short, two-act play dramatizing some event in Queen Hatshepsut's life.
- As performed, the students' short play effectively conveys an event, leaving the audience with a clear picture of something that happened in the life of Queen Hatshepsut.

Mathematics/Art
Do-It-Yourself Pyramid

- The student, using his or her own calculations, constructs a scale model of a pyramid using blocks made from clay, plastic foam, or other suitable material.
- The student maintains a record of the calculations used to build the scale model.
- The student may choose to sketch a diagram or blueprint of the pyramid before building the model.
- The student's execution of the work results in a scale model of a pyramid.

CHAPTER 4

The People of the Book
The Ancient Hebrews 2000 B.C.–A.D. 70

Deborah
from *Women of the Bible*
by CAROLE ARMSTRONG
(student text page 103)

CONTENT-AREA CONNECTION
HISTORY ●

Reading Level: Average

Text Summary
This excerpt from *Women of the Bible* recounts an incident in the life of Deborah, the only woman ever to serve as a judge for the ancient Hebrews (also known as Israelites). Israelite leaders consulted with Deborah in hopes that she could help them overthrow the oppressive rule of the Canaanites. Deborah assured them that God was on their side and ordered the Israelite military leader Barak to fight the heavily armed Canaanites. Frightened, Barak insisted that Deborah accompany him and his ten thousand men into battle. She did, and the Israelites defeated the larger and more heavily armed forces of the Canaanites and won their freedom.

BEFORE READING

Make the Connection
Lead students in a brief discussion about what makes someone a hero. [Heroes overcome hardship, make great sacrifices for the common good, and so on.] What qualities do heroes possess? [Heroes are brave, decisive, willing to sacrifice, and so on.] What modern day heroes can you think of? [Sports figures, family members, political leaders, and so on.]

Build Background
■ More About the Topic
The Canaanites were farmers and city dwellers who lived in an area called Canaan. The name Canaan is believed to be related to an ancient Semitic word meaning "reddish purple," the color of a popular dye produced in the region. Scholars credit the Canaanites with developing an alphabet that was a precursor to the Phoenician, Greek, and Latin alphabets. The Canaanites practiced a polytheistic religion that focused on agriculture and fertility. They worshiped El as their main god and Baal as their god of rainfall and fertility. The Israelites and Canaanites lived close together and but did not adopt aspects of each other's religions. The two groups also came into conflict, as detailed in this excerpt from *Women of the Bible*.

Vocabulary Development
The following words are underscored and defined in the student text.
oppressed: treated harshly and unjustly.
plight: bad or dangerous state or condition.
refuge: safety or shelter.
sympathized: shared or understood the feelings or ideas of another.
brutally: in an unfeeling, cruel, or direct manner.
Before assigning the reading, you may want to introduce students to any words that could cause pronunciation or definition problems.

┌─ *Vocabulary Tip* ─────────────
Using Inflected Endings Remind students that changing the ending can change the tense of a word and can indicate when actions occur. For example, the ending *–ed* changes a word from present tense *(oppress* or *sympathize)* to past tense *(oppressed* or *sympathized)*. Understanding the tense of a word can help students decipher the meaning of a sentence by indicating the proper chronological context.

Although the following words are important to an understanding of the text selection, some of them may be unfamiliar to students.

general*: a high-ranking military officer.
military: of or relating to war or soldiers.
commander: the person in charge of an army.
chariots: two-wheeled carts pulled by horses and used in battle.
triumph: victory or success.

* Although students may be familiar with other meanings of this word, the word as used in the selection has a specific meaning that pertains to the content area.

Reading Informational Material

Reading Skill:
Taking Notes

Explain to students that taking notes during reading can help them monitor their comprehension, as well as identify important details and main ideas in a text.

Reading Strategy
Taking Effective Notes (Strategy 10)

Strategy 10 described in Content-Area Reading Strategies helps students monitor comprehension by using note taking to respond to the text as they read. Provide students with a blank transparency sheet, a blank sheet of paper, or some self-adhesive notes so they can mark the text without writing in their books. Students may also find a Key Points and Details Chart (Graphic Organizer 5) or a Cluster Diagram (Graphic Organizer 3) useful in organizing their notes after the reading process.

▶ **Teaching Tips**
Multiple Symbols Often a single statement in a selection will call for the use of more than one symbol. For example, students who read the "You Need to Know . . ." feature before reading the selection may put a check mark next to the first sentence to indicate that they already knew that Deborah was the only woman to serve as a judge. They may also mark the first sentence with asterisks if they feel that it is important information or with plus signs if they feel that it is a supporting detail.

Alternative Note Taking Using symbols as described in Strategy 10 allows students to make quick notations without interrupting the flow of their reading. However, some students may be overwhelmed by having to learn a new reading skill and a set of symbols for marking text. Feel free to allow students to develop their own symbols or shorthand for marking the text. In this case, learning to conduct a conversation with the text while reading is more important than learning a specific set of symbols.

DURING READING

Differentiating Instruction
■ Learners Having Difficulty

Struggling readers often have difficulty comprehending the overall text if they have to pause often to take notes or ask questions while reading. These students may benefit from reading the entire selection once without stopping, then pausing to ask questions and take notes while re-reading the text. Students who have taken few notes during their reading may also benefit from teaming with a skilled reader who can explain the notes he or she took while reading.

AFTER READING

✓ Reading Check

The following are sample answers to the questions on student text page 105.

1. People flocked to Deborah because she was a wise judge.

2. Sisera led the Canaanite military. He had oppressed the Israelites for twenty years.

3. Barak was afraid because Sisera had nine hundred chariots of iron and an army that far outnumbered the Israelite army.

4. Deborah was not afraid because she had received God's promise that the Israelites would win.

5. Sisera was murdered in his sleep by Jael, who secretly sympathized with the Hebrews. She was the wife of Heber, one of Sisera's friends.

Reteaching

If students are still struggling with the concept of engaging in a conversation with the text, model the process using the first few sentences of the selection. Read the first sentence aloud, and then pause and model a conversation with the text. ["I had already read that in the 'You Need to Know . . .' feature, so I'll mark that with a check because I already knew it."] Write the appropriate symbol on the chalkboard, and then read the second sentence aloud, pausing for additional comments. ["That's interesting that she would sit under a palm tree. That sounds like a supporting detail."] After marking the appropriate symbol on the chalkboard, proceed by reading the next sentence aloud. This time, pause to solicit comments from students.

Connecting to Language Arts

▪ Writing

Here Comes the Judge Lead students in a brief discussion about how Barak, the military commander of the Israelites, felt about the possibility of attacking the heavily armed Canaanite army. Then, have students work independently to write a diary entry from Barak's perspective describing the day that he was called before Deborah. Students may base their diary entries on information provided by the selection, or you may wish to have them do additional research.

▪ Speaking and Listening

You Are There Have students in small groups discuss the notes they took while reading the selection. What details in the selection supported the plan to attack the Canaanites? [The Canaanites were oppressing the Israelites. The Israelites could rely on God's help.] What details indicated that an attack might not be a good idea? [The Canaanites had a strong army with superior weapons.] Then, have each group write a "you are there" historical scene recreating the meeting between Barak and Deborah and act out their scenes before the class.

Connecting Across the Curriculum: History

A Chariot in Every Garage Have students research the design and uses of chariots in ancient times. Where and when did they originate? [Chariots apparently originated in Mesopotamia around 3000 B.C.] How were they used? [Chariots were used in parades, warfare, hunting, racing, and so on.] What did they look like? [They were open vehicles with two or four wheels that were pulled by animals.] After students have finished their research, they may work independently or in pairs to complete one of the following assignments:

- a written research report detailing the evolution of the chariot
- a diorama of a parade, battle, or race featuring chariots
- a scale model of a chariot or of different kinds of chariots
- a brochure advertising a new line of chariots
- a series of drawings of various kinds of chariots

Further Resource
Book

The Illustrated History of the Jewish People edited by Jane S. Gerber and Nicholas De Lange.

Assessment

Turn to page 142 for a multiple-choice test on the selection.

Test Answers
1. c   2. b   3. a   4. d   5. b
6. c   7. d   8. a   9. d   10. b

Judaism

from *One World, Many Religions*
by MARY POPE OSBORNE
(student text page 106)

Reading Level: Average

Special Considerations

Students who have different religious beliefs may be confused or upset that the selection recounts the stories of Abraham and Moses in a factual manner. Assure students that the book from which this selection is excerpted discusses other religions in a similar manner. Lead students in a brief discussion about religious tolerance. How should people treat those who have different religious beliefs? Is it more important to stress the differences between various religions or the similarities? [Opinion responses to both will vary.]

Text Summary

This excerpt from *One World, Many Religions* tells the stories of Abraham, the founder of Judaism, and Moses, who led the Israelites out of slavery. Judaism began 4,000 years ago when Abraham promised everlasting faithfulness to God. In return, God promised Abraham and his descendants a land called Canaan. Many years later, Abraham's people were enslaved in Egypt. God told Moses to take his people back to Canaan and then sent a series of plagues to Egypt. Then, Moses helped his people escape.

BEFORE READING

Make the Connection

Ask students what they know about the Biblical stories of Abraham and Moses. [Abraham entered into a covenant with God, Moses led the Israelites out of slavery, and so on.] What other stories from the Bible do they know? [Adam and Eve, Cain and Abel, Noah's ark, Jonah and the whale, and so on.]

Build Background

■ More About the Topic

Abraham is an important figure in all three of the world's major monotheistic religions—Judaism, Christianity, and Islam. Much of what we know

about him comes from Genesis, the first book of the Bible. Genesis paints Abraham as a brave and compassionate man with many positive qualities, as well as a few human weaknesses. The greatest test of Abraham's faith came late in his life when God demanded that Abraham sacrifice his only son Isaac. Abraham proved his willingness to make the sacrifice, so God spared Isaac.

Vocabulary Development

The following words are underscored and defined in the student text.

descendants: people who trace their families back to a certain ancestor.

stunning: striking or remarkable.

plagues: great troubles sent as divine punishment; calamities.

infestation: destructive swarming.

Before assigning the reading, you may want to introduce students to any words that could cause pronunciation or definition problems.

┌─ *Vocabulary Tip* ─

Using Etymology Tell your students that learning about the etymology of a word can help them remember the word's meaning. Ask students to consult dictionaries to find the derivation of *infestation*. [*Infest* comes from the Latin word *infestus*, which means "hostile."] Point out to students that they can better remember the definition of *infestation* by thinking of "destructive swarming" as a "hostile" action.

CONTENT-AREA VOCABULARY

Although the following words are important to an understanding of the text selection, some of them may be unfamiliar to students.

worshiped: engaged in practices expressing belief in a divine being.

faithful: showing loyalty.

prayed: implored or begged, especially in addressing God.

holy: divine or sacred.

Reading Informational Material

Reading Skill
Using Prior Knowledge

Tell students that spending just a few minutes organizing their thinking and setting goals before reading can help them connect with their prior knowledge and better understand the ideas and concepts presented in the writing.

▶ Teaching Tip
Previewing Reading Check Tell students that previewing the Reading Check comprehension questions that follow the selection can help them in several ways. Previewing these questions can help establish a purpose for reading. These types of questions also give readers insight into the main idea and additional information that may spark a connection to readers' prior knowledge. Reading the comprehension questions first will also make students more alert for the answers as they read the text.

Reading Strategy
Previewing Text (Strategy 1)

To help students connect to their prior knowledge about the subjects of this selection, use Strategy 1 described in Content-Area Reading Strategies. Previewing text allows students to establish a purpose for reading, to identify important ideas, and to connect with their prior knowledge. You may find it helpful to provide students with a KWL chart (Graphic Organizer 6) to help them organize their thinking during the reading process.

▶ Teaching Tip
Prior Knowledge Some students may have little prior knowledge of Judaism. These students may benefit from a class discussion of the text's subjects and ideas. Having some students share what they know about the subject can provide more context for other students with less prior knowledge.

DURING READING

▶ Teaching Tip
Adjusting Focus Remind students to check occasionally, as they read, to see if the assumptions they made during the Before Reading exercises are holding up. Students may have to adjust their purpose for reading or rethink their notions of which ideas are most important. The purpose of the Before Reading exercises is not to come up with correct answers, but to help students focus on the text and better understand and remember the material they read.

Viewing the Art
Pharaoh's Army

Refer students to the painting of Pharaoh's army being swallowed by the Red Sea on page 108. Ask students to describe the scene depicted in the painting and discuss how the picture affects them. [Opinion responses will vary.] Ask them why they think the painter chose to depict the scene in this manner. [for dramatic reasons, to make a point, and so on]

Differentiating Instruction
■ Learners Having Difficulty

Some students may lack the patience or focus to carefully preview a selection before they begin reading. These students may benefit from a more structured approach. Create a checklist based on the description of Strategy 1 in Content-Area Reading Strategies. [Look at the text structure; note special features (summaries or guiding questions); look at the table of contents, glossary, and index; think about your purpose for reading; note headings; read key vocabulary; think about what you already know about the topic; and so on.] Distribute the list to students having difficulty, and have them check off each item as they preview that portion of the text.

AFTER READING

✓ Reading Check

The following are sample answers to the questions on student text page 110.

1. God promised to bless Abraham and Sarah and to lead them to Canaan. Abraham promised that he and his family would always be faithful to God.

2. The Israelites left Canaan because of a shortage of food.

3. The Israelites became unhappy in Egypt because they were forced into slavery.

4. The Ten Commandments were carved on the stone tablets God gave Moses.

Reteaching

If students are having trouble connecting with their prior knowledge, write a purpose for reading on the chalkboard. [to gather information to correctly answer comprehension questions] Flip through the selection with the entire class, pointing out the illustrations and the vocabulary words defined in the margins and footnotes. Ask students to discuss what they already know about Abraham and Moses. Then, read aloud the "You Need to Know . . ." and the "Sidelight" features. Ask students if the information presented in these features sounds familiar or reminds them of anything they may know about Abraham and Moses. Finally, have each Reading Check question read aloud and ask students to predict the answers. Explain to students that connecting to their prior knowledge in this manner can help them better understand and remember the information presented in the text.

Connecting to Language Arts

▪ Writing

Moses Have students research the childhood of Moses. How was he separated from his parents? [They floated him down the Nile in a reed basket to save him because Egypt was killing all firstborn Hebrew sons.] How did he wind up being raised as an Egyptian? [He was found by the pharaoh's daughter and raised in the Egyptian court.] What subjects did he study? [religious, military, and civil matters] Students can present their information in a classic-style comic strip, a script for a play or movie scene, or a written proposal for a documentary.

Connecting Across the Curriculum: Art

The Many Faces of Moses Instruct students to research a variety of paintings and/or sculptures of Moses by different artists. How does the physical appearance of Moses differ with each artist? What, if anything, is Moses doing in the artwork? Is there anything in the paintings or sculptures that hints at the divine nature of Moses? After students have finished their research, they may work independently or in pairs to complete one of the following assignments:

- a script for a slide show of artwork depicting Moses
- a painting, drawing, or sculpture of Moses using some of the themes or events depicted in the artwork
- a design of a catalog for an exhibit featuring famous artwork about Moses
- costume design based on the artwork for a movie about the life of Moses

Further Resource
Online

Direct students to the Web site for the Jewish History Museum in New York City. The museum houses one of the world's largest collections of art and artifacts documenting 4,000 years of Jewish cultural history. Check out the tour of the museum's permanent collection titled *Culture and Continuity: The Jewish Journey.*

Assessment

Turn to page 143 for a multiple-choice test on the selection.

Test Answers
1. b   2. a   3. c   4. d   5. a
6. c   7. b   8. a   9. c   10. a

from The Writings

from *A Treasury of Jewish Literature:*
From Biblical Times to Today
by GLORIA GOLDREICH
(student text page 111)

Reading Level: Average

Text Summary

This excerpt from *A Treasury of Jewish Literature: From Biblical Times to Today* discusses the third section of the Hebrew Bible, the *Writings*, or *Ketuvim* in Hebrew. The books that make up the Writings present a variety of literary forms, including poems, hymns, histories, and proverbs. The Book of Psalms consists of lyrics conveying sorrow, joy, disappointment, and blessings. The Book of Proverbs is made up of sayings that offer advice on living a moral and just life. The Book of Job addresses the moral question of why bad things happen to good people. The Book of Ecclesiastes discusses the relevance of life. The Song of Songs is a series of love poems that celebrate the end of winter and the beginning of spring.

BEFORE READING

Make the Connection

On the chalkboard, write the last proverb from Selected Proverbs on student text page 116. Read the proverb aloud, and then ask students what they think it means. [The words of a just person are valuable, but the desires of a wicked person have little value.] Lead students in a discussion about this proverb and about proverbs in general. How does the proverb apply to their lives? [Answers will vary.] What purposes do proverbs serve? [Proverbs tell people how to live properly.]

Build Background
- More About the Topic

The Bible consists of combinations of the books of the Hebrew Bible, called the Old Testament, and Christian literature produced after the life of Jesus Christ, called the New Testament. Many religions consider the Bible a holy book; different religions recognize different versions of the Bible. For example, the Roman Catholic and Eastern Orthodox versions include material in the Old Testament that Protestant religions do not believe to be authentic. Jewish scripture includes only the books of the Old Testament and presents them in a different order than the Bible used by other religions. Today, publishers produce Bibles for a variety of people. There are Bibles with supplemental material aimed specifically at teenagers, college students, fathers and mothers—all kinds of readers. Bibles are published in every way that books can be published: in hardback, in paperback, in leather-bound special editions, on CD-ROMs, on the Internet, and so on.

- Building Prerequisite Skills

Point out the word *individual* (page 112 in the phrase "The individual psalmist . . .") Write the word on the chalkboard, and ask students if they know what it means. [Responses will vary] Divide the word into its parts [in•dividu•al], and have students guess at the meanings of the word parts. [The root word –*dividu*– derives from the Latin word *dividere*, which means "to divide." The prefix *in*– means "not." The suffix –*al* means "of" or "relating to."] Ask students to guess the meaning of the word based on the meanings of its parts. [*individual* means "relating to something that cannot be divided"] This process, called structural analysis, is a valuable tool to use in determining the meanings of unfamiliar words.

Vocabulary Development

The following words are underscored and defined in the student text.

legislates: brings about by making laws.

implores: asks earnestly.

just: upright; virtuous.

affirmation: act of declaring to be true.

integral: essential.

Before assigning the reading, you may want to introduce students to any words that could cause pronunciation or definition problems.

Vocabulary Tip

Using Structural Analysis Tell students that guessing at a word based on an analysis of familiar prefixes, suffixes, and root words can be tricky. For example, the root word of *implores* derives from the Latin *–plorare–*, meaning "to cry out." The prefix *im–* usually means "not." [*im–* is how the prefix *in–* is spelled when added to a word that starts with *b, m,* or *p*] A structural analysis of *implore* could produce the definition "not to cry out," which is opposite of the word's actual meaning. Explain that when a word's structural analysis does not make sense in the context of the reading assignment, they might consider consulting a dictionary.

(**CONTENT-AREA VOCABULARY**)

Although the following words are important to an understanding of the text selection, some of them may be unfamiliar to students.

exaltation: the act of glorifying something.
hymns: songs that glorify God.
narratives: stories that are told.
lyric*: expressing a great deal of emotion, as in a song.
verses: portions of a poem or song.

*Although students may be familiar with other meanings of this word, the word as used in the selection has a specific meaning that pertains to the content area.

(**Reading Informational Material**)

Reading Skill
Using Context Clues

Explain to students that context clues can help them determine the meaning of unfamiliar words. Context clues include how a word is used in a sentence, the main idea of the text, the topic of the paragraph, familiar word parts (prefixes, root words, and suffixes), and so on.

Reading Strategy
Developing Vocabulary Knowledge (Strategy 11)

To help students use context clues and structural analysis to discover the meaning of unfamiliar words, use Strategy 11 described in Content-Area Reading Strategies. You may find it helpful to

provide students with a Contextual Redefinition Chart (Graphic Organizer 4) to help them organize their thoughts on unfamiliar words, context clues, and word structure during the reading process.

▶ **Teaching Tip**
Stopping to Look Up Words The best way to determine the exact meaning of a word is to look it up in a dictionary. However, stopping often to consult a dictionary can disrupt the flow of the story. Explain that students should first determine if they really need to know the exact definition of a word in order to understand the main ideas presented in the text. If so, they should pause and look up the word. If not, they can jot down the word, guess at the meaning, and look up the word later.

DURING READING
Differentiating Instruction
- English-Language Learners

Vocabulary presents additional problems for English-language learners. These students are likely to encounter more unfamiliar words, have difficulty breaking these words into morphemes that are meaningful to them, and struggle with identifying context clues. Consider allowing English-language learners to team with native English speakers to discuss unfamiliar words and to brainstorm ways of arriving at definitions of those words. Students may find some words with roots that are also found in their native language.

▶ **Teaching Tip**
Structural Analysis Tell students that not every word lends itself equally well to structural analysis. When a word lacks morphemes that are meaningful to students, they will have to depend more on context to guess at the definition of the word. To determine context, students often will have to look beyond the sentence level to the larger context of the paragraph, the passage, and/or the entire text.

AFTER READING

✓ Reading Check

The following are sample answers to the questions on student text page 116.

1. The books in the Writings that contain poetry are the Book of Psalms, Lamentations, and the Song of Songs.

2. Proverbs, Ecclesiastes, and the Book of Job offer philosophy, wisdom, and guidance.

3. The books of Ruth and Esther tell the stories of great women.

4. Hemingway's title *The Sun Also Rises* is from the Book of Ecclesiastes.

5. Psalm 8 marvels at God's creation of human beings.

Reteaching

If students are still having trouble with contextual redefinition, you may want to introduce them to a parallel strategy called Wordbusting, also known as CSSD for Context, Structure, Sound, Dictionary. Draw a five-column organizer with two rows on the chalkboard, and label it as follows:

Word	Context	Structure	Sound	Dictionary

Point out to students the word *incomprehensible* (page 113), and ask students to guess its meaning. Write some of their guesses under "Word." Then, briefly discuss *The Writings* before reading aloud the paragraph containing *incomprehensible* (pages 112–113). Have students guess again at the word's meaning, and write their answers under "Context." Next, break down the word into its parts [*in•comprehens•ible*], and have students guess at the meanings of the word parts. [*in–* means "not"; *–comprehens–* means "comprehend" or "understand"; *–ible* means "capable of being"] Write their guesses under "Structure." Have students say the word aloud to see if it sounds like any words they already know. Write student responses under

"Sound." Lead the students in guessing a final definition based on the information in the chart, and write it on the chalkboard. Lastly, have a student find the word in a dictionary and write the definition under "Dictionary" in the chart.

Connecting to Language Arts

- Writing

Passover Have students research the Jewish holiday of Passover. Why is Passover celebrated? [to mark the escape of the Israelites from slavery in Egypt] What practice is observed during Passover? [eating unleavened bread] What does this practice symbolize? [the deliverance of the Israelites from slavery] Students can present their findings in a short poem or as a children's story.

Connecting Across the Curriculum: History

The Life of David Have students research the life of King David, one of the authors of the Psalms. What were his major accomplishments as king? Why does the selection refer to him as a "poet-warrior"? After students have finished their research, they may work independently or in pairs to complete one of the following assignments:

- a series of trading cards featuring scenes from King David's life
- a dramatic monologue featuring King David looking back on his life
- a diorama illustrating a moment from King David's life
- a time line of important events in King David's life

Further Resource

Online

Students can learn more about *The Writings* at the Web site for the Jewish Virtual Library. The Web site's Religion section features a link to the Holy Scriptures, which includes the entire text of the *Ketuvim*. The Biography section includes biographies of such figures as David and Solomon.

Assessment

Turn to page 144 for a test on the selection.

Test Answers
1. b   2. c   3. a   4. a   5. d
6. d   7. c   8. a   9. d   10. b

The Mystery of Qumran and the Dead Sea Scrolls

FROM *MUSE* BY HERSHEL SHANKS
(*student text page 117*)

Reading Level: Average

Text Summary

This magazine article tells of the mystery surrounding the Dead Sea Scrolls, which are ancient writings about the Bible, early Judaism, and the origins of Christianity. Even the discovery of the first of the scrolls in a cave near the Dead Sea is in doubt, with several people claiming to be the shepherd who stumbled across them. Eventually, hundreds of scrolls were found in eleven caves in the vicinity. Archaeologists, hoping to find clues about who wrote the scrolls and why, began excavating a nearby ancient Jewish settlement called Qumran. Scholars disagree about whether Qumran was a religious community, a military fortress, a hotel, or different things at different times. There is also mystery about who lived in Qumran. The most likely possibility is that Qumran was occupied by a Jewish sect called the Essenes.

BEFORE READING

Make the Connection

Ask students whether they think it is important to study artifacts from ancient civilizations. Why do people go through so much trouble to dig up broken pottery and shredded scrolls? [to learn about the past] What can such objects teach us? [how ancient people lived, where they settled, and so on]

Build Background

■ More About the Topic

The Dead Sea is a salt water lake that straddles the border of Israel and Jordan. It is the lowest body of water on Earth, averaging some 1,300 feet below sea level. The Dead Sea is far too salty to support animal and plant life. Bacteria can live in the saline waters, but fish brought in by fresh water tributaries die instantly. Because the Dead Sea does not supply fish and cannot be used for agriculture, the shores around the Dead Sea are generally deserted.

Vocabulary Development

The following words are underscored and defined in the student text.

tatters: rags; shreds.
distractions: things that draw attention away.
communally: sharing together as a group.
fortress: stronghold; fort.
fortified: strengthened against attack by using walls or forts.

Before assigning the reading, you may want to introduce students to any words that could cause pronunciation or definition problems.

Vocabulary Tip

Using Etymology Have students look up the etymologies of the words *fortress* and *fortified* and explain how they are related. [Both are derived from the Latin *fortis,* meaning "strong."] Ask students to look up the meanings of the suffix *–ify* and the inflected ending *–ed* and explain how adding these endings to fort changes its meaning. [*Fort–*"strong" + *–ify–*"to make" + *–ed–*"having features of" creates *fortified,* an adjective meaning "having features of something made strong."]

(CONTENT-AREA VOCABULARY)

Although the following words are important to an understanding of the text selection, some of them may be unfamiliar to students.

Bedouin: a nomadic Arab who lives in the desert.
archaeologists: scientists who study the remains of ancient human civilizations.
excavate: to expose by digging out or uncovering.
scholars: people who have advanced learning in a particular area of study.
settlement*: a place where a small group of people live together.

* Although students may be familiar with other meanings of this word, the word as used in the selection has a specific meaning that pertains to the content area.

Reading Informational Material

Reading Skill:
Making Inferences

Explain to students that an inference is an educated guess based on their experiences and on clues in the text or in the visuals that accompany the text, such as charts, diagrams, photographs, maps, illustrations, and so on.

Reading Strategy
Building Background (Strategy 6)

To help students make inferences about what they will read, use Strategy 6 described in Content-Area Reading Strategies. Students may find the Predictions and Confirming Activity organizer (Graphic Organizer 8) helpful for organizing their inferences before reading and for checking the accuracy of their inferences after reading.

▶ **Teaching Tip**

Confirming Inferences After students finish reading the selection, have them review the inferences they made to confirm which of their inferences were accurate. Skipping this step increases the likelihood that students will remember as facts inferences that turn out to be inaccurate as well as those inferences that are confirmed by the text.

DURING READING

Using the Side-Margin Feature
▪ An Ancient Treasure Map?

Ask students if they have read other stories that involve maps to hidden treasures. [*Treasure Island, The Road to El Dorado*, and so on] How do those stories differ from the story of the Copper Scroll? [Stories of treasure maps often involve stolen pirate booty. In the case of the Copper Scroll, it appears that the treasure was hidden to prevent it from being stolen.]

▶ **Teaching Tip**

Using Visuals Students can enhance their comprehension of the text by studying the accompanying visuals while they read. Previewing the visuals may help students in their pre-reading predictions, as well.

Differentiating Instruction
▪ Advanced Students

Give your advanced learners a mystery to try to solve. Propose that these students, working individually or in small groups, examine the mysteries and controversies surrounding the Dead Sea Scrolls, their contents or discovery, or Qumran. With the facts that they can "dig up" in hand, ask them to propose a possible solution to the mystery. (One group may wish to present several solutions and show what is right or wrong about each.) Let them choose how to present their project: as a panel report, a series of informative posters, a videotaped program, and so on.

AFTER READING

✓ Reading Check

The following are sample answers to the questions on student text page 122.

1. The Dead Sea Scrolls may have been found by a Bedouin shepherd who was looking in a cave for one of his sheep. However, several different men with different stories have claimed to be the shepherd who found the Dead Sea Scrolls.

2. Qumran may have been a religious settlement because it's in a remote location in the desert and because there are several large rooms of the type that would be found in a communal settlement.

3. Qumran may have been a military fortress because some arrowheads and a fortified tower were found at the site.

4. Other archeologists think that Qumran could have served as a hotel or retreat center.

5. The Dead Sea Scrolls are important because they tell a lot about the Bible, the origins of Christianity, and early Judaism.

Reteaching

If students are still having difficulty making inferences, guide them through the visual information. Direct them to the picture on page 118. What does this picture show? [caves near the Dead Sea] Why would such a picture be used to illustrate this article? [The Dead Sea Scrolls were found there.] How could such a picture enhance a reader's understanding of the text? [Readers can visualize the site of the discovery.] Then, direct students to the map on page 120. What does the map show? [the area around the Dead Sea in modern times] How can a map help readers better understand a reading selection? [by placing the selection in a geographical context] Finally, direct students to the picture on page 121. What does this picture depict? [a fragment of the Dead Sea Scrolls] How does this picture help a reader better understand the selection? [by showing what the scrolls look like, since the author described only their condition and not their appearance] Have students use self-adhesive notes to mark places in the text where the visual information enhances or clarifies the text.

Connecting to Language Arts

- Writing

A Shepherd's Diary The selection begins with an account of the discovery of the first of the Dead Sea Scrolls. Have students think about what it must have been like for shepherds to make such a discovery. What would have been their first thought when they heard the jar break? How would they have reacted when they realized that the jars contained ancient scrolls? Have students write a ten-word message to a family member or the press from the perspective of one of the shepherds on the day that the scrolls were discovered.

- Speaking and Listening

The Essene Life Have students research the Essenes, the religious sect believed by some scholars to have written the Dead Sea Scrolls. How were they expected to conduct their lives? [Follow the law of Moses, refuse to take part in public life, live in seclusion, do manual labor, share all property.] What were some of their beliefs? [celibacy, immortality, divine punishment of the sinful] What was their day of worship like? [daylong prayer and Torah reading] Students can present their findings as an oral history, an audio recording of an informational speech, or a skit about an orientation tour for new Essenes.

Connecting Across the Curriculum: Archaeology

Digging Up Qumran Have students research the archaeological excavations that have taken place at Qumran since the discovery of the Dead Sea Scrolls. When did excavations begin? What structures did they find? What sort of construction materials were used? After students have finished their research, they may work independently or in pairs to complete one of the following assignments:

- a scale model of the Qumran complex
- a script for a documentary film describing Qumran
- an architectural drawing and floor plan of the Qumran complex
- an informational article for a travel magazine
- a museum display about the Dead Sea Scrolls

Further Resource
Online

Check out the Web site for the Orion Center for the Study of the Dead Sea Scrolls at the Hebrew University of Jerusalem. The site offers a photographic tour of the Qumran caves and essays about the discovery of the scrolls and their significance. The Web site's Resources page includes links to outside Web sites that discuss the scrolls.

(Assessment)

Turn to page 145 for a multiple-choice test on the selection.

Test Answers

1. c **2.** b **3.** c **4.** a **5.** d
6. d **7.** c **8.** b **9.** a **10.** d

To Every Thing There Is a Season

Ecclesiastes 3:1–8

from THE KING JAMES BIBLE
(student text page 123)

Reading Level: Average

Text Summary

The selection consists of the first eight lines of chapter three from the Book of Ecclesiastes. These lines amount to a philosophical essay about the nature of life. The writer says that everything in life has its time, then uses pairs of opposites to illustrate the point. Just as the phrase "a place for everything and everything in its place" describes an orderly house, these lines from Ecclesiastes describe the author's notion of an orderly existence.

BEFORE READING

Make the Connection

Ask students to express their opinions about war, killing, and hate. Do these things have a place in the world? Should they? Is it possible to do away with them? Why or why not? [Responses will vary.]

Build Background
■ More About the Topic

Ecclesiastes is one of the books that comprise the section of the Hebrew Bible known as *The Writings*. Jewish tradition calls for Ecclesiastes to be read aloud in the synagogue on the Sabbath of the week of Sukkoth, a festival of thanksgiving held in autumn. It is not certain who wrote the book, but tradition ascribes its authorship to King Solomon, who also is credited with writing the *Song of Songs* and *Proverbs*. However, scholars believe the book was written long after Solomon's reign. Ecclesiastes is a philosophical work consisting of skeptical observations about life, the unpredictability of the fate of humankind, and the inscrutability of God's methods.

■ Motivate

If students have not heard the song "Turn! Turn! Turn!" sung by The Byrds or by Pete Seeger, play one or both for the class. What is their opinion of

the song? [Responses will vary.] What is the theme of the song? [that life encompasses both positive and negative things] What other styles of music do students think the lyrics lend themselves to? [Responses will vary.]

Reading Informational Material

Reading Skill:
Determining the Main Idea

Explain to students that the main idea is the message, opinion, or insight that is the focus of an article or another piece of writing.

Reading Strategy
Constructing Concept Maps (Strategy 4)

To help students determine the main idea of the selection, use Strategy 4 described in Content-Area Reading Strategies. Some students may find helpful a Cloze Concept Map, in which you have filled in some information.

▶ **Teaching Tip**
Modifying the Diagram Make sure students realize that the Cluster Diagram (Graphic Organizer 3) is just a suggestion. They may use only some of the circles, or they may add to the diagram according to their needs and the requirements of the text. Students should feel free to use lines, arrows, circles, triangles, squares, or any other marks that work for them.

DURING READING

Differentiating Instruction
■ English-Language Learners

The Bible has been translated into many different languages, so this selection offers an opportunity to allow English-language learners to practice a reading skill with a selection written in their native language *and* in English. Consider allowing students to locate this passage in a Bible printed in their language and then to compare it with the English version presented in the selection. Students should, however, fill out their concept maps in English to allow for teacher and peer evaluation.

AFTER READING

✓ Reading Check

The following are sample answers to the questions on student text page 124.

1. Verse 1 states the theme of the poem.

2. Verses 2 through 8 use pairs of opposites to illustrate the theme.

Reteaching

This selection lends itself well to remedial instruction on constructing concept maps. The main idea of the selection is stated in the first line, with the remainder of the poem supplying supporting statements. If students are still having problems identifying the main idea, write the main idea in the center of a Cluster Diagram (Graphic Organizer 3). Distribute copies of the diagram to students having difficulty. Ask them to identify statements in the selection that support the main idea. [Students may cite any of the pairs of opposites that the writer uses to illustrate the main idea.] Students may want to go further by adding their own examples to the cluster diagram. [a time to study, a time to relax, and so on] Discuss with students how the supporting statements in a piece of writing often lead directly to the main idea.

Connecting to Language Arts
▪ Writing

To Every Song, There Is a Rhythm Have students research the lyrics to Pete Seeger's song "Turn! Turn! Turn!" in a book or on the Internet, and then compare those lyrics to the lines from Ecclesiastes that are printed in the selection. How do the two differ? [Seeger's version adds the refrain "turn, turn, turn," deletes some words, and changes others.] Then, have students write two verses of their own to add to either the Ecclesiastes version or to "Turn! Turn! Turn!"

Connecting Across the Curriculum: Journalism

The Daily News Divide students into seven groups and assign each group one of the verses in "To Every Thing There Is a Season." Have each group search the library's newspapers and magazines for examples of current events that echo their verse from Ecclesiastes. [birth announcements for "a time to be born," an obituary for "a time to die," and so on] After students have finished their research, groups may present the results of their investigations in one of the following forms:

- a collage of photocopies of the articles and the words from their line
- a bookmark with their line accompanied by an appropriate illustration
- an editorial showing a link between their line and modern conditions
- a fact book or sheet with examples of their line echoed in current events
- a magazine cover linking their line with a current event

Further Resources
Audio
- "Turn! Turn! Turn!" by The Byrds.
- *The World of Pete Seeger* by Pete Seeger.

Assessment

Turn to page 146 for a multiple-choice test on the selection.

Test Answers
1. c **2.** a

The following criteria can help you evaluate each student's success in completing the activities prompted by the Cross-Curricular Activities feature in the student textbook.

Art/Geography
How Did They Get There from There?
- The student conducts research to find maps showing Abraham and Sarah's route from Mesopotamia to Canaan or the route that Moses and the Israelites' took on their journey from Egypt to Canaan.
- The student uses the research to create his or her original map showing one of these routes. The student also illustrates, with words or symbols, where key events occurred.
- The student's map is clearly drawn and labeled. In addition, appropriate legends or keys that provide information about the map's scale and interpretation of symbols on the map are included.

Music
Singing a Bible Song
- The student does research to find various musical versions of Psalm 23 and a recording of The Byrds' "Turn! Turn! Turn!"
- The student reviews the various musical arrangements to determine his or her favorite version(s).
- The student sings or plays his or her favorite version(s) for the class.

History/Science
Arms Racing
- The student conducts research to find inventions that were specifically developed for warfare.
- The student chooses one invention and determines how it was employed in warfare and some of the consequences of its use (the student may examine how the invention changed warfare and what nonmilitary consequences the invention had).

History/Speech
You Can Say That Again!
- The student brainstorms about locations where critical historic events occurred.
- The student chooses one of the places and reads about the historic event associated with this location.
- The student writes a slogan that captures the symbolic importance of the historic event that occurred at this location.
- The student presents a brief speech to the class about the historic importance of the location chosen and clearly explains how the slogan he or she wrote relates to this place and event.

Art/History
Archaeological Art
- The student locates additional information about Qumran or the Dead Sea Scrolls, especially illustrations of ruins and objects associated with them.
- The student chooses to draw or paint an item from the archaeological site or to create a modern treasure scroll.

Home Economics
Nice Threads
- The student conducts research about the types and styles of clothing worn by the ancient Hebrews.
- The student draws or paints a costume in this style or creates an actual costume for display to the class.

CHAPTER 5

Early Civilizations in Asia
Ancient India and China 2500 B.C.–A.D. 250

Cities of the Indus Valley

from *Weird and Wacky Science: Lost Cities*

by JOYCE GOLDENSTERN
(*student text page 129*)

CONTENT-AREA CONNECTIONS

HISTORY •
SCIENCE •

Reading Level: Above Average

Text Summary

In the 1920s, an important archaeological find was made in the Indus Valley of India. Two cities—Harappa and Mohenjo-daro—were uncovered, providing new theories about who first brought civilization to the valley. Excavations revealed that the inhabitants of these two cities were artisans who had a strong sense of ownership and a writing system that has yet to be decoded. The streets were laid out in grids, and both cities had advanced drainage and sewer systems. What happened to this civilization is a mystery, although most scholars believe that its sudden end was due to environmental negligence and Aryan raids.

BEFORE READING

Make the Connection

Ask students to imagine that an ancient city is discovered near their hometown and that excavations are underway. What might be found in the lost city? Have students create theories about the people who lived there. Who were they and what kind of culture did they have? What caused their culture to disappear? Write student suggestions on the chalkboard or on an overhead transparency.

Build Background

• More About the Region

Indus Valley civilizations, also known as the Harappan civilization, covered several thousand miles of what is now northwestern India and southern Pakistan. The cultures that lived there around 2,500 B.C. were highly skilled and artistic. The cities were well-organized, interdependent commercial centers. As the Sarasvati River (which ran parallel to the Indus River) dried up, the civilizations seem to have disappeared as well. More information about trade routes and the impact of the vanishing rivers needs to be gathered before conclusions can be reached as to what happened to these advanced civilizations. Other Harappan sites include Dholavira, Rakhigarhi, and Lothal, all in India; Ganeriwala and Chanudarho in Pakistan; and Sutkagen Dor, near Iran.

Vocabulary Development

The following words are underscored and defined in the student text.

gruesome: causing horror or disgust; repulsive.

decipher: to interpret the meaning of something.

circumference: distance bounding an area of a circle or an area suggesting a circle.

anthropologists: scientists who study human origins, including physical and cultural development.

ecology: pattern of relationships between living things and their surroundings.

Before assigning the reading, you may want to introduce students to any words that could cause pronunciation or definition problems.

Vocabulary Tip

Using Semantic Mapping To help students incorporate challenging vocabulary into their own speech and writing, have them create a semantic map. Students should begin by finding how the word is used in the text. Next, have them define the word. Using a thesaurus, have them find synonyms or antonyms for the word. Finally, have them use the word in a sentence. They may want to create their semantic maps using a Cluster Diagram (Graphic Organizer 3).

CONTENT-AREA VOCABULARY

Although the following words are important to an understanding of the text selection, some of them may be unfamiliar to students. Present this list of words and definitions to students. Ask students to use both vocabulary lists to predict what the selection will be about.

inhabitants: people who live in a particular area.
seals*: stamps with designs or letters that make impressions.
inscriptions: markings; words or symbols.
nomadic: moving or traveling constantly.
citadel: fortress; safe place.

*Although students may be familiar with other meanings of this word, the word as used in the selection has a specific meaning that pertains to the content area.

Reading Informational Material

Reading Skill
Identifying Text Structure: Cause and Effect
Explain to students that cause-and-effect explanations show how one event is connected to another.

▶ **Teaching Tip**
Using Text Features This selection uses subheads to indicate major themes. Have students scan the text, taking note of the subheads, the photographs, and the questions at the end of the selection. Then, ask students to write one sentence predicting what the selection will be about.

Reading Strategy
Previewing Text (Strategy 1)
To help students find the main idea of this selection, use Strategy 1 in Content-Area Reading

Strategies. Provide students with a Cause-and-Effect Chart (Graphic Organizer 2) to help them recognize ideas or actions that caused certain events to occur.

DURING READING

▶ **Teaching Tip**
Using Quotations to Capture Attention This selection begins with a quote by Sir Mortimer Wheeler. Ask students how this technique captures the interest of the reader. Are there any more details in the selection about this "gruesome scene"? How does the quote tie in with the rest of the selection? Encourage students to engage readers' attention with startling information in their own writing.

Using the Side-Margin Feature
Everything Old Is New Again
Ask students to find an invention, a way of doing something, or another feature of city life that originated in the past. Have each student present his or her ancient find to the class, compare the modern version with the ancient one, and discuss the changes that have occurred over time.

Differentiating Instruction
■ English-Language Learners
Before students read each section, have them skim the material to identify words they do not know. Have them use a dictionary or thesaurus to find words that are more familiar or to clarify the definition, or pair them with more proficient English speakers as partners to help them learn the new words. Then, after students have read the section, have them summarize it in one or two sentences before reading on. You may want to pose questions for each section to guide them in their summaries.

AFTER READING

✓ Reading Check

The following are sample answers to the questions on student text page 133.

1. Mohenjo-daro was in the Indus Valley of India. We know about the violent death of the people because their skeletons were found exactly

where they died, and two had sword marks on their bones.

2. The Indus Valley civilizations flourished due to commerce, river trade, and agriculture.

3. The seals were used to show ownership of items. The seals show that the people had developed writing.

4. Indra was the main god of the Aryans. *Purmamdara* means "fort destroyer."

5. Ecological factors also led to the decline of these civilizations. The people may have destroyed the forests, which caused flooding and soil erosion.

Reteaching

If students are still struggling with the concept of cause and effect, tell them they are trying to find evidence that solves the mystery: What happened to the cities of Harappa and Mohenjo-daro? Write this question in the center of a Cluster Diagram (Graphic Organizer 3) and distribute copies to the class. Ask students to work in pairs and write their answers on the chart. [Aryan raids, inhabitants destroyed the forests] Ask students to go a step further; for example, under "inhabitants destroyed the forests," students can add that the bare hills allowed the water to rush into the river, the river flooded, the people fought the floodwaters, they became tired, and so on. Have students add arrows from each event that caused another event to happen so that they can visualize the relationship. If, for example, students had the statement "the inhabitants needed wood to bake the bricks," the arrow would point to "inhabitants destroyed the forests."

Connecting to Language Arts

▪ Writing

Playtime The writer mentions that the inhabitants of the Indus Valley enjoyed leisure time. He mentions dice, board games, and toys. Have students create a new board game about ancient cities and write the rules to the game. Students may want to develop their games around the Indus culture. If time allows, students may want to share their game with the class.

▪ Speaking and Listening

Presentation The writer describes Harappa—its dimensions, the citadel, streets laid out in a grid,

and the granaries. He also mentions Mohenjo-daro's public bath. Have students search for a replica of the cities in the library or on the Internet. Then, have them create their own visual representation. Using their visual aid, have students present their findings to the class.

Connecting Across the Curriculum: Science

Trees, Trees, Trees Assign students to find out more about deforestation. Although the role of deforestation in the decline of Mohenjo-daro and Harappa is not clear, have students find out the general causes for deforestation [demand for farmland, need for timber] and its effect on the environment. [rising temperatures, soil runoff, floods] Students should focus on the role of forests in the ecosystem. After students have completed their research, they may work with a partner or independently to present the results of their investigations. They might create one of the following projects:

- a flowchart, illustrating the water cycle and how forests play a role
- a children's book, explaining how deforestation affects the environment
- a recommendation that offers solutions to deforestation

Further Resources

Book

Ancient India: Land of Mystery (Lost Civilizations) by Time-Life Books, Dale M. Brown, ed.
Map of the Indus Valley

Online

The *Harappa* Web site demonstrates how archaeologists and scholars share their work on ancient Harappa.

The *Wide Horizon Education Resources* Web site provides teachers with ideas, resources, and links to other support material relevant to a study of India.

(Assessment)

Turn to page 147 for a test on the selection.

Test Answers

1. d **2.** b **3.** c **4.** d **5.** a
6. b **7.** c **8.** a **9.** b **10.** c

A Vow to Conquer by Dhamma

from *Calliope*

by JEAN ELLIOTT JOHNSON

(student text page 134)

Reading Level: Above average

Text Summary

Ashoka is a famous emperor of India who changed his method of ruling from rule by force to rule by *dhamma*. Two things effected this change—his battle against the city of Kalinga and his conversion to Buddhism. Although he did not want everyone to convert to Buddhism, he did want everyone to practice *dhamma*—nonviolence toward others and proper treatment of everyone. Ashoka's contributions include the construction of hospitals, roads, and water wells for his people. He is also remembered for planting trees and growing medicinal herbs.

BEFORE READING

Make the Connection

Have students create a two-column chart. Ask them to list the qualities of a peaceful ruler in one column and those of a warring ruler in the other. Encourage students to provide names of rulers who fit in either category. [Most students will know warriors, such as Napoleon, Hitler, Mussolini, and so forth. Some may name Mohandas K. Gandhi and Dr. Martin Luther King, Jr. as peacemakers.] Ask students if they think it is possible for someone to change from being a violent ruler who uses force to a peaceful, spiritual ruler.

Build Background

• More About the Time Period

After the death of Alexander the Great, a new dynasty emerged in ancient India. The Mauryan Empire was the first to rule most of the Indian subcontinent under one authority. Chandragupta, who ruled from 322 to 296 B.C., expanded his empire by conquering territories to the north. His son, Bindusara, extended the empire to the south during his rule from 296–273 B.C. When Ashoka, Bindusara's son, assumed control, he also embraced military strikes, attacking and gaining control of Kalinga. However, this battle changed Ashoka's attitude toward warfare, and the ruler adopted a nonviolent approach. After Ashoka's death in 232 B.C., the Mauryan Empire gradually broke up due to its vast size, weak rulers, and disunity within the empire. The last Mauryan king was killed by Pushyamitra Sunga, who then founded the Sunga dynasty.

Vocabulary Development

The following words are underscored and defined in the student text.

ethical: in keeping with moral standards and values.

diverse: made up of various people or things.

compassionate: feeling or showing sympathy for the sorrow or suffering of others.

principles: rules of conduct.

prosperous: successful.

Before assigning the reading, you may want to introduce students to any words that could cause pronunciation or definition problems.

⌐ *Vocabulary Tip* ─

Recognizing Homophones Remind students that some words are homophones—words that are pronounced the same but whose meanings are different. *Principle* and *principal*, for example, are homophones that are often confused. In fact, their meanings are completely different. *Principle* is a noun only. In this reading the author refers to Buddhist principles, reflecting the usual meaning of the word as referring to rules or standards. *Principal* is both a noun and an adjective. As a noun, it generally refers to a person who holds a high position, such as the principal of a school. As an adjective, it has the sense of "chief" or "leading," as in: "The weather was the principal factor in our move from Minnesota to California."

Although the following words are important to an understanding of the text selection, some of them may be unfamiliar to students. Present this list of words and definitions to your students. Have students use each of the following words to write a sentence about someone they know or have read about.

righteousness: goodness; honor.
virtue: fairness; decency; goodness.
tolerant: open-minded.
moral: just and good; noble.
harmoniously: in agreement; peaceably

Reading Informational Material

Reading Skill
Summarizing the Text
Explain to students that summarizing means rephrasing the ideas of a text in fewer words.

▶ **Teaching Tip**
Finding Out Word Meaning Have students read the title. Do they know what *dhamma* means? Ask them to find the word in the selection. Point out that the word appears in italics. Then, have students read Ashoka's definition of *dhamma* on page 135. Based on this definition, discuss the meaning of the title before students begin reading.

Reading Strategy
Taking Notes (Strategy 10)
To help your students summarize the text, use Strategy 10 in Content-Area Reading Strategies. Provide students with a Key Points and Details Chart (Graphic Organizer 5) to help them organize their notes as they read the selection.

DURING READING

▶ **Teaching Tip**
Using Examples to Clarify Meaning Point out that examples can provide more clarity than the definition itself. On page 135, the text defines *dhamma* by comparing it to *dharma*. If students do not know what *dharma* means, the definition is not helpful. However, as students read on, they are given concrete examples. Review the examples to make sure students understand the concept of dharma.

Using the Side-Margin Feature
• Two Great Men, One Principle
Ask students to find out more about Mohandas K. Gandhi and Dr. Martin Luther King, Jr. and their use of nonviolent means to achieve their goals. As a class, discuss examples of nonviolent action, focusing on the positive and negative aspects as well as possible results.

Differentiating Instruction
• Learners Having Difficulty
Students may have difficulty reading the selection because it is about a philosophy, not about a story with a beginning, middle, and an end. Have students work with a partner and list the main points they understand. Suggest that they begin with concrete examples. [Parents make the rules and the children obey them, Ashoka built hospitals, and so on] Have them write each idea as a sentence on a strip of paper. Then, have them arrange the strips in the order that information is presented in the selection. Students may use these sentences in their summaries of the selection.

AFTER READING

✔ Reading Check

The following are sample answers to the questions on student text page 138.

1. Unlike other rulers, Ashoka used morals and ethics rather than force.

2. Ashoka was influenced by Buddhism. Followers of Buddha practice compassion toward all living things and do not steal, lie, gossip, envy, or perform work that harms others.

3. Ashoka hoped that his kingdom would be united and that everyone would be content.

4. To support his policies, Ashoka built hospitals, grew herbal medicines, constructed roads and resthouses, planted trees, and dug wells.

5. Ashoka wanted to be a *chakravartin* so that he and his empire would be peaceful and prosperous. He wanted his reign to be associated with that of the Golden Age.

Reteaching

If students are still struggling with the concept of summarizing, have them answer the *5W-How?* questions (Who? What? Where? When? Why? and How?) using a two-column organizer. Tell students to write the questions in the left column and their answers in the right column. They should not focus on details, as a summary should not be too specific. Once they have completed their charts, allow students to work in pairs to write a one-paragraph summary. Have each pair read their summary to the class.

Connecting to Language Arts

• Writing

Bumper Stickers The writer describes some of the actions Ashoka took to practice his rule by *dhamma*. Have students choose a principle of *dhamma* or a project that Ashoka undertook and create a slogan for a bumper sticker. Students may decorate their stickers and display them on the bulletin board.

• Speaking and Listening

Making an Appeal Have students work in pairs to write a short persuasive speech that promotes Ashoka's ideas. They may use either logical or emotional appeals. Once students have written and practiced their speeches, have them give their speeches to the class.

Connecting Across the Curriculum: Art

Wayside Rest Ask students to design a resthouse, a well, and a garden for pilgrims in Ashoka's kingdom. The garden should include medicinal herbs and the resthouse can be decorated to further Ashoka's principles. Students can submit their designs as a plan on paper, a model, or a diorama.

Further Resources
Book

King Asoka and Buddhism edited by Anuradha Seneviratna, ed., Vipassana Research Publications.

Map of Mauryan Empire

Assessment

Turn to page 148 for a multiple-choice test on the selection.

Test Answers

1. c **2.** a **3.** d **4.** b **5.** d
6. a **7.** c **8.** d **9.** b **10.** c

Siddhartha Gautama: The Buddha

from *Buddhism*

by JOHN SNELLING
(student text page 139)

Reading Level: Average

Special Considerations

Remind students that the emphasis of this selection is on its historical aspects, that is, Siddhartha Gautama's life and his influence on Indian culture and people.

Text Summary

This selection provides a brief overview of the life and teachings of Siddhartha Gautama. Prince Siddhartha, curious about the world outside the palace where he lived, journeyed into the world and was shocked by the suffering he saw there. Hoping to find a way to end suffering, the prince left his home and family and went seeking answers from other people who had gone in search of truth. When he realized that they did not have the answers, the prince sat in meditation and looked within himself. By doing so, he reached enlightenment, thus becoming the Buddha. With this knowledge, he traveled in northern India, teaching dharma and the Eightfold Path.

BEFORE READING

Make the Connection

Ask students what they think would end human suffering. Allow students to work in small groups to outline their solutions. Write their ideas on the chalkboard or on an overhead transparency, and refer to them after students have finished reading the selection.

Build Background

■ More About the Topic

The Buddha's first sermon was given to his former companions at Deer Park. The Buddha began by stating that two extremes must be avoided—overindulging in sensual pleasures and tormenting the body. He then taught the Four Noble Truths—suffering, its cause, its end, and the way to its end. The Buddha then outlined the Eightfold Path as

the way to end suffering. The steps of the Eightfold Path are Right Understanding—to know and understand the Four Noble Truths; Right Thought—to have thoughts of renunciation, goodwill to others, and kindness; Right Speech—to not tell lies or gossip; Right Action—to not kill or steal; Right Livelihood—to avoid trading in weapons, living beings, alcohol, or poison; Right Effort—to clear evil thoughts and develop good thought; Right Mindfulness—to be mindful of the body and thoughts; and Right Concentration—to keep the mind focused as in meditation.

Vocabulary Development

The following words are underscored and defined in the student text.

privilege: special favor.

forsaken: cast aside; abandoned.

quest: search or pursuit, usually of knowledge or some important goal or object.

reluctant: hesitant.

compounded: made up of various elements; complex.

Before assigning the reading, you may want to introduce students to any words that could cause pronunciation or definition problems.

Vocabulary Tip

Using Context Clues (Synonyms) Remind students that familiar words in a sentence can help them determine the meaning of an unfamiliar word. For example, on page 141, the first sentence under the subhead Enlightenment states that Gautama was alone and *forsaken*. If students do not know the meaning of *forsaken*, they should know what *alone* means. By looking for clues that show how an unfamiliar word is similar in meaning to a more familiar word, students can learn the meaning of a word and increase their vocabulary.

Although the following words are important to an understanding of the text selection, some of them may be unfamiliar to students. Present this list of words and definitions to your students.

holy man: a person devoted to religion, usually living a simple life.

reality: that which is true; based on fact.

nirvana: a state of great peace; paradise; pure bliss.

enlightenment: a state of knowing truths; knowledge.

devote: to give up time or self for some sacred cause; dedicate.

strive: to expend great effort to do something.

Using the two vocabulary lists, have students predict what the selection will be about.

Reading Informational Material

Reading Skill
Identifying Text Structure: Chronological Order
Explain to students that a story about the events in a subject's life is typically presented in chronological, or time, order.

▶ **Teaching Tip**
Using Subheads This selection is divided into four major sections. Point out the subheads to students [The Quest, Enlightenment, Turning the Wheel of *Dharma, Parinirvana*]. Have students read each section and list the events in each section before moving on.

Reading Strategy
Understanding Text (Strategy 2)
To help your students summarize the main events in this selection, use Strategy 2 in Content-Area Reading Strategies. Provide students with a Sequence or Chronological Order Chart (Graphic Organizer 10) to help them arrange the events in the selection in the order in which they happened.

DURING READING

Using the Side-Margin Feature
▪ Buddhist Art: Mandalas
Ask students if they know of another design or art form that a religion uses to represent an ideal. Students may mention a cross, a fish sign, a star, a menorah, or the yin/yang symbol.

▶ **Teaching Tip**
Recognizing Figures of Speech Point out to students that figures of speech are often used to make imaginative comparisons. In the selection, a reference is made to those who had "just a little dust in their eyes." Ask students what they think this means. [Some people are not open to new ideas. These people would be "blinded"—their eyes closed. Others are more willing to hear new ideas and look at the world differently.]

Differentiating Instruction
▪ Learners Having Difficulty
Ask students to re-read each section. Then, tell them to draw two or three pictures that depict major events in that section. Ask them to write a sentence telling about the event. As a class, students can arrange the drawings in chronological order and bind them into a booklet.

AFTER READING

✔ Reading Check

The following are sample answers to the questions on student text page 144.

1. Siddhartha Gautama was born twenty-five hundred years ago; he was the son of a king in northern India; he lived a life of luxury.

2. The Buddha left his family and privileged life when he set out on his quest to find a way to end suffering.

3. The Buddha went seeking answers with the holy men of India. He studied their ways, practiced exercises, lived in forests, and starved himself. However, he realized that these acts were not answering the questions he had and that if he did not take better care of his body, he would not live to find the truth.

4. The Buddha reached enlightenment by sitting in meditation and looking within himself. After he became enlightened, he walked all over northern India, teaching and helping people.

5. The teaching of Buddha is called the *Dharma*. It is often symbolized by an eight-spoked wheel.

Reteaching

If students are still struggling with the concept of chronological order, have each work with a partner and draw a series of boxes on a sheet of paper. The boxes should meander across the page, like a path. Students should write "Enlightenment" in the middle of the path and "Parinirvana" at the end of the path. Tell students that they will record in the boxes the steps the Buddha took to find a way to end suffering. Ask the pairs of students to list on another sheet of paper the steps the Buddha took. Then, have them number these steps in the order in which they occurred in the selection. Finally, have them write each step in the appropriate box. Students can add symbols or color to their depictions of the Buddha's path.

Connecting to Language Arts
- Writing

Parable Have students read the parable of "The Burning House" on page 143. Remind them that a parable is a brief story that teaches a lesson about life. Unlike a fable that uses animal characters, a parable uses human characters. Have students choose a life lesson and create a parable to illustrate it. For example, they might write a parable about not stealing or cheating. Allow students to work in small groups to brainstorm their ideas and to write their parable. Put the parables together in a booklet and place it in the classroom or library.

- Speaking and Listening

Sharing Life's Lessons Have students think of an experience that taught them or someone else a lesson. They should list the details of the event in the order in which they occurred and include any special details, dialogue, or images that would make the story interesting. Once students have made notes about the experience, have them tell the story to the class. Suggest that they practice telling their stories a few times before they make their presentations.

Connecting Across the Curriculum: Geography

The Path of Enlightenment Assign students to locate on a map where the Buddha was born, where he lived with his family, where Budh Gaya and Deer Park are, and the towns he visited to spread his message. Additionally, students can research how far-reaching Buddhism is today. How many countries claim Buddhism as their country's religion? How important is Buddhism in the United States? What are the main principles of Buddhism? Have students read some of the Buddha's parables. After students have completed their research, they may work with a partner or independently to present the results of their investigations. They might create

- a pin map by placing a pin in each city or town that the Buddha traveled through or a call-out map by writing two or three sentences for each major city, describing the major events that occurred there.
- a map showing the countries to which Buddhism has spread. They can color-code the countries based on how many practicing Buddhists each country claims.
- a traveler's report, paraphrasing and interpreting the Buddha's parables.
- a mandala, discussing the materials used to create the artwork and the reason behind destroying the art upon its completion.

Further Resources
Books

Prince Siddhartha: The Story of Buddha by Jonathan Landaw.

Buddha by Demi.

The Prince Who Became a Beggar (Tales of Heaven and Earth) by Maina Okada, et al.

Assessment

Turn to page 149 for a multiple-choice test on the selection.

Test Answers

1. a **2.** d **3.** c **4.** b **5.** c
6. b **7.** d **8.** a **9.** d **10.** c

Confucianism and Taoism
from *One World, Many Religions*
by MARY POPE OSBORNE
(student text page 145)

Reading Level: Advanced

Text Summary
This excerpt examines two influential philosophers who shaped Chinese culture—Confucius and Lao-tzu. Dismayed by the violence and turmoil of the times, Confucius wanted to change the social order in China. He stressed the importance of family, tradition, and obedience. Lao-tzu, on the other hand, was more concerned with living a life of humility and simplicity. Neither one of these philosophers was interested in creating a religion. Nevertheless, both of these teachings were practiced as religions—Confucianism and Taoism—in China until the Chinese Communists intervened in 1949.

BEFORE READING

Make the Connection
Life is busy and stressful. People often react to this in a negative way—they may act rudely or say mean things. Ask students to work together in pairs and to suggest ways to make life easier and simpler. Some may suggest listening to music, taking a walk in a park, playing with their pet, or sitting by a river or the ocean. Ask students to share their ideas with the entire class, and write their suggestions on the chalkboard. Keep this list for reference during the reading of the selection.

Build Background
■ More About the Topic
Confucius was born in 551 B.C. in the Chinese state of Lu, an area noted for maintaining the traditions of the Chou civilization. Confucius was a teacher at heart, hoping to make education available to all people, not just the wealthy. Unhappy with his political involvement, Confucius left China at age fifty-six in self-imposed exile. He returned to his homeland eleven years later and continued teaching until he died at the age of seventy-three.

Few facts are known about Lao-tzu. He was born in China in the sixth century B.C. and was a curator of the Imperial Chinese archives. He is considered the founder of Taoism and the author of the *Tao Te Ching*. However, some historians question whether Lao-tzu actually wrote the text.

Vocabulary Development
The following words are underscored and defined in the student text.

courteous: polite and considerate.
relied: depended on; trusted.
infinite: having no limits; vast.
humble: modest.
revere: to feel deep respect toward; to worship.

Before assigning the reading, you may want to introduce students to any words that could cause pronunciation or definition problems.

Vocabulary Tip

Using Etymology Remind students that knowing the origin of a word's root will help them better understand its meaning. For example, the Latin root for *humble* is *humilis*, which means "low." Therefore, a humble person is not high and mighty, but down-to-earth. The author of this selection uses it to describe Confucius. Interestingly, there is a different Latin root for the word *humble* when it is used in the phrase, "to eat humble pie." Originally, this was "umble pie" where *umble* means "deer organs," which can be traced back to the Latin *lumbus*. Since a person who ate humble pie was thought to be of a lower status, "to eat umble [humble] pie" came to mean "to apologize under humiliating circumstances."

CONTENT-AREA VOCABULARY

Although the following words are important to an understanding of the text selection, some of them may be unfamiliar to students. Present this list of words and definitions to your students.

transmitter*: someone who communicates a message.

sages*: wise and knowing people, usually elders.

tradition: customs or practices that have been used for many years.

veneration: feeling of admiration and respect.

spiritual: religious; holy.

*Although students may be familiar with other meanings of these words, the words as used in the selection have specific meanings that pertain to the content area.

Reading Informational Material

Reading Skill
Identifying Text Structure: Comparison and Contrast
Explain to students that information is often presented by comparing and contrasting the subjects; that is, by seeing how the subjects are similar and how they are different. This skill helps the reader draw conclusions, make inferences, and determine cause and effect.

Reading Strategy
Using Graphic Organizers (Strategy 3)
To help students note the similarities and differences between each philosopher, use Strategy 3 in Content-Area Reading Strategies. Provide students with a Venn Diagram (Graphic Organizer 11) to help students organize their thoughts as they move through the reading process.

DURING READING

Using the Side-Margin Feature
• The Yin and Yang
One story that explains the circle that encloses this symbol is that the circle represents a legendary hen's egg from which the first man, P'an Ku, was born. After eighteen thousand years had passed, the egg enclosing P'an Ku opened out, or hatched.

The yang element separated itself from the yin; the elements of light were separated from the elements of earth; P'an Ku grew taller and taller and held heaven above the earth. Another source attributes the circle to the shadow cast by the eight-foot pole used by the ancient Chinese to track the sun's cycle through the year. The final sun track and its shadow formed the yin and yang symbol, containing the cycle of the year and the four seasons. The two small circles mark the positions of the summer and winter solstices. Ask students to investigate other meanings attributed to the yin and yang symbol.

Teaching Tip
▶ *Organizing Text* Point out to students that a writer may organize an article that compares and contrasts two subjects by using the block method (writing about one subject first and then the other) or the point-by-point method (comparing and contrasting the subjects point by point). The writer of this text uses the block method, first discussing Confucianism and then Taoism, with similarities stated at the end of the selection.

Differentiating Instruction
• Advanced Learners
Have students read some sections of the *Tao Te Ching* and choose several to paraphrase. Students may work with a partner, as these writings are difficult to understand. Have students use a modern example of how the philosophy can be implemented. Students may present their findings to the class.

AFTER READING

✓ Reading Check

The following are sample answers to the questions on student text page 149.

1. The sages were wise men of ancient times. Confucius taught the wisdom of the sages because society had fallen into chaos, and greed and violence had taken over.

2. Confucius said that government leaders should care for the people just as a good father cares for his family.

3. "Never do to others what you would not like them to do to you." Responses will vary, but most religions practice this simple philosophy.

4. "The Tao" is usually translated as "the way" or "the road." People who live in harmony with the Tao live a quiet, simple life and are humble and compassionate.

5. Chinese folk tradition teaches that the ancestors connect the world of the living with the world of the gods. The spirits of the ancestors can protect people by interceding with the gods.

Reteaching

If students are still struggling with the concept of comparison and contrast, divide the class in half—one half to define and clarify the concepts of Confucianism and the other half to do the same for Taoism. To encourage discussion, ask each half to break into groups of three or four. Once students have made their notes and have a full understanding of their philosophies, pair a Confucian expert with a Taoism expert. Ask them to work together to complete a Venn Diagram (Graphic Organizer 11).

Connecting to Language Arts

▪ Writing

Anthology of Wisdom Have students read some of *The Analects of Confucius*. They can find the book at the library or they can find translations of the Analects on the Internet. Have students choose their favorites and make a poster that captures the messages. Students may either paraphrase the sayings or create their own messages that restate the underlying principles. Students can put their posters together in a book for the classroom or the library.

▪ Speaking and Listening

Sharing Chinese Folk Tales The selection mentions folk traditions and the importance of keeping these traditions alive. One Chinese folk tradition is the art of storytelling. Ask students to find a short Chinese folk tale in the library and get together with three classmates to prepare a group reading. If the story contains dialogue, remind students to suit their voices to the roles. Have students present their folk tales to the class and, at the same time, record the folk tales on audiotape to place in the library.

Connecting Across the Curriculum: Art and Culture

Chinese New Year Festival Ask students to find out about the Chinese New Year and how it is celebrated. Then, tell students that working independently or with another student, they are going to use their research to plan a Chinese New Year celebration for the class. For the celebration, students might create one of the following:

- a poster of their animal signs from the Chinese zodiac, including an analysis of whether the animals' characteristics fit their personalities
- a poster that provides information about the current year according to the Chinese zodiac
- a traditional Chinese New Year dish
- fortune cookies with fortunes

Students could also create "booths" or centers to teach one of the following skills:

- Chinese mask painting
- Chinese checkers or mah-jongg
- how to make shadow puppets for acting out a Chinese folk tale
- how to make a Chinese paper lantern
- how to make a Chinese kite

Further Resources
Books

The Analects of Confucius by Confucius; D.C. Lau, translator.

Tao Te Ching (Everyman's Library) by Lao-tzu; D.C. Lau, translator.

Taoism (World Religions) by Paula R. Hartz.

Pooh and the Millennium: In Which the Bear of Very Little Brain Explores the Ancient Mysteries at the Turn of the Century by John Tyerman Williams.

Assessment

Turn to page 150 for a multiple-choice test on the selection.

Test Answers

1. c **2.** d **3.** b **4.** a **5.** d
6. c **7.** b **8.** c **9.** a **10.** d

from **The Great Wall of China**

from *Walls: Defenses Throughout History*

by JAMES CROSS GIBLIN
(student text page 150)

Reading Level: Average

Text Summary

This selection describes the building of the Great Wall of China, primarily focusing on its construction under the supervision of Emperor Shih Huang-ti. In addition to providing statistics about the length of the wall, how long it took to build, how many people were involved in its erection, and unique features of the wall, the author also provides details about Emperor Shih's harsh rule.

BEFORE READING

Make the Connection

Ask students why people construct walls. [to keep pets safely in a yard, to provide privacy, for protection, to hide something] Then, ask students to look at the illustrations and read the title of the selection, the Sidelight, and the side-margin feature. Ask students what they already know about the Great Wall of China and what they think they will find out by reading this selection. Record their comments on the chalkboard. Conclude the discussion by asking students to propose theories as to why the Chinese constructed the wall.

Build Background

• More About the Topic

The Great Wall was built over a period of 1,000 years by different dynasties. Three dynasties, however, made significant contributions. During the Qin dynasty, the oldest section of the wall was built. Under the Han dynasty, workers restored portions of the wall that had collapsed and added another three hundred miles across the Gobi desert. During the Ming dynasty, accomplished builders not only extended the wall, but also added more elaborate features. Emperor Shih of the Qin dynasty, known for his ruthless tactics, supervised the building of three thousand miles of the wall. He also designed his own tomb, a burial site guarded by an army of clay soldiers.

Vocabulary Development

The following words are underscored and defined in the student text.

ruthless: showing no mercy; cruel.

embarked: set forth; began.

ambitious: requiring great skill or effort for success.

priority: something that is first in importance or order.

restored: brought back to a former condition.

Before assigning the reading, you may want to introduce students to any words that could cause pronunciation or definition problems.

─ *Vocabulary Tip* ─

Using Suffixes The common suffix *–less* means "without." For example, *homeless* means without a home, *formless* means without form or shape, and *powerless* means without power. *Ruthless* is a little different from most other words with this suffix in that the base word *ruth* is seldom used. But *ruth*, from early Middle English *ruethe* meaning "to rue," is a perfectly good English word, meaning "feeling compassion or sorrow for another person." You could describe a person as either ruthful or ruthless, but *ruthless* is much more commonly used.

(**CONTENT-AREA VOCABULARY**)

Although the following words are important to an understanding of the text selection, some of them may be unfamiliar to students. Present this list of words and definitions to students. Have students think of other homographs—words that are spelled the same but have different meanings and pronunciations. [wind (to twist)—wind (breeze); bass (a musical instrument)—bass (a fish); sow (to disperse seeds)—sow (a female pig); pre*sent*—pre*sent;* and so on] Post a chart in the classroom and encourage students to add other homographs.

rampart: a wall used for defense against attack.

wind*: to extend in a twisting or zigzag manner.

siege: a drawn-out attack or assault of a place.

mortar*: mixture of cement used as a plaster to hold bricks or stones in place.

incline: a sloped surface or grade.

*Although students may be familiar with other meanings of these words the words as used in the selection have specific meanings that pertain to the content area.

Reading Informational Material

Reading Skill

Using Text Structures: Description

Explain to students that description is a technique authors use to develop an idea. They use specific details to create a clear picture of an object or an event.

▶ Teaching Tip

Understanding Text Structure This selection provides a chronology of the building of the Great Wall. Point out to students that texts often have more than one structure. Even though a writer may be telling the history of an event in the order in which it happened, he or she is also interested in describing the event colorfully.

Reading Strategy

Activating and Using Prior Knowledge (Strategy 8)

To help your students think about ideas while reading, use Strategy 8 in Content-Area Reading Strategies. Provide students with a KWLS Chart (Graphic Organizer 7) to help them set a purpose for reading based on what they already know about the Great Wall.

DURING READING

Using the Side-Margin Feature

• Protection or Prison

Ask students if they know of other famous walls that have been built in other parts of the world. Students might mention the Berlin Wall, Hadrian's Wall, the Wailing Wall, or the Vietnam Memorial Wall. Discuss the purpose for building these different walls. Are walls a good or bad idea? Ask students to support their opinions with examples.

Reading Informational Material

▶ Teaching Tip

Engaging the Reader Point out to students that a startling fact or statistic used at the beginning of a text can engage a reader's interest. What startling fact or facts are included in the first paragraph? [The Great Wall can circle the globe at the equator with an eight-foot-high wall. It is the only man-made structure visible with the naked eye from the moon.]

Differentiating Instruction

▪ English-Language Learners

To help these students get an idea of the subject matter before reading and to make reading easier, work with students to complete their KWLS Charts by looking at the photo on page 151. Encourage students to look at photographs and illustrations of the Great Wall in books from the library. After determining that students understand the subject of the selection, ask them to fill in their KWLS Charts.

AFTER READING

✓ Reading Check

The following are sample answers to the questions on student text page 156.

1. The difference in length depends on whether the measurement is taken from beginning to end, or whether it includes all of the loops and offshoots.

2. Emperor Shih Huang-ti was cruel, ambitious, power-hungry, and proud of his empire. He burned books and buried people alive if they disobeyed his commands. He also built roads and canals.

3. Over one million people worked on the Great Wall. Working conditions were very poor. It was either too hot or too cold, and the people had little shelter and food. They were also attacked by nomads. People were often buried in the wall.

4. The author compares the Great Wall to a giant stone snake.

5. The Great Wall is studied by scientists today who are interested in gathering information about the effect of earthquakes that occurred in the past. Archaeologists also search for artifacts to understand more about the people who built it.

Reteaching

If students are still struggling with the concept of description, ask them to make a drawing, diorama, or model of a particular aspect or stage in the building of the Great Wall. Tell them to include detailed labels and full descriptions in their work. These details will be from the selection, their previous knowledge, and their research from other sources. Display the students' work in the library, along with the resources they used for research.

Connecting to Language Arts

■ Writing

Letter Writing Have students write a letter to Emperor Shih Huang-ti, expressing their views on the Great Wall and its construction. Was building the Great Wall a good idea? Did it fulfill expectations? What do they think of the emperor's treatment of his subjects? Encourage students to read their letters to the class.

■ Speaking and Listening

Sharing Life's Lessons Emperor Shih had a problem: The villages on the northern border of his empire were ravaged by nomads. The Great Wall was his solution to this problem. What other solutions were available to the emperor? In groups of three or four, ask students to arrive at another solution to the problem of the ravaging nomads. The solution must be described in detail and reasons for choosing it must be given. Have each group present its solution to the class and rate the solutions for practicality and creativity.

Connecting Across the Curriculum: History

Ancient Inventions The Chinese were great inventors. Assign students to choose one invention by the ancient Chinese, such as paper, the harvesting of silk, porcelain, kites, compasses, or wheelbarrows. Students should find out when the invention was created, what led to the invention, and the effect the invention had on the world. After students have completed their research, they may work with a partner or independently to present the results of their investigations as:

- a drawing or working model of the invention, explaining how it works, its importance in history, and its impact on society
- an advertisement for the invention, highlighting its main features
- a story about the invention, describing its unique qualities and characteristics
- a sales pitch, verbally persuading the audience to try the new invention

Further Resources

Books

The Great Wall of China (Aladdin Picture Books) by Leonard Everett Fisher.
The Great Wall: The Wonders of the World Book by Elizabeth Mann.
The Great Wall of China (Building History Series) by Tim McNeese.
Map of China showing the Great Wall

Online

- Discovery Channel's Web site gives a history of the Great Wall on *Secrets of the Great Wall.*
- The China Vista Web site offers a virtual tour of the Great Wall.

Assessment

Turn to page 151 for a multiple-choice test on the selection.

Test Answers

1. b **2.** c **3.** a **4.** a **5.** c
6. d **7.** b **8.** a **9.** c **10.** d

March of the Terra-Cotta Soldiers

from *Archaeology's Dig*

by VICTORIA C. NESNICK
(student text page 157)

Reading Level: Above Average

Text Summary

The author tells about a visit to the tomb of Emperor Shihuangdi in China. The site was discovered in 1974 when local farmers were digging a well. At the foot of Mount Li, archaeologists have unearthed seven thousand clay warriors, horses, and chariots. These life-sized soldiers were created to protect the emperor's tomb and assist him in the afterlife. The excavations continue today, and an effort is being made to uncover Shihuangdi's burial tomb, allegedly filled with palace models, and decorated with diamonds and pearls that represent the night sky, gold ducks, and trees made of jade.

BEFORE READING

Make the Connection

Ask students why someone would want to be buried with his or her possessions. Write their responses on the board. Then, ask students to name cultures that bury the dead with their treasures. [Most students will mention the Egyptians.] Have students consider what a powerful ruler would take with him or her to the afterlife. Why might he or she take an entire army?

Build Background

■ More About the Topic

Shihuangdi was China's first emperor. He took the throne at age thirteen, but did not assume real power until the age of twenty-one. Although his dynasty lasted only fifteen years, he managed to unite China, construct roads and fortresses (including the Great Wall), and standardize Chinese writing, measures, and law. However, this unification did not come without a price. Shihuangdi executed Confucian scholars, burned books, and ruled with malice. He is often remembered for his inhumane treatment of his people.

Vocabulary Development

The following words are underscored and defined in the student text.

massive: huge.

catastrophe: a widespread misfortune or disaster.

souvenirs: things kept as reminders of the past.

conservation: careful use and protection; preservation.

disintegrate: to break apart into small pieces; to crumble.

Before assigning the reading, you may want to introduce students to any words that could cause pronunciation or definition problems.

CONTENT-AREA VOCABULARY

Although the following words are important to an understanding of the text selection, some of them may be unfamiliar to students. Present this list of words and definitions to students. Before reading the selection, ask students if they can determine the connection between these words, based on the title of the selection and the photographs.

terra cotta: brown-red baked clay, used for making pottery or sculptures.

sculpted: carved or shaped.

infantry: soldiers trained specifically to fight on foot.

cavalry: troops who ride on horses.

fired*: baked in a kiln or oven.

*Although students may be familiar with other meanings of this word, the word as used in the selection has a specific meaning that pertains to the content area.

Recognizing Multiple Meanings *Fire* has many meanings, both as a noun and as a verb. In this selection, the past tense verb form has a special-ized meaning. You can easily tell which meaning of *fired* an author intends if you pay attention to the context. In this selection clay pottery was *fired* in a kiln, a special oven that makes the clay hard and durable. If a gun is *fired*, it is being dis-charged. If a ball is *fired*, it is thrown or hit with great speed. If a person is *fired*, he or she is dis-missed from a job. And if a person is *fired up*, he or she excited or upset about something.

Reading Informational Material

Reading Skill
Finding the Main Idea
Explain to students that the main idea is an overall topic that is developed in an article or in part of an article. The main idea includes the most important ideas expressed in the article.

▶ **Teaching Tip**
Finding the Main Idea This selection is from a magazine article. Point out to students that the selection is divided into three sections ["How Were They Found?" "Why Were They Made?" and "The Last Puzzle Piece?"]. Have students take notes as they read to summarize the main idea in each section.

Reading Strategy
Building Background Information (Strategy 6)
To help your students make predictions before reading, use Strategy 6 in Content-Area Reading Strategies. Provide students with a Predicting and Confirming Activity (Graphic Organizer 8) to help them set a purpose for reading based on their pre-dictions.

DURING READING

▶ **Teaching Tip**
Making Inferences This article provides informa-tion about the terra-cotta warriors and the emperor who ordered them created. While the warriors are an amazing accomplishment, the clay figures are also a reminder of Shihuangdi's cruelty. Ask stu-dents to express their opinion about Shihuangdi after they read about the workers at the burial site being buried alive in order to keep the site's loca-tion a secret. Why do they think the author included this information? [Students will probably state that the emperor was extremely harsh. Killing people to keep a secret is proof of this. Spending so much time and resources on a burial complex for one's self is also extreme. As this article focuses on the burial site as an archaeological find, the author may want to make the reader aware of its human cost.]

Differentiating Instruction
■ English-Language Learners
Divide students into four groups, one group for the introduction and each of the three sections of the selection. Ask students to listen as one of their group reads an assigned section aloud. Then, have each student write one sentence on a strip of paper. The sentence should be about something in the section they found interesting. Then, each group will arrange their sentence strips in order of importance and tape them to a sheet of paper. Finally, have all the groups share their findings.

AFTER READING

✔ Reading Check

The following are sample answers to the questions on student text page 162.

1. The first people who saw the ancient terra-cotta soldiers were farmers who were digging a well. They thought they had discovered a ghost.

2. Over six thousand statues were excavated in the first pit. In the second pit, archaeologists found fourteen hundred foot soldiers, cavalry, and the remains of ninety war chariots.

3. Shihuangdi may have had these soldiers created in order to protect his tomb, to escort him in the afterlife, or to celebrate his military victo-ries. Sculptors, others who worked on the tomb, and anyone who knew about it were buried alive.

4. Sima Qian wrote that Shihuangdi's tomb had diamonds and pearls used to represent the night sky, silver and gold ducks, and jade trees. Experts believe there may be some truth to this as they have verified other things Sima Qian wrote.

5. The Chinese have learned that the tomb must not be opened right away as exposure to air may cause delicate items, such as paper and silk, to disintegrate. Once the tomb is opened, workers must be ready to take proper care of the artifacts. Lack of money and the presence of booby traps may also delay excavation.

Reteaching

If students are still struggling with the concept of main idea, have them create a four-column chart. Tell students to label the first column "Introduction" and the next three columns with the subheads of the three sections. Students may work in pairs to summarize each section. Ask students to look for important details, in particular those that answer the question of the subhead. [For example, under **How Were They Found?** Students can add details such as "farmers digging a well, found head of clay warrior, excavations begin, found six thousand statues, some beheaded," and so on.] Once students have identified the important details of their section, they can work on writing the section's main idea. Encourage students to write the main idea of the section using only one or two sentences. Share main ideas with the class.

Connecting to Language Arts

▪ Writing

Free Verse Have students write a poem in free verse, without a regular meter or rhyme scheme. The poem should be written from the point of view of one of the sculptors and include the following elements: the sculptor's mood or feeling about the terra-cotta warrior he or she is sculpting, a description of the tomb or building site (students may use the photos in the selection, from library resources, or from the Internet to get ideas), a figure of speech (simile, metaphor, hyperbole, or personification), and a message the sculptor has for those reading the poem. Students may wish to illustrate their poems and publish them by displaying them in the classroom.

▪ Speaking and Listening

Apology Qin Shihuangdi was a brutal ruler. In fact, when he died, the Ch'in dynasty collapsed and the imperial family was killed. Have students research Shihuangdi's regime to learn about his harsh rule. Then, have students write an apology—from Qin to the people of China—expressing his remorse for treating his people so badly. Students will read their apologies to the class. Consider voting on the most sincere, most heartfelt apology.

Connecting Across the Curriculum: Science

Weathered Warriors The writer mentions that exposure to the air has erased some of the colors of paint from the clay warriors. She also states that if Shihuangdi's tomb is found, exposure to air may cause disintegration of certain items, such as paper and silk. Assign students to investigate how exposure to external forces such as rain and wind is affecting many ancient structures. What can be done to protect them and conserve ancient structures? Why does air alone have such a detrimental effect? After students have completed their research, they may work with a partner or independently to present the results of their investigations. They might create:

- ▪ an illustration that demonstrates how weather causes erosion
- ▪ a clay figurine, demonstrating how water can easily crumble its shape
- ▪ a flip book of ancient structures that have been affected by erosion and steps that have been taken to preserve them

Further Resources
Book
> *The Incredible Story of China's Buried Warriors (Frozen in Time, Set 2)* by Dorothy Hinshaw Patent.

Map of China

> ### (Assessment)
>
> Turn to page 152 for a multiple-choice test on the selection.
>
> *Test Answers*
> **1.** d **2.** a **3.** c **4.** b **5.** a
> **6.** c **7.** d **8.** b **9.** c **10.** a

The following criteria can help you evaluate each student's success in completing the activities prompted by the Cross-Curricular Activities feature in the student textbook.

Science/History
Made in China
- The student researches some of the technological, scientific, or medical contributions of the ancient Chinese by using the Internet or other tools.
- The student makes a list of important discoveries or advancements made by the ancient Chinese, including approximate dates of each innovation.
- The student may choose to create a visual time line of Chinese inventions.
- The student discusses the findings with classmates.

History/Geography
Map It Out
- The student researches Mohenjo-daro and Harappa and finds photographs of the excavations.
- The student uses the photos to draw his or her own map of these cities and includes the positions of homes, granaries, public baths, and other structures or important sites.

Language Arts
Sum It Up
- The student re-reads the selections about the Great Wall and the terra-cotta soldiers to gather more information about the first emperor of China, Shihuangdi.
- The student does further research by using Internet or library sources on the life and accomplishments of the emperor.
- The student writes an epitaph that summarizes the emperor's life.

History/Art
Cartoon Characters
- The student brainstorms about the ways that a comic book's words and pictures work together to tell a story.
- The student chooses one key event in Ashoka's life to write about in a comic-book history.
- The student draws cartoon pictures and writes speech bubbles to reveal the characters' thoughts and words.

Language Arts
Three of a Kind
- The student writes an essay comparing and contrasting Ashoka, Mohandas K. Gandhi, and Dr. Martin Luther King, Jr.
- The student addresses these questions: What did they each want for their people? What obstacles stood in their way, and how did they overcome them? What were key aspects of their philosophies?

Drama/Music
Scenes from a Life
- The student chooses two scenes from the life of either Confucius or the Buddha.
- The student rewrites the scenes as scripts and finds music to accompany them.
- The student performs the script as a member of a small group or as a partnership.
- The performance is relatively free of performance errors. Props, costumes, music, sound effects, and other enhancements contribute to the overall effectiveness of the students' performance.

CHAPTER 6

The Classical World
Ancient Greece and Rome
1000 B.C.–A.D. 350

---

from The Ancient Olympics

from *The Olympic Games*
by THEODORE KNIGHT
(student text page 167)

CONTENT-AREA CONNECTIONS

HISTORY •
PHYSICAL EDUCATION •

Reading Level: Average

Text Summary

This excerpt recounts the evolution of the ancient Olympic Games from a handful of footraces to a five-day athletic competition accompanied by pageants, parades, feasts, and rituals. At first, participation in the games was limited to male Greek citizens who had enough money to train, travel, and host victory celebrations; eventually, women were allowed to compete. The games went into decline after Rome conquered Greece. After more than twelve hundred years of competition, the games were banned in A.D. 393.

BEFORE READING

Make the Connection

Ask students for their memories of recent Olympic Games that they may have seen on television. What events did they most enjoy? Who were their favorite athletes? What is necessary to compete in the Olympics?

Build Background
■ More About the Modern Olympics

The Olympic Games have changed considerably since they were revived in 1896. From thirteen nations competing in ten sports that year, the Games have grown into an event involving hundreds of countries and thousands of competitors. Originally, the Games were held every four years. That changed in 1994, when the Winter Games were held early to put them on an alternating two-year schedule with the Summer Games. Another monumental change occurred in 1986, when the governing body of the Olympics revoked the rule that limited the Games to amateur athletes.

Vocabulary Development

The following words are underscored and defined in the student text.

anonymous: not known by name.
initiating: starting; beginning.
barred: kept out; banned.
spectators: onlookers.
confined: restricted.
hostilities: warfare.
pageants: colorful shows or entertainments.
spectacle: dramatic public display.
negotiate: to bargain with others in hope of reaching agreement.
bribery: giving money to someone to do something illegal.

Before assigning the reading, you may want to introduce students to any words that could cause pronunciation or definition problems.

CONTENT-AREA VOCABULARY

Although the following words are important to an understanding of the text selection, some of them may be unfamiliar to students. Ask students what the words in the list have in common. [All the words are related to athletes and athletic events.]

trained*: practiced for an athletic event.

sprint: a short footrace run at top speed.

hippodrome: a stadium where horse and chariot races were held.

contestants: people who take part in an athletic competition.

*Although students may be familiar with other meanings of this word, the word as used in the selection has a specific meaning that pertains to the content area.

Reading Informational Materials

Reading Skill
Using Prior Knowledge
Explain to students that they will better understand the main points of a reading selection if they think about what they already know about the subject before beginning to read.

▶ **Teaching Tip**

A Reason to Read If students are having difficulty focusing on prior knowledge that applies to this particular reading selection, write a reading purpose statement on the chalkboard. [for example, *to learn about the ancient Olympic Games*] If students understand their purpose for reading, they can avoid getting bogged down in discussions of the modern Games.

Reading Strategy
Activating and Using Prior Knowledge (Strategy 8)
To help students activate their prior knowledge about the subject of a reading selection and increase their understanding of the text, use Strategy 8 described in Content-Area Reading Strategies. To help students organize their prior knowledge before they begin reading and to use that knowledge as they read, you may wish to provide them with a KWLS Chart (Graphic Organizer 7).

DURING READING

Viewing the Art
■ Chariot Race

Direct students to the drawing [a chariot race] on page 170 and have a student read the caption aloud. Why would this picture be used to illustrate a story about the ancient Olympic Games? [Chariot racing was a popular event in the Games.] What differences exist between ancient chariot racing and modern horse racing? [Chariots are not used or have given way to sulkies (small, lightweight carriages used in harness racing); horses and jockeys rarely die; horses are usually monitored for humane treatment.]

Differentiating Instruction
■ Learners Having Difficulty

Vowel combinations in the Greek names in the selection may intimidate some students. Emphasize to students that these names are not critical to their understanding of the text's main idea. Discuss with them how skipping names or assigning a "nickname" to replace a difficult name in their minds can be a strategy for understanding a new text.

AFTER READING

✓ Reading Check

The following are sample answers to questions on student page 173.

1. Only male Greek citizens were allowed to compete at first. They needed to be rich in order to pay for the cost of ten months of training, of

traveling to the games, and of hosting banquets to celebrate their victories.

2. Women competed in the 128th Olympics. A woman named Belisiche won the chariot race that year.

3. The festival included pageants, parades, feasts, and religious rituals as well as athletic events. On the third day, one hundred cattle were sacrificed to the gods.

4. The religious significance was lost; athletes began to demand prizes and money; cheating and bribery increased; real athletic competition died out.

5. Emperor Theodosius I banned the games in A.D. 393 because Christians considered them a pagan ritual.

Reteaching

If students had difficulty organizing their prior knowledge, create and work through a three-column PIC organizer. Label the columns *P, I, C*. Put the chart on a transparency, and ask students to explain why people would want to read the selection. Fill in their answers under the *Purpose* column. Ask them to tell you the important ideas from the selection as you fill in the middle column of the chart. Now that they know more about the ancient Olympics, ask them to explain how the article expanded their prior knowledge. Record their answers on the transparency in the *Connection* column.

Connecting to Language Arts
- **Writing**

Politics and the Games The Olympics are supposed to be apolitical, but politics have intervened on more than one occasion. Have students research the history of the modern Olympic Games to find occasions when political controversy intruded on the Games. Students should also research the results of the situation. [the 1936 Games held in Nazi Germany, the 1972 hostage incident, and the cold war boycotts of 1980 and 1984] Students can present their findings in a birth announcement or an obituary, writing of the rebirth or death of the Olympic spirit.

Connecting Across the Curriculum: History

A Man with a Plan Have students research Baron Pierre de Coubertin, the Frenchman who revived the Olympics. Who was he? [a member of the French aristocracy who was interested in education reform] How long did it take for the Olympics to be revived? [Coubertin made a public plea for an Olympics in 1892; the first games were held in 1896.] What did he think the Games could accomplish? [peace and increased communication among nations] After students have completed their research, they can pool their findings or work independently to present the results of their investigations. They might complete one of the following assignments:

- a biographical sketch or informational article about Coubertin
- a presentation speech for an award to Coubertin for his work on the Olympics
- a postage stamp commemorating Coubertin's work on reviving the Olympics
- a design proposal for a statue honoring Coubertin
- a magazine cover for a story about Coubertin and the revival of the Olympics

Further Resources
- **Video**

100 Years of Olympic Glory, directed by Bud Greenspan (1996; PBS documentary).

Chariots of Fire, directed by Hugh Hudson (1981, rated PG).

- **Books**

The Original Olympics (Ancient Greece), Stewart Ross and Peter Bedrick.

The Ancient Olympic Games, by Judith Swaddling.

Assessment

Turn to page 153 for a multiple-choice test on the selection.

Test Answers

1. c	2. b	3. a	4. c	5. d
6. b	7. g	8. c	9. f	10. a
11. d	12. f	13. c	14. a	15. e

The Spartan Way

from *Junior Scholastic*

by SEAN PRICE
(student text page 174)

Reading Level: Average

Text Summary

This magazine article details the harsh and disciplined life in the ancient Greek city-state of Sparta. Rising to power on the strength of its brutal army, Sparta held sway over the Greek world for more than two hundred years. Spartans despised comfort and luxury and valued order, discipline, and obedience.

BEFORE READING

Make the Connection

Ask students why a society would offer people food which is intentionally made to taste bad. [Students might suggest that the society is trying to keep people from being pampered and to prepare them for a rigorous life.] What purpose could be served by not allowing children to wear shoes even in winter? [Some students might say such behavior could lead to illness; others might say it would strengthen the immune system and make people appreciate better treatment.] Why might children be taught not to show pain? [Failure to show pain might make them seem invincible and might intimidate their enemies.]

Build Background

■ More About Thebes

Ancient Greeks, while very loyal to their particular city-states, felt little unity with one another; city-states were as likely to go to war with one another as with outsiders. One city-state with a history as turbulent as that of Sparta was Thebes. It was destroyed in 1200 B.C., shortly before the Trojan War. By the time of the Peloponnesian War, Thebes had returned to power and sided with Sparta against Athens. Soon after the war ended, Thebes and Sparta were fighting each other. After crushing the Spartan army in 371 B.C., Thebes reigned as Greece's supreme military power for ten years before falling into civil discord and eventually

being taken over by Philip II of Macedon, the father of Alexander the Great. In a revolt against Philip in 338 B.C., Thebes suffered an overwhelming defeat. Two years later, after the assassination of Philip, the city rebelled against Alexander and was nearly destroyed. It never regained its former power.

Vocabulary Development

The following words are underscored and defined in the student text.

deceit: misleading by telling lies.
dominated: controlled; ruled over.
endure: to put up with quietly.
provisions: food and other supplies.
overbearing: arrogant or domineering.

Before assigning the reading, you may want to introduce students to any words that could cause pronunciation or definition problems.

> ― *Vocabulary Tip* ―
>
> **Using Context Clues** Tell students that they often must look for context clues beyond the sentence in which an unfamiliar word appears. For example, there are few context clues for the word *deceit* in the sentence in which it appears. However, the first paragraph tells how the boy misled his questioners about the fox and showed fearlessness about his injuries. By pairing those context clues with the sentence in which *deceit* appears, students can guess that *deceit* suggests behavior that fools or misleads.

―(**CONTENT-AREA VOCABULARY**)―

Although the following words are important to an understanding of the text selection, some of them may be unfamiliar to students.

qualities: traits or behaviors.
discipline: adhering to strict rules under threat of punishment.

secretive: inclined to keep things secret.

customs: practices or behaviors that are common to a certain area.

restrictions: limitations.

Encourage students to predict what the selection might be about based on these words. [Students may say the selection is probably about the values and behavior of a strict society.]

Reading Informational Materials

Reading Skill
Determining the Main Idea

Explain to students that the main idea is the message, opinion, or insight that is the focus of an article or a piece of writing and that the details are included to support that idea.

Reading Strategy
Constructing Concept Maps (Strategy 4)

To help students determine the main idea of the selection, use Strategy 4 described in Content-Area Reading Strategies. You may want students to develop their own concept maps, but if some students have difficulty with a free-form activity, you could offer them a Cluster Diagram (Graphic Organizer 3) or create a Cloze Concept Map on which you have filled in some of the spaces.

▶ **Teaching Tip**
Organizing Versatility Tell students that the Cluster Diagram (Graphic Organizer 3) can be modified to suit their needs and the requirements of the text. Students can use only some of the circles, or they can add lines, arrows, triangles, squares, or more circles.

DURING READING

Using the Side-Margin Feature
■ Athens and the Golden Age

Ask students to identify differences between Sparta and Athens. [In Athens, citizens voted on city matters; Sparta was ruled by rich families. Athenians admired art and philosophy; Spartans admired order and discipline.] How were the cities similar? [Both were Greek city-states; both left legacies for the modern world.]

Reading Informational Materials

▶ **Teaching Tip**
The Importance of Re-reading Tell students not to panic if they have not identified the main idea and all the supporting details after reading the selection once. After reading the selection, students may benefit from reading the selection a second time, using different-colored self-adhesive notes to mark main points and supporting details as they read.

Differentiating Instruction
■ English-Language Learners

Figurative language may create special problems for English-language learners. Examples of figurative language in this selection include "…shape the modern world," "built the foundations of Western culture," and "opposing armies crumbled at the very sight." Have a volunteer draw pictures of each of these examples. [Show someone creating a globe of clay, someone placing brick and mortar under the word *culture*, armies collapsing like a hill of dry sand.] Explain to students that the images created here are not to be taken literally, but as colorful ways of creating memorable comparisons. Ask native English speakers to supply simple phrases to replace the figurative ones. [influence the modern world; developed the ideas that are basic to Western culture]

AFTER READING

✔ Reading Check

The following are sample answers to questions on student text page 179.

1. Qualities the Spartans held dear included strength, discipline, the ability to trick the enemy, and fearlessness about pain and death.

2. Spartan boys were taught only the basics of reading and writing, while boys in Athens received a much fuller education.

3. During their free time, Spartan men talked, exercised, hunted, and attended dances, festivals, and feasts.

4. The Spartans feared a slave revolt because slaves outnumbered Spartans ten to one.

5. By the time it was conquered by Rome, Sparta was reduced to being a tourist attraction.

Reteaching

Students having difficulty constructing concept maps can benefit from teacher modeling of the process using the "You Need to Know…" feature on page 174. Read the feature aloud, then write a statement of the main idea in the center of a cluster diagram. [Sparta's relationship with Messenia fueled the need for a strong army.] Re-read the feature aloud, pausing to allow students to add supporting details to the cluster diagram. [Sparta demanded half of Messenia's food; Messenia's resistance caused Sparta to focus on military training; that focus increased Sparta's need for Messenia's food; that need for food made military training more important.] Discuss with students how details throughout the reading support the main idea.

Connecting to Language Arts

▪ Writing

Pro and Con Have students work in groups to discuss the Spartan way of life. Do they agree or disagree with the Spartan emphasis on military training and harsh discipline? Should a society be ruled by a small number of wealthy families? Should the roles of men and women be so rigidly defined? After their discussions, each group should write a letter to the editor of a fictional newspaper in ancient Athens supporting or disagreeing with the Spartan way of life. Writers should support their opinions with details and finish with a strong statement of their beliefs.

Connecting Across the Curriculum: History

Slaves of Sparta Have students research the practice of slavery in Sparta and ancient Greece. Who was forced into slavery? How did slavery affect Spartan society? After students have completed their research, they may want to pool their findings or work independently to present the results of their investigations. They might complete one of the following assignments:

- a pamphlet written by a Spartan slave calling for a revolt against the slaveholder
- a letter smuggled out of Sparta to the family of a person forced into slavery (the letter should include how the person was captured)

- the step-by-step actions, including maps or diagrams, of a slave leader planning to escape or lead a slave rebellion
- a time-traveling journalist's interview with a Spartan slave

Further Resources

▪ **Book**

The Spartans (Osprey Military Elite Series, 66), written by Nicholas Victor Sekunda and illustrated by Richard Hook.

Assessment

Turn to page 154 for a multiple-choice test on the selection.

Test Answers
1. a **2.** c **3.** b **4.** d **5.** b
6. c **7.** a **8.** b **9.** d **10.** a

from In the Footsteps of Alexander the Great

based on the Maryland Public Television series

by MICHAEL WOOD

(student text page 180)

Reading Level: Above average

Text Summary

This excerpt from "In the Footsteps of Alexander the Great" details the author's travels from Greece to Asia as he filmed a public television documentary series about Alexander III of Macedon. The author and his film crew followed the route taken by Alexander as he built one of history's greatest empires. Along the way, the author gained insight into the contradictory aspects of Alexander's personality while enduring the same hardships and rugged terrain that confronted the commander and his army.

BEFORE READING

Make the Connection

Ask students to name some of the great empires in history. [the British Empire, the Roman Empire, the Ottoman Empire, and the Byzantine Empire] How do the students feel about a country conquering its neighbors in order to expand its boundaries? [Opinions will vary.]

Build Background

■ Motivate

If possible, acquire a videotape copy of "In the Footsteps of Alexander the Great" or another feature about Alexander the Great or the empire he built. Preview the video, and select a segment that you feel is appropriate for your students and interesting enough to spark discussion. Show the segment in class before you begin the prereading portion of your instruction. After students have watched the segment, have them brainstorm a list of questions that they would like answered about Alexander and his quest for an empire.

Vocabulary Development

The following words are underscored and defined in the student text.

vindictive: desiring revenge.
dynamic: strong and energetic.
melancholy: sad; gloomy.
vindicated: cleared of blame or suspicion; justified.
eroded: worn or eaten away.

Before assigning the reading, you may want to introduce students to any words that could cause pronunciation or definition problems.

┌─ *Vocabulary Tip* ─

Word Histories Tell students that understanding the etymology of a word can help them guess the meaning of words that share the same roots. For example, *vindicate* comes from the Latin *vindicare*, meaning "to avenge." Knowing that, readers can guess that *vindictive* has something to do with revenge. Pairing this guess with the context in which *vindictive* appears in the selection, the reader can guess that Alexander desired revenge.

CONTENT-AREA VOCABULARY

Although the following words are important to an understanding of the text selection, some of them may be unfamiliar to students. Ask students to use this list of words to predict what the selection will be about. [The selection will probably feature a powerful leader involved in military battles for land.]

crusade*: a military journey carried out with great passion.
visionary: one who has great foresight and imagination.
tyrant: one who rules using fear and brutality.

trek: journey.

conquest: the act of defeating and taking over another group.

*Although students may be familiar with other meanings of this word, the word as used in the selection has a specific meaning that pertains to the content area.

Reading Informational Materials

Reading Skill
Making Predictions

Explain to students that making predictions before reading a text can help them access their prior knowledge of the subject of the text and better understand the points the author is trying to make.

▶ **Teaching Tip**

Previewing When selecting words that represent important concepts in the text, look for words that are italicized or boldfaced, that are defined in the margins or in footnotes, or that are included in pull-out quotes or headlines. When composing a general question for your students, look for questions the author asks in the text or browse the questions in the Reading Check.

Reading Strategy
Building Background Information (Strategy 6)

To help students make predictions about the selection, check the accuracy of their predictions, and set a purpose for reading, use Strategy 6 described in Content-Area Reading Strategies. You may wish to provide students with a Predicting and Confirming Activity (Graphic Organizer 8) to help them track their predictions as they read.

DURING READING

Viewing the Art
▪ Alexander Mosaic

Direct students to the photograph on page 185. What does the picture show? [Alexander in battle] Why do they think the artist chose to depict Alexander in this way? [because he won his fame in battle]

Differentiating Instruction
▪ Advanced

Read the following statement to your more advanced students: "There was destruction and loss of life, to be sure, but great things occurred which advanced the history of humanity." (Ahmed Dani) Are destruction and loss of life justifiable if they advance "the history of humanity" under all, some, or no circumstances? Have students explain their answers.

AFTER READING

✔ Reading Check

The following are sample answers to questions on student page 185.

1. The author describes Alexander as a man of contradictions. Alexander was cruel and brutal, but he could also be kind and generous.

2. A temple to Alexander and a small chapel in his honor had been discovered near Bahariya Oasis. This pleased the author because it supported his theory that Alexander had passed through the area.

3. Cleitus was one of Alexander's commanders and had once saved his life. Cleitus said that all of Alexander's glory was due to his father's efforts.

4. Alexander poured his water out because he felt it would be wrong to drink when his men had no water.

5. The author thinks Alexander must have been suprised that he had not yet found the end of the earth.

Reteaching

If students are having difficulty making predictions based on the word list and your general question, have a student read aloud the first section of the selection. [The first section ends with the sub-head "The Journey" on page 181.] Then, ask students what this portion of the selection is about. [the author's reasons for his journey; Alexander's impact on history] How do students think Alexander will be portrayed based on the section read aloud? [as a man with a complex and contradictory personality] What do students predict that the author will say about his efforts to film the documentary? [Responses may vary.] Review the word list and your question with students; then, conduct a round of brainstorming to come up with additional predictions.

Connecting to Language Arts
▪ Writing
Hero or Villain? Divide students into groups to discuss the question, *Was Alexander a hero or a villain?* What evidence from the selection indicates that Alexander was a hero? [He led his men through tough circumstances. He was chivalrous, generous, and shared his men's toughest situations.] What evidence paints him as a villain? [He killed thousands or even millions of people, including his best friend.] After the discussion, students may compose either a funeral speech praising Alexander or an election campaign ad denouncing him.

▪ Speaking and Listening
Court for the King Divide students into groups to discuss the incident in which Alexander killed Cleitus. Then, have each group assign half its members to prosecute Alexander for murder, with the other half assigned to defend him. Students can use the information presented in the article or do additional research. After students have completed their preparation, have a representative for each side present closing arguments for a mock trial. Afterward, the class can act as the jury and decide on Alexander's guilt or innocence.

Connecting Across the Curriculum: Art
Alexander in Art Have students research depictions of Alexander the Great on coins, statues, paintings, mosaics, and so on. How do artists tend to depict Alexander? In what kinds of settings do artists choose to place Alexander? Is he always shown as a hero, or does art ever reflect his meaner side? If so, how and by whom? After students have completed their research, they may want to work independently or together to present the results of their investigations. They might complete one of the following assignments:
- a panel discussion comparing contemporary and later works of art featuring Alexander
- notes for a lecture on artistic depictions of Alexander
- a guidebook entry for a museum display of art and artifacts featuring Alexander

Further Resources
▪ Video
In the Footsteps of Alexander the Great, directed by Michael Woods (Not rated, PBS).
▪ Book
In the Footsteps of Alexander the Great, by Michael Woods.

Assessment

Turn to page 155 for a multiple-choice test on the selection.

Test Answers

1. c   **2.** b   **3.** a   **4.** d   **5.** d
6. c   **7.** a   **8.** b   **9.** d   **10.** c

Science in a Hellenistic World

from *Calliope*

by LOUISE CHIPLEY SLAVICEK
(student text page 186)

Reading Level: Average

Text Summary

This magazine article provides an overview of the contributions of Hellenistic scientists to mathematics, physics, astronomy, and medicine. The sciences flourished during the Hellenistic period, in part because the conquests of Alexander the Great brought Greek scientists into contact with scientists from other cultures. In addition, Hellenistic rulers like the Ptolemies of Egypt competed with each other in offering financial support to the sciences. After the death of Cleopatra VII, the last Ptolemy to rule Egypt, scientific advances were put aside for centuries.

BEFORE READING

Make the Connection

Ask students if they have ever looked up into the night sky and wondered how many stars exist. Perhaps they have sometimes wondered how they caught a cold. Discuss with students how curiosity has sparked many scientific advances.

Build Background

■ More About the Topic

Ancient scientists believed that human health, behavior, and temperament were determined by the relative levels of four bodily fluids, which they called "humors." An excess of one of the four fluids—blood, phlegm, choler (yellow bile), and melancholy (black bile)—was thought to produce specific results. For example, a person who was sad and depressed was thought to be suffering from melancholy, or an excess of black bile. Despite the advances made by Erasistratos, the belief that human behavior was dictated by humors continued until the Middle Ages and beyond.

Vocabulary Development

The following words are underscored and defined in the student text.

maneuvering: skillfully moving, managing, or manipulating.
buoyancy: ability of something to float.
comprehensive: of wide scope; complete.
anatomy: science dealing with structure of the body.
innovative: new and different.

Before assigning the reading, you may want to introduce students to any words that could cause pronunciation or definition problems.

Vocabulary Tip

Using Suffixes Tell students that the Hellenistic scientific legacy extends to the names of various fields of study. For example, names of scientific fields that end in *–nomy* derive in part from the Greek word that means "a system of rules or laws." *Astronomy* combines *–nomy* with the Greek word for "star." Names of mathematical fields that end in *–metry* derive in part from the Greek word that means "to measure." *Geometry* combines *–metry* with the Greek word for "earth" or "soil."

CONTENT-AREA VOCABULARY

Although the following words are important to an understanding of the text selection, some of them may be unfamiliar to students. Present this list of words and definitions to students, and have students predict the subject of a selection using the words. [The words are all related to scientific or mathematical investigation.]

geometry: the mathematical study and measurement of points, lines, angles, and surfaces.
experiment: a test or trial used by scientists attempting to prove or disprove something.

astronomers: scientists who study stars and planets.

observations: facts noted in the course of scientific study.

research: the search for facts through careful study or examination.

Reading Informational Materials

Reading Skill
Listing or Enumerating Details

Tell students that listing or enumerating details in a reading selection can help them identify important information and better remember the main ideas presented in the text.

▶ **Teaching Tip**

The Once-Over Allow students to read the selection straight through once; then, have them read it a second time while pausing to assign symbols, take notes, and ask questions about the text. Allowing a straight read-through of a text provides some students a better chance to grasp the overall message before concentrating on the specific details.

Reading Strategy
Taking Effective Notes (Strategy 10)

Strategy 10 described in Content-Area Reading Strategies can help students learn to take effective notes while they read. Students can use a blank transparency sheet, a blank sheet of paper, or self-adhesive notes to indicate important points in the text.

If students have difficulty deciding which symbols to assign to specific pieces of information, model the strategy using the first few sentences of the selection. Read the first sentence aloud, then pause and model a conversation with the text. ["This sounds like a topic sentence. That's important information, so I'll mark it with asterisks."] Mark the sentence; then read the second sentence aloud and pause for comments. ["These details support the statement in the first sentence, so I'll mark them with plus signs."] Mark the sentence, and then read the third sentence aloud. This time, ask students which symbol to assign to the sentence. [asterisks for important information]

▶ **Teaching Tip**

Adjusting the Strategy The purpose of Strategy 10 is to help students think critically while reading.

Rather than having students focus on learning a specific set of symbols, allow them to develop their own symbols or shorthand for marking the text. Students can also mark a single statement with more than one symbol when the situation requires.

DURING READING

Correcting Misconceptions
Some students might consider the practice of dissecting human bodies to be an indicator of a less-advanced civilization. These students may be surprised to learn that human dissection continues to be widely used today. For example, forensic scientists dissect human bodies to determine a cause of death, and medical students dissect cadavers to learn about human anatomy.

Viewing the Art
■ Hellenistic Thinkers

Direct students to the painting on page 188. Ask what clues about the content of the article are provided in this painting and its caption. [It probably has something to do with Hellenistic thinkers and the sciences, specifically astronomy.] Why do students think the caption refers to this illustration as an "idealized image of Hellenistic achievements in astronomy"? [Opinions will vary.]

Differentiating Instruction
■ Learners Having Difficulty

If students find that using symbols and self-adhesive notes interferes with their ability to comprehend the text, consider allowing them to organize their note taking with a concept map. Students can use different shapes to indicate different types of information. For example, a square box could indicate important information and a round box could indicate a supporting detail.

AFTER READING

✔ Reading Check

The following are sample answers to questions on student page 190.

1. Euclid worked in geometry; Archimedes developed a new physical law.

2. Aristarchos and Hipparchos were two great Hellenistic astronomers.

3. The idea that arteries carried air, not blood, and the belief that all disease resulted from an imbalance of "humors" were two old beliefs about the human body that Hellenistic physicians rejected.

4. The conquests of Alexander allowed close contact between Greeks and non-Greeks.

5. Royal patrons supported and promoted the work of many leading Hellenistic scientists through financial assistance and by founding a library and museum in Alexandria.

Reteaching

Students may find that a Key Points and Details Chart (Graphic Organizer 5) can help them organize the notes they took while reading. Provide copies of the chart, and have students add the appropriate symbols to each column. Students may also find a concept map a useful way to organize the information they gleaned from the article.

Connecting to Language Arts
▪ Writing

Dear Diary Have a student read aloud the Sidelight feature (on page 189) about Pytheas and his sailing adventures. Then, conduct a brief class discussion about the feature and lead students in speculating about Pytheas's reactions to the comments of his contemporaries regarding his stories of adventures. Finally, have students write a journal entry in which Pytheas discusses his discoveries and his feelings about people who did not believe him.

▪ Speaking and Listening

Government Support: Pros and Cons Scientific advances were greatly aided by support from Hellenistic rulers. Divide students into groups to discuss the pros and cons of government support of the sciences. [Some students may say government support is appropriate because scientific advances benefit all; others may argue that the support should come from businesses and organizations that benefit financially from the advances.] After their discussions, students can present their opinions in a panel discussion or a debate.

Connecting Across the Curriculum: Mathematics/Philosophy

Researching Hypatia Have students research the life of Hypatia. Where was she from? [Alexandria] What was she known for? [She was a leading philosopher, scientist, and mathematician.] Why was she controversial in her time? [She was a female intellectual and a pagan in an increasingly Christian environment.] After students have completed their research, they may want to pool their findings or work independently to present the results of their investigations. They might detail Hypatia's accomplishments by

- writing and delivering a script for a television news obituary for her
- writing a biographical sketch about her
- creating an acrostic puzzle with the letters of her name
- writing and/or performing an imaginary interview with her

Further Resources
▪ **Book**

Archimedes and the Door to Science (*Living History Library*), by Jeanne Bendick and Laura M. Berquist.

Assessment

Turn to page 156 for a multiple-choice test on the selection.

Test Answers
1. c **2.** a **3.** c **4.** b **5.** d
6. a **7.** d **8.** b **9.** c **10.** c

Doing the Impossible: Hannibal Crosses the Alps

from *Calliope*
by GLENNA DUNNING
(student text page 191)

Reading Level: Average

Text Summary

This magazine article describes how Hannibal and his army crossed the Alps to attack Rome during the Second Punic War. The Roman navy's control of the Mediterranean Sea forced Hannibal to lead thousands of troops and thirty-seven war elephants across Europe's greatest mountain barrier. Although the perilous fifteen-day journey cost Hannibal half his troops and many of his elephants, it is considered one of the greatest military feats in history.

BEFORE READING

Make the Connection

Ask students to cite examples of people who did something that everyone else thought was impossible. [Students might think of Charles A. Lindbergh's first nonstop solo flight across the Atlantic, feats by astronauts such as walking on the moon, battles such as David defeating Goliath, the development of vaccines such as the ones for polio, or even athletic accomplishments such as the breaking of the four-minute mile or the conquering of Mount Everest.] What qualities would a person have to possess in order to achieve something that most people think is impossible? [persistence, confidence, skill, and so on]

Build Background

■ More About Carthage

Settled by Phoenicians from Canaan, Carthage was a powerful city-state on the shore of the Gulf of Tunis in North Africa, just across the Mediterranean Sea from Italy. In the sixth century B.C., Carthage controlled the entire Mediterranean coast of North Africa, as well as several islands and part of Sicily. Carthage fought three wars with Rome, called the Punic Wars. The Third Punic War ended with the army of Carthage defeated, the city leveled, and the ground salted to prevent new habitation. Today, Carthage is a suburb of the city of Tunis in the country of Tunisia.

Vocabulary Development

The following words are underscored and defined in the student text.
translated: led to or resulted in.
ally: partner, especially in a formal agreement or alliance.
chronicles: records of events as they happened in time; histories.
replenished: provided with a new supply; restocked.
allegiance: loyalty.

Before assigning the reading, you may want to introduce students to any words that could cause pronunciation or definition problems.

— Vocabulary Tip —

Using Prefixes Tell students that the prefix *re–* means "to do (something) again." For example, *plenish* means "to stock up." Adding the prefix *re–* produces *replenished*, or "to stock up again." Explain to students that understanding the meaning of prefixes can help them guess the meanings of unfamiliar words.

CONTENT-AREA VOCABULARY

Although the following words are important to an understanding of the text selection, some of them may be unfamiliar to students. Present this list of words and definitions to students.

invasion: the entering of a country by military force.
formation*: an array of military troops.
securing: taking possession of something and making it safe.
advance: forward movement.

*Although students may be familiar with other meanings of this word, the word as used in the selection has a specific meaning that pertains to the content area.

Reading Informational Materials

Reading Skill
Determining the Meanings of Unfamiliar Words

Explain to students that using context clues or affixes and roots to determine the meanings of unfamiliar words can increase their comprehension of the text and make reading easier and more enjoyable.

▶ **Teaching Tip**
Multiple-Meaning Word Parts Tell students that trying to determine the meaning of unfamiliar words by associating them with similar words can be risky. Sometimes words that appear to be related are not. For example, *infantry* and *invasion* may appear to share a prefix, but in fact they do not, because the prefix *in–* can have more than one meaning. Students who try to determine the meaning of one of these words based on the meaning of the other could run into difficulties.

Reading Strategy
Developing Vocabulary Knowledge (Strategy 11)

Strategy 11 described in Content-Area Reading Strategies can help students develop ways of determining the meanings of unfamiliar words encountered during reading. You may wish to provide students with a Contextual Redefinition Chart (Graphic Organizer 4) to help them organize their thoughts on the meanings of unfamiliar words as they read.

DURING READING

Using the Side-Margin Feature
■ Elephants in Battle: Pros and Cons

Question students about the pros and cons of using war elephants. What advantages did war elephants offer? [Their size and speed terrified the enemy; archers and javelin throwers could be positioned in towers on the elephants' backs.] What was the one great disadvantage of using war elephants? [One possibility is that elephants endangered friendly troops by panicking when injured;

some students may consider using animals in battle to be cruel or immoral.]

Differentiating Instruction
■ Advanced Learners

Advanced students can be an important resource for teaching skills to learners having difficulty and English-language learners. Consider having advanced students work with struggling learners to discuss unfamiliar words and ways of arriving at a working definition of those words.

AFTER READING

✓ Reading Check

The following are sample answers to questions on student text page 195.

1. Hannibal entered Italy from the north, which the Romans did not expect because a mountain crossing was considered impossible.

2. We learn much about Hannibal through reports of Greek war correspondents he hired to go with him. Later, Roman historians used the Greek reports to write their own history books.

3. Many of the elephants panicked while crossing the river on large rafts and overturned them. They then crossed by walking along the bottom of the shallow river.

4. The steep, narrow, slippery passes were very dangerous since the army could not march in regular formation. It was also very cold and there was little to eat. In addition, the Gauls attacked them.

5. Rome planned to oppose the Carthaginians in Africa and Spain.

Reteaching
If students are still having trouble with contextual redefinition, write the word *overland* on the chalkboard. Ask students to guess what the word means. [Some students may guess at the definition based on the meanings of *over* and *land.*] Begin presenting context clues by reading aloud the second part of the sentence in which *overland* appears on page 191. Have students guess the meaning of *over-*

land based on the context clues. [The context clues indicate that *overland* is a kind of route or way of getting somewhere.] Read the entire sentence containing the word, and lead students in continuing to refine their guesses. [The additional context clues indicate that an overland route is one that does not involve the sea.] Finally, look up *overland* in the dictionary and share the definition with the class. ["by land" or "across land"]

Connecting to Language Arts

▪ Writing

Hannibal: Man, Myth, Legend Have students research the life of Hannibal. What early experiences shaped his life? Why did he dislike Rome so much? How did he come to lead an army? What strengths did he have as a leader? Students can present their findings in an obituary or as a letter of recommendation to a possible employer.

▪ Speaking and Listening

The Punic Wars Hannibal's attack on Saguntum sparked the Second Punic War, but what caused the first and third wars? Have students research all three wars. Why was the First Punic War fought? [to determine who would control two Mediterranean islands] Who won? [Rome] What caused the Third Punic War? [Carthage broke a treaty with Rome.] Who won that war? [Rome.] Students can present their findings by staging a series of mock television news reports on the wars.

Connecting Across the Curriculum: Geography

Mapping a Route Have students locate and study maps of the Mediterranean area during the conflict between Rome and Carthage. What areas did Rome control? Over what areas did Carthage have influence? What route did Hannibal take to reach Italy? After students have completed their research, they may want to pool their findings or work independently to present the results of their investigations. They might show Hannibal's route and the areas controlled by Rome and Carthage by

- drawing a two-dimensional map
- making a three-dimensional map
- using a computer program to design an interactive map
- writing an informative report
- delivering an oral report

Further Resources

▪ Magazine article:

"'Carthage Must Be Destroyed,' But Must It Be Forgotten?" by David Soren in *Archaeology Odyssey,* December 2000.

▪ Books:

Hannibal (First Book), by Robert Green.

The History Atlas of Europe, by Ian Barnes and Robert Hudson.

Assessment

Turn to page 157 for a multiple-choice test on the selection.

Test Answers

1. c **2.** a **3.** d **4.** b **5.** c
6. d **7.** a **8.** d **9.** a **10.** c

from Stadium of Life and Death

from *National Geographic World*
by JERRY DUNN
(student text page 196)

Reading Level: Average

Text Summary

This excerpt describes how the Roman Colosseum was built and used. The stone structure was erected by slaves and master craftsmen and was designed to handle large crowds efficiently. Spectators were seated according to social class and protected from the sun by canvas awnings. Beneath the stadium, builders created rooms for gladiators and cages for animals. The Colosseum has deteriorated over time, but restoration efforts are underway.

BEFORE READING

Make the Connection

Ask students if they have ever seen a movie or read a book about gladiators in ancient Rome. Where did the gladiators fight? [in amphitheaters] What was the most famous amphitheater in the Roman Empire? [the Colosseum]

Build Background

▪ More About the Colosseum

The Colosseum was the brainchild of the Roman Emperor Nero, who planned to include an amphitheater in the enormous imperial complex he was building around an artificial lake in the heart of Rome. Nero died before work began on the amphitheater, leaving the actual construction to his successor, Vespasian. The resulting structure was officially called the Flavian Amphitheater, since Vespasian was the founding member of the Flavian dynasty of Roman emperors. Before long, however, Romans were calling the enormous amphitheater the "Colosseum" after a colossal statue of Nero that stood nearby.

Vocabulary Development

The following words are underscored and defined in the student text.

majestic: impressive; grand.
feat: achievement.

collapsed: fell down or caved in.
efficiently: in a manner that does not waste time, energy, money, or materials.
sloping: slanting upward or downward.

Before assigning the reading, you may want to introduce students to any words that could cause pronunciation or definition problems.

┌ *Vocabulary Tip* ─

Using Suffixes One suffix that students will encounter often in their reading is *–ly,* which means "in a manner similar to" or "having an appearance similar to." For example, the word *efficiently* means "in an efficient manner." Tell students that understanding the meanings of a variety of prefixes, root words, and suffixes can help them determine the meanings of unfamiliar words.

(CONTENT-AREA VOCABULARY)

Although the following words are important to an understanding of the text selection, some of them may be unfamiliar to students. Present this list of words and definitions to them.

construction: the act of making or building something.
arches: curved frameworks that act as supports.
structure*: a building.
constructed: built.
chambers: rooms.

*Although students may be familiar with other meanings of this word, the word as used in the selection has a specific meaning that pertains to the content area.

(Reading Informational Material)

Reading Skill
Establishing a Purpose for Reading
Tell students that establishing a purpose for reading can help them focus on the points that an author is trying to communicate.

▶ Teaching Tip

Purposes for Reading Explain to students that there are many purposes for reading. One purpose for reading expository text is to gain information about the topic. Other reasons are to form an opinion, to identify topics for research papers, or simply for entertainment.

Reading Strategy

Previewing Text (Strategy 1)

To help students increase their understanding of a text by establishing a purpose for reading, identifying important ideas, and connecting to their prior knowledge, use Strategy 1 described in Content-Area Reading Strategies. Students may find a KWL or KWLS Chart (Graphic Organizers 6 and 7) helpful in organizing their thoughts.

DURING READING

Differentiating Instruction

▪ Advanced Students

Advanced students usually have little difficulty establishing a purpose for reading but may be reluctant to adjust that purpose once they start reading. Remind students that establishing a purpose for reading often involves a bit of guesswork. As they read, students should feel free to adjust their purpose for reading. Assure students that monitoring and adjusting their reading strategies is an important part of the reading process.

AFTER READING

✔ Reading Check

The following are sample answers to questions on student text page 198.

1. The builders used arches because solid stone walls would have collapsed under their own weight.

2. The ringside seats were reserved for the emperor, his friends, and priestesses. Women and the very poor sat in the seats farthest from the action.

3. The builders stretched a canvas awning over the crowd.

4. It took eight years to build the Colosseum. Most of the work was done by slaves and craftsmen.

5. The Colosseum seated fifty thousand people. The crowd was seated within ten minutes of arriving.

Reteaching

Tell struggling students that their purpose for reading is related to the author's purpose for writing and that a common purpose for writing expository text is to explain or amplify a main idea using supporting details. Then, make and distribute copies of a Cluster Diagram (Graphic Organizer 3) with the main idea written in the center. [The Colosseum is an amazing achievement.] Have students re-read the selection and fill out the cluster diagram with details that support the main idea. [It was majestic; the only large machine used was a hoist; it took only eight years to build; it handled crowds efficiently; and so on.]

Connecting to Language Arts

▪ Writing

A Day at the Colosseum Have students research the Colosseum and the gladiatorial games held there. How did a day of games usually begin? [with a parade of gladiators] What kinds of games were held? [Gladiators fought each other or animals.] What role did spectators play? [They decided whether an injured gladiator lived or died.] Students can present their findings by writing a "you are there" script set at the Colosseum during a day of games.

▪ Speaking and Listening

Rebuilding the Colosseum The success of dramatic productions and staged gladiatorial contests in 2000 sparked talk of a full restoration of the Colosseum. Have students in groups discuss restoring ancient structures. What are the pros? [prevent further deterioration, increase tourism, and so on.] What are the cons? [cost, wear from increased use, and so on] Students can then present their views in a town meeting.

Connecting Across the Curriculum: History

Caution: Romans at Work The Roman Empire's architectural achievements extended far beyond the Colosseum. Assign students to research Roman architecture. What materials did they use? [volcanic rock, limestone, marble, bricks, stucco, concrete, and so on] What were the common architectural elements? [arches, columns, piers, vaults, domes, and so on] After students have completed their research, they can pool their findings or work independently to present the results. Students could complete one of the following projects:

- build an architectural model of a typical Roman building
- narrate a slide show describing aspects of Roman architecture
- produce an architectural drawing of a typical Roman building
- write a "how-to" article explaining how Romans built an arch, vault, or dome

Further Resources

▪ Books

The Colosseum (Great Buildings), by Peter Chrisp.

The Roman Colosseum (Inside Story), written by Fiona MacDonald and illustrated by Mark Bergin and Peter Bedrick.

The Roman Colosseum (Wonders of the World), written by Elizabeth Mann and illustrated by Michael Racz.

▪ Video

Secrets of Lost Empires (Nova Classroom Field Trips), (2000, not rated).

Assessment

Turn to page 158 for a multiple-choice test on the selection.

Test Answers

1. c   **2.** a   **3.** d   **4.** b   **5.** c

6. d   **7.** b   **8.** d   **9.** a   **10.** c

Who Were the Gladiators?

from *Gladiator*

by RICHARD WATKINS

(student text page 199)

Reading Level: Average

Text Summary

This book excerpt discusses the kinds of people who fought in the Roman gladiatorial games. Most gladiators were prisoners of war, criminals, slaves, or poor and desperate volunteers who had no choice except to fight. However, as the games grew ever more popular, the glory of the arena also lured noblemen, senators, and even emperors.

BEFORE READING

Make the Connection

Ask students if they know where Rome got the gladiators who fought to their deaths in amphitheaters such as the Colosseum. [Some students may know that gladiators were slaves, criminals, or prisoners of war.] Ask if any of them would want to be gladiators. Why or why not? Ask them to consider what a day in a gladiator's life might have been like. Tell them to watch the text to see if their predictions are supported by the selection.

Build Background

■ More About Commodus

Commodus, the emperor who scandalized Rome by fighting as a gladiator, became sole ruler in A.D. 180 at the death of his father, Marcus Aurelius. After his sister and a group of senators tried to kill him two years later, Commodus became vindictive. He ordered the execution of senators who opposed him and then confiscated their riches. Eventually, the emperor slid into madness. He renamed Rome "Colony of Commodus," and he became convinced that he was the god Hercules. Commodus was strangled on New Year's Eve in A.D. 192, and the stable empire he inherited from his father descended into civil war.

■ Motivate

Ask students if they have seen movies about gladiators. Then, lead students in a discussion about the games and the gladiators. What is their opinion of games in which people fight to the death for the entertainment of others? [Responses will vary.] Do they think the games diminish the accomplishments of the Roman Empire? [Opinions will vary.]

Vocabulary Development

The following words are underscored and defined in the student text.

conquest: act of conquering and acquiring territory.

auctioned: sold to the highest bidder.

deterrent: something that prevents or discourages someone from acting in a certain way.

dispose: to get rid of.

exhibition: display; public showing.

Before assigning the reading, you may want to introduce students to any words that could cause pronunciation or definition problems.

┌─ *Vocabulary Tip* ─

Using Suffixes Point out to students that adding a suffix to a word sometimes changes the way the word is spelled. For example, *−ed* is added to *auction* without changing the spelling. However, when *−ent* is added to *deter,* an extra *r* is added between the root and the suffix.

(**CONTENT-AREA VOCABULARY**)

Although the following words are important to an understanding of the text selection, some of them may be unfamiliar to students. Present this list of words and the definitions to your students.

captives: people who have been taken and held against their wishes.

convicted: found guilty by a court or some other authority.

sentence*: to penalize or punish for committing a crime.

frenzy: wild, uncontrolled activity.

intensity: the quality of possessing great purpose and
    energy.

* Although students may be familiar with other meanings of this word, the word as used in the selection has
a specific meaning that pertains to the content area.

Reading Informational Materials

Reading Skill
Drawing Inferences

Tell students that to draw an inference, they combine information from the text with their own
knowledge to form a conclusion.

▶ **Teaching Tip**
  Interpreting Visual Information Tell students
  that whenever they encounter visual information in
  a text, they should ask themselves, "How does this
  information relate to the text?" or "Why was this
  information included with the text?" These questions
  help students create a link between the visual information and the subject matter covered by the text.

Reading Strategy
Visualizing Information (Strategy 5)

To help students draw inferences from visual information, have them use Strategy 5 in the Content-
Area Reading Strategies. You may wish to have
students create their own visuals based on their
reading of the chapter.

DURING READING

Using the Side-Margin Feature
■ Animals in the Arena

Ask students if they can think of any modern
sporting events that involve animals. [Students
may cite horse or dog racing, rodeos, bullfighting,
and so on.] What do students think about using
animals in this way? [Opinions will vary.] How do
modern uses of animals in sporting events compare to the ways ancient Romans used animals?
[Roman games usually involved the death of an
animal; most modern games do not.]

▶ **Teaching Tip**
  Sketch It If the visual information that accompanies a text is a chart or diagram, it can be useful to
  have students sketch the visual from memory after
  reading the selection. In addition to providing
  important clues about the effectiveness of the visual
  information, this activity can help students process
  the information and move it to long-term memory.

Differentiating Instruction
■ English-Language Learners

Since visual information involves few if any words,
students with limited English proficiency may find
that previewing the chapter's images is a good
alternative to other prereading strategies that focus
on textual information. English-language learners
who are struggling with other prereading strategies
can use Strategy 5 to help them preview text, make
predictions, build background information, or
activate prior knowledge.

AFTER READING

✓ Reading Check

The following are sample answers to questions on
student text page 203.

1. Most gladiators were prisoners of war, slaves, or
   criminals.

2. They were sent to gladiator schools to be
   trained by former gladiators.

3. Anyone who survived three years as a gladiator
   would be very skilled and could train others to
   fight well.

4. The *rudius* was a wooden baton awarded to a
   gladiator who was then allowed to retire from
   fighting.

5. Some volunteers were poor people who wanted
   regular meals and the glory; some were noblemen
   and even emperors who wanted a thrill.

Reteaching

If students are still having difficulty analyzing visual
information, direct their attention to the mosaic
reproduced on page 201. Ask students to identify the
mosaic's subject. [a gladiator fighting a leopard]

How does this mosaic relate to the text? [Gladiators fought animals.] Write these two study questions on the chalkboard: What use would Romans have for wild animals? Where did they get these animals? Have students read the selection and write short answers to the questions. [Romans used the animals in gladiatorial games. They got the animals from all corners of the Roman Empire.] Afterwards, have students share their answers and discuss whether the mosaic accurately reflects the text. [Opinions will vary.]

Connecting to Language Arts
▪ Writing
The Revolt of Spartacus What happened when slaves who were forced to become gladiators did not submit meekly? Have students research the life of Spartacus. What is he famous for? [leading gladiators in a revolt against Rome] How did he become a gladiator? [He was sold as a slave.] Was his rebellion successful? [He succeeded briefly, but he was eventually defeated.] After students have completed their research, they can present their findings in a diary entry written from the perspective of Spartacus.

▪ Speaking and Listening
Post-Game Show Ancient Romans did not have television, but if they had, you can bet that gladiators would have been interviewed after their victories. Have students work in teams to prepare questions and answers for an imaginary post-game interview between a gladiator and a sports journalist. After preparing their questions and answers, students can practice and present their mock interviews to the class.

Connecting Across the Curriculum: History
Gladiator for a Day Have students meet in groups to discuss the phenomenon of emperors and noblemen becoming gladiators. Why might these people have wanted to be gladiators? [to hear the cheers of the crowd, to shock people around them] Why were some Romans scandalized by this behavior? [Gladiators were usually from the lower classes.] What unfair advantages might an emperor or nobleman have in the arena? [Gladiators

might fear attacking them; special rules might protect them.] After students have completed their discussions, they can pool their findings or work independently to complete one of the following projects:

- draw a cartoon strip about an emperor or nobleman who wants to be a gladiator
- write an editorial for an ancient Roman newspaper arguing for or against allowing emperors and noblemen to be gladiators
- prepare and deliver an oral commentary on the practice of Roman emperors and noblemen becoming gladiators
- write a confession from the perspective of an emperor or nobleman who wants to be a gladiator
- prepare and stage a daytime talk show on emperors and noblemen who want to be gladiators

Further Resources
▪ Video
Gladiators—Bloodsport of the Colosseum (not rated, 2000).

(Assessment)

Turn to page 159 for a multiple-choice test on the selection.

Test Answers
1. a   **2.** c   **3.** d   **4.** b   **5.** d
6. c   **7.** b   **8.** c   **9.** a   **10.** d

The Spread of Christianity

from *Calliope*

by PAMELA PALMER
(student text page 204)

Reading Level: Average

Text Summary

This magazine article tells about the early years of a new religion that came to be called Christianity. The religion began with a small group of followers spreading the teachings of Jesus of Nazareth. As the religion grew, the followers established a structure for the church and formalized their belief system and ordinances like baptism and the Eucharist.

BEFORE READING

Make the Connection

Ask students what they know about the early days of Christianity. Was it a popular religion? [It began small, but it spread quickly.] Where did it begin? What were its roots? How did it spread? Can they imagine a time when one of the world's great religions may have had only a few followers?

Build Background

■ More About Jerusalem

Jerusalem, also called the Holy City, is venerated by three major monotheistic religions. Christians revere Jerusalem as the scene of Jesus's crucifixion and triumph over death. Jews see the city as symbolic of their covenant with God. The city is also the site of one of the Muslims' most sacred shrines. Scholars believe that the heart of Jerusalem, a walled-off area of ancient buildings called the Old City, has been inhabited for some five thousand years. Outside the walls, Jerusalem is a modern city with high rises, restaurants, apartments, businesses, and schools.

Vocabulary Development

The following words are underscored and defined in the student text.

imminent: about to happen.
invalid: very sick person.
diversity: variety.

converts: people who change from one religion to another.
decreed: established by command.
precedent: example to be followed.
authoritative: official.
heritage: beliefs or traditions handed down from the past.
envious: jealous.
commemorated: marked or celebrated the memory of.

Before assigning the reading, you may want to introduce students to any words that could cause pronunciation or definition problems.

Vocabulary Tip

Understanding Suffixes Tell students that the suffix *–ous* means "filled with." For example, adding *–ous* to *envy* produces *envious,* which means "filled with envy." [You might want to point out to students that the *y* in *envy* is changed to an *i* before *–ous* is added.] Explain to students that understanding the meaning of suffixes like *–ous* can help them determine the meanings of unfamiliar words.

CONTENT-AREA VOCABULARY

Although the following words are important to an understanding of the text selection, some of them may be unfamiliar to students. Present this list of words and definitions to students. Ask students to consider what a selection using the words is likely to concern.

sermon: a speech on religious matters.
salvation*: the state of having been forgiven for committing sins.
spiritual: concerned with sacred matters.
scripture: sacred writings.
sacred: holy.

*Although students may be familiar with other meanings of this word, the word as used in the selection has a specific meaning that pertains to the content area.

Reading Informational Materials

Reading Skill
Summarizing
Remind students that a summary is a short restatement of the important ideas and details presented in a piece of writing. A good summary always contains the main idea of a selection and includes some supporting details.

Reading Strategy
Constructing a Concept Map (Strategy 4)
To help students organize their thoughts, use Strategy 4 described in Content-Area Reading Strategies. Students can create Concept Maps or use a Cluster Diagram (Graphic Organizer 3). Then, have them use the completed organizer to write a summary of the selection.

DURING READING

Using the Side-Margin Feature
▪ From Victims to Victors
Ask students what they think the burning cross was telling Constantine to conquer. [Some may say he was supposed to conquer the opposing general; others may say he was supposed to conquer religious intolerance.] Why might Constantine consider a burning cross a significant sign? [The cross is a Christian symbol.]

Differentiating Instruction
▪ Learners Having Difficulty
Because struggling readers often have difficulty categorizing and labeling words, they can benefit from a quick example of these skills. Make a list of four words that clearly fit into two distinct categories. [baseball, history, basketball, literature] Write the words in no particular order on the chalkboard, and then ask students to identify which words go together. [baseball and basketball; history and literature.] Then, ask students to label both groups of words. [baseball and basketball are sports; history and literature are school subjects.]

AFTER READING

✔ Reading Check

The following are sample answers to questions on student text page 208.

1. Most early Christians were ordinary people without any high position in society. Most of the earliest believers were Jews.

2. Paul believed that the church needed moral leaders who were strong in both their religious lives and their personal lives.

3. The Jerusalem Council ordered that Gentile converts were not required to follow Jewish law to become Christian, and that believing in salvation by faith was more important than following rituals.

4. People were baptized in order to identify themselves with the death and resurrection of Jesus. Baptism symbolized dying to sin and rising to a new life.

5. All Christian communities emphasized living a strictly moral life and observing a set worship service.

Reteaching
If students are still having difficulty turning their Concept Maps or Cluster Diagrams into summaries, divide them into groups and help them narrow their focus by briefly discussing the selection's main idea. [Early Christians established the foundations of their religion.] Then, have each group discuss the details in the selection that support the main idea. [Early Christians established a structure for the Church, formalized their belief system, developed rituals, and so on.] After the discussion, have each group vote on the three most important supporting details. Students can then work independently to develop their summary statements based on the main idea and the three supporting details.

▶ **Teaching Tip**
Keep It or Lose It? If students are having difficulty deciding whether to mention a detail in a summary, remind them of the main idea of the selection. [Early Christians established the foundations of their

religion.] Tell them that before adding any detail to their summaries, they should ask "Is this information absolutely necessary for me to understand the main idea?"

Connecting to Language Arts

■ Writing

Sketching Nazareth Have students research the ancient town of Nazareth. Where is it located? [northern Israel] What is it known for? [being the boyhood home of Jesus] Who lived there during Jesus' time? [mostly Jews] What are the major industries of modern Nazareth? [trade, tourism, manufacturing] Students should create a newspaper article for the travel section briefly describing the area as a historical and tourist site.

Connecting Across the Curriculum: Art

The Art of the Sacred Have students search the library or the Internet for paintings or sculptures of important people from the early days of Christianity. How did the artists choose to depict their subjects? What similarities do the various works of art share? How are they different? [Student responses will vary depending on the art they find.] After students have completed their research, they can pool their findings or work independently to present the results. They might complete one of the following assignments:

- create an original work of art in a similar style.
- write a brochure for a museum display featuring the art.
- write a review of an imaginary museum display featuring the art.

Further Resources

■ Books

The Atlas of the Bible Lands: History, Daily Life and Traditions, written by Andrea Due and Matteo Chesi and illustrated by Paola Ravalgia and Peter Bedrick.

The Life of Jesus: In Masterpieces of Art by Mary Pope Osborne.

Assessment

Turn to page 160 for a multiple-choice test on the selection.

Test Answers

1. a	**2.** d	**3.** c	**4.** a	**5.** b
6. f	**7.** d	**8.** a	**9.** c	**10.** g
11. f	**12.** a	**13.** e	**14.** g	**15.** b

from The Buried City of Pompeii

by SHELLEY TANAKA
(student text page 209)

Reading Level: Average

Text Summary

This book excerpt describes the volcanic explosion that buried the ancient Roman city of Pompeii almost 2,000 years ago and details modern efforts to excavate the city. The city was abandoned after it was covered by pumice and ash from the explosion of Vesuvius, a volcano on the Bay of Naples. Archaeological excavations of Pompeii in modern times have revealed much about the lives of people living under Roman rule.

BEFORE READING

Make the Connection

Ask students if they have ever heard of a volcano called Vesuvius. Where is it located? [on the Bay of Naples in Southern Italy] What incident is Vesuvius associated with? [an eruption that buried the ancient city of Pompeii] What other natural disasters are students familiar with? How have the disasters affected peoples' lives? [Students may cite the eruption of Mount St. Helens or mention hurricanes, earthquakes, and tornadoes that have left many people homeless. They may not know of any disaster that has wiped out an entire city.]

Build Background

■ More About Vesuvius

Vesuvius had been sitting dormant on the shores of the Bay of Naples in southern Italy for centuries when it roared to life in A.D. 79. That fiery eruption buried the unsuspecting towns of Pompeii, Herculaneum, and Stabiae. Another major eruption in 1631 kicked off some three hundred years of fairly regular activity. Although the last major eruption occurred in 1944, the volcano remains active. Today, some two million people live in its shadow.

Vocabulary Development

The following words are underscored and defined in the student text.

summit: highest point or top.
suffocated: smothered or choked.
earnest: in a serious manner or with sincere effort.
archaeologist: a person trained in scientific study of earlier peoples, mainly done by digging up and examining remains of cultures.
renovations: repairs.

Before assigning the reading, you may want to introduce students to any words that could cause pronunciation or definition problems.

┌─ *Vocabulary Tip* ──────────────────
Using Roots Tell students that *archaeologist* derives from the Latin word *archaio,* which means "belonging to an earlier period." Combining *archaio* with the suffix –*logy,* which means "the study of," produces *archaeology,* or "the study of things that belong to an earlier period." Adding the suffix –*ist,* which means "one who does a specific thing," produces *archaeologist,* or "one who studies things that belong to an earlier period."
└──────────────────────────────────────

(**CONTENT-AREA VOCABULARY**)

Although the following words are important to an understanding of the text selection, some of them may be unfamiliar to students. Present this list of words and definitions to students, and ask them to consider what a selection using the words is likely to concern. [excavating areas where a natural disaster has occurred]

earthquake: powerful tremors caused by volcanic activity or by the release of stress along a fault line.
eruption*: the violent release of volcanic material.
excavation: the act of digging archaeological artifacts out of the ground.
archaeological: related to the study of things from an earlier period.

* Although students may be familiar with other meanings of this word, the word as used in the selection has a specific meaning that pertains to the content area.

Reading Informational Materials

Reading Skill
Using Text Structure: Chronological Order
Tell students that identifying text structure can prepare them to think in a way that will increase their understanding of the text. Chronological order uses a straightforward time order and is often used for historical accounts or news reports.

Reading Strategy
Understanding Text (Strategy 2)
Strategy 2 described in Content-Area Reading Strategies can help students identify text structure and better understand a reading selection. You may wish to provide students with a Sequence or Chronological Order Chart (Graphic Organizer 10) to help them organize their thoughts on the sequence of events as they move through the reading process.

▶ **Teaching Tip**
First Things First Tell students that texts written in chronological order use repeated references to time. Explain to students that before writing an event in their chronological organizers, they should ask, "Is this event an important step toward the outcome of the reading selection, or is it is simply a supporting detail?" By restricting chronology to important steps, students can keep their eyes on the big picture and avoid getting bogged down in supporting details.

DURING READING

Using the Side-Margin Feature
■ **An Eyewitness to Disaster**
Ask students to list some qualities that they associate with heroes. [bravery, concern for others, the ability to act quickly, and so on] Was Pliney the Elder a hero? [Opinion responses will vary.] How do students think they would have behaved in the same situation? [Student responses will vary.]

Differentiating Instruction
■ **English-Language Learners**
English-language learners may have difficulty recognizing that context affects the meaning of some signal words. For example, *on* coupled with a date becomes a chronological indicator. Proficient readers are often able to make inferences based on similar constructions. For example, a student might see *on* (date) in a list of signal words and infer that *at* (time of day) also signals chronological structure. These inferences are an important part of determining text structure because no list can include every inference for every signal word and phrase. Provide English-language learners with mentors proficient in English and willing to help them investigate the inferences created by context.

AFTER READING

✔ Reading Check

The following are sample answers to questions on student text page 212.

1. Most of the people tried to run away. Others hid in their homes.

2. Serious digging began in 1748, but the work was disorganized.

3. When Pompeii was uncovered, the buildings began to crumble and the paintings began to fade.

4. Fiorelli made detailed maps, carefully recorded each find, and began restoring the buildings and art.

5. The House of Menander was a grand residence that was uncovered in Pompeii. Diggers found farm tools, coins, jewelry, and dishes, as well as the bodies of several people and a dog.

Reteaching
If students are still struggling to identify chronological order in this selection, give them a fresh start. Find a short news article that deals with a sequence of events. Read aloud the first two paragraphs in the article. Then, ask students to identify the signal words or phrases in the two paragraphs. Write these

words and phrases on the chalkboard as students identify them. Then, ask students which structure uses these words or phrases. [chronological order] You may wish to repeat this process with additional paragraphs, or have students analyze paragraphs individually, in teams, or in small groups.

Connecting to Language Arts

■ Writing

The Last Days of Pompeii The citizens of Pompeii had no idea that they were living at the base of an active volcano until it was too late. Based on their reading of the selection and additional research, have students consider what the last days of Pompeii must have been like. Students can present their findings by writing a series of diary entries from the perspective of a Pompeii teenager shortly before the eruption of Vesuvius.

■ Speaking and Listening

To Tour, or Not to Tour Tourist traffic poses a major threat to Pompeii and other ancient archaeological sites. Have students separate into groups and discuss the benefits and risks of tourism in archaeological sites. What are some benefits? [Tourism is educational; it can raise money for maintenance, and so on.] What are some risks? [accidental damage, increased motor traffic, increased pollution, and so on] Have students write and deliver to the class slogans to promote their stand on the issue.

Connecting Across the Curriculum: Archaeology

Uncovering Pompeii Have students research the excavation of Pompeii. Why are archaeologists so interested in Pompeii? What types of structures were uncovered during excavations? [temples, private homes, villas, bakeries, restaurants, inns and so on] What other evidence of ancient Roman culture was uncovered? [frescoes, mosaics, statues, and so on] Students can pool their findings or work independently to present the results of their research. They might do one of the following assignments:

- draw a map of the city indicating the location of major buildings
- build an architectural model of a structure typical of ancient Pompeii

- write a research paper on the excavation of Pompeii or an aspect of life in Pompeii
- create a slide show or scrapbook showing the ruins of Pompeii
- write a diary entry from the perspective of an early Pompeii archaeologist

Further Resources

■ **Book**

Pompeii by Peter Connolly.

■ **Video**

In the Shadow of Vesuvius, directed by Nicolas Noxon and Aram Boyajian (National Geographic, 1983).

Assessment

Turn to page 161 for a multiple-choice test on the selection.

Test Answers

1. d **2.** b **3.** a **4.** d **5.** c
6. b **7.** a **8.** a **9.** d **10.** c

The following criteria can help you evaluate each student's success in completing the activities prompted by the Cross-Curricular Activities feature in the student textbook.

Note: Activities marked with an asterisk allow the involvement of more than one student. For these activities you may wish to evaluate each student on his or her specific and individual contribution to the activity and then give the partners or group an overall rating.

Health/Visual Art
Classic Good Looks

- The student conducts research using Internet or library resources on ancient Greek or Roman clothing (materials, colors, styles) and accessories (jewelry, hair adornments, and so on); grooming aids (at home and at public baths); or beauty treatments.
- The student prepares drawings or a short talk for the class.

Language Arts
Gladiators of Yesterday and Today

- The student chooses a popular spectator sport of today that may be a descendent of Roman gladiator fights, such as a rodeo, professional wrestling, or boxing.
- The student writes a comparison-contrast essay explaining how the contemporary spectator sport is similar to and different from the gladiator entertainments of ancient Rome.
- The student considers and may include information about the topics of costumes, training and discipline, danger level, popularity, and entertainment value.

Geography/History
Covering Ground

- The student draws or traces a map that includes the places mentioned in either "Doing the Impossible: Hannibal Crosses the Alps" (page 194) or *from* "In the Footsteps of Alexander the Great" (page 183).
- The student conducts more research on either journey and adds details, such as the route taken and important mountain ranges and rivers, to the map.
- The student may include illustrations with his or her map.

*History/Speech
Let's Hear the Pros and Cons

- The student makes notes about what it would be like to live in a society that valued discipline, strength, and military might.
- The student becomes part of one of the two debate teams (one pro-Spartan and the other anti-Spartan) and helps choose a panel of three judges.
- The student focuses the debate on specific questions, such as the following: Should any Spartan values be part of our educational system today? Which Spartan values are dangerous or useful? Is it better to have life decisions made by the state or the individual?
- The judges decide which team made the strongest presentation and explain their decision.

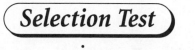

The Permafrost Crumbles
from *Raising the Mammoth,*
a Discovery Channel Web site
by DIRK HOOGSTRA

COMPREHENSION QUESTIONS

Circle the letter of the best answer to each of the following items. *(50 points)*

1. How did scientists learn about the Jarkov mammoth?
   a. They used radar to detect frozen animals
   b. They were looking for extinct animals
   c. The Dolgan nomads found the mammoth
   d. Wild animals exposed a piece of the creature

2. Which of the following items did scientists find in the stomach of the mammoth that was discovered in 1902?
   a. a human leg
   b. 33 pounds of grass
   c. a strange virus
   d. 25 pounds of peanuts

3. Once excavated, the mammoth will be transported to
   a. an ice cave in Khatanga
   b. a museum in Khatanga
   c. a storage warehouse near a river
   d. a science lab in Moscow

4. What do scientists hope to discover by slowly defrosting the Jarkov Mammoth?
   a. organs that can be used for transplants
   b. bone marrow
   c. the cause of death
   d. information about the mammoth's world

5. The mammoth's tusks are reattached to the frozen block of earth
   a. so they won't be misplaced
   b. so people can visualize the mammoth's position in the block
   c. to balance the load for transport in the helicopter
   d. to honor the religious beliefs of the Dolgan nomads

VOCABULARY

Using your knowledge of the underlined word, circle the letter of the word or phrase that best completes each statement. *(50 points)*

6. A <u>preserved</u> carcass is rare because it is
   a. extinct
   b. commonplace
   c. dehydrated
   d. undamaged

7. To <u>estimate</u> how much a load will weigh, you
   a. compute the exact number
   b. make a rough calculation
   c. make an uneducated guess
   d. put the object on scales

8. An <u>ambitious</u> scientist is one who is
   a. doubtful
   b. stubborn
   c. determined
   d. famous

9. The smell of the mammoth's hair was <u>pungent</u>, or
   a. sharp
   b. dull
   c. foul
   d. sweet

10. To have a <u>specimen</u> of something means that you have a/an
    a. discovery of something rare
    b. design of the object
    c. animal bone
    d. sample of the object

Selection Test

Summer in the Pits—Going for the Goo
from Discovery.com
by MARK WHEELER

COMPREHENSION QUESTIONS

Circle the letter of the best answer to each of the following items. *(50 points)*

1. The "tar" in the Rancho La Brea Tar Pits is actually
   a. loose rock
   b. fossils
   c. asphalt
   d. quicksand

2. Which of the following animals was **not** excavated at the Rancho La Brea Tar Pits in 1997?
   a. a horse
   b. a lion
   c. a coyote
   d. a dog

3. Animals trapped in the tar pits probably died from being eaten by predators or from
   a. suffocation
   b. slow starvation
   c. internal injuries
   d. poisoning

4. Excavation is done during the summer because that's when
   a. students are out of class
   b. the angle of the sun is right for viewing
   c. the tar is most viscous
   d. more tourists can observe

5. Entire skeletons are seldom found intact for all the following reasons **except**
   a. predators destroyed part of the prey
   b. the tar dissolved part of the bones
   c. the rains washed the bones downstream
   d. earthquakes caused the asphalt to shift

VOCABULARY

Using your knowledge of the underlined word, circle the letter of the word or phrase that best completes each statement. *(50 points)*

6. Jerry Smith was trying to extract the bones of a dire wolf, or
   a. date them
   b. pry them loose
   c. arrange them into a skeleton
   d. preserve them

7. If an excavation team were called to do a job, what would they do?
   a. build a museum
   b. demolish a building
   c. train others
   d. dig something up

8. A building that is intact is one that is
   a. complete
   b. under construction
   c. ruined
   d. unfinished

9. If you leave a legacy, you leave
   a. a scar
   b. something from the past
   c. a footprint in stone
   d. mysterious clues

10. When researchers found protruding bones, the bones were
    a. sticking out
    b. hidden
    c. shocking
    d. mysterious

Name _____ Class _____ Date _____

Selection Test

Mary Leakey, 1913–1996
from *Newsweek* magazine
by SHARON BEGLEY

COMPREHENSION QUESTIONS
Circle the letter of the best answer to each of the following items. *(50 points)*

1. Mary Leakey's discovery of the footprints seemed to suggest that the ability to walk on two feet came before the development of
   a. the jaw bone
   b. the larger brain
   c. the arms
   d. teeth

2. What characteristic about the footprints impressed Leakey?
   a. one was of a child
   b. all were extraordinarily large
   c. one seemed to pause and turn
   d. they were in volcanic ash

3. According to the obituary, Mary Leakey's discovery of a piece of skull helps support the notion that _____ was the cradle of humankind.
   a. Africa
   b. Asia
   c. Europe
   d. America

4. From reading this obituary, you can conclude that Mary Leakey's discoveries were
   a. unimportant
   b. lucky
   c. fake
   d. extremely significant

5. According to the obituary, Mary Leakey was primarily interested in
   a. writing books
   b. creating theories
   c. fame
   d. adding to the fossil record

VOCABULARY
Using your knowledge of the underlined word, circle the letter of the word or phrase that best completes each statement. *(50 points)*

6. When Leakey found an underline{impression} in the rock, she saw
   a. a painting
   b. an opinion
   c. a visible mark
   d. a skull

7. When something is underline{encased}, it is
   a. closed on all sides
   b. open to the elements
   c. under water
   d. endangered

8. A behavior that underline{transcends} time is one that
   a. lags behind
   b. goes beyond time
   c. is inherited
   d. lacks tradition

9. The footprints indicated that the hominids underline{ambled} across the plain, or
   a. walked
   b. crawled
   c. ran
   d. struggled

10. When Darwin had a underline{notion} about the location of humankind's origin, he had
   a. a misconception
   b. a feeling
   c. a dream
   d. a belief

(**Selection Test**)

Swimming into the Ice Age
from *Muse*
by DAVE GETZ

COMPREHENSION QUESTIONS
Circle the letter of the best answer to each of the following items. *(50 points)*

1. Where was the cave that Henri Cosquer discovered?
   a. in the Mediterranean Sea
   b. in the Caspian Sea
   c. in the Atlantic Ocean
   d. in the Black Sea

2. Cosquer believed that he was not the first modern person in the cave when he saw
   a. engravings
   b. handprints
   c. mineral deposits
   d. geometric shapes

3. The prehistoric paintings were determined to be authentic based on carbon dating and
   a. the nonexistence of bones in the cave
   b. the now extinct animal artwork
   c. the unusual drawings of shapes
   d. the calcite sheets covering the artwork

4. Based on the evidence the researchers found, they concluded that the paintings were probably
   a. created for leisure
   b. simply cave decorations
   c. part of a religious or magic ceremony
   d. made when the cave was still underwater

5. All of the following images were found inside the Cosquer Cave **except**
   a. a hand with missing fingers
   b. a reindeer
   c. a red foot
   d. a seabird

VOCABULARY
Using your knowledge of the underlined word, circle the letter of the word or phrase that best completes each statement. *(50 points)*

6. An <u>extinct</u> animal is one that
   a. has not been classified
   b. has unusual markings
   c. has migrated to warmer climates
   d. is no longer alive and has no descendants

7. When the researchers found a <u>depiction</u> of a killing, they found
   a. a representation
   b. a dramatic performance
   c. evidence
   d. a weapon

8. When Cosquer <u>emerged</u> into the cave, he was
   a. escaping from the cave
   b. coming out of the tunnel
   c. sinking into the cave
   d. lowering himself into the cave

9. If an object is <u>transparent</u>, it is
   a. muddy   c. prehistoric
   b. clear   d. bleary

10. When researchers found <u>geometric</u> designs, they probably saw
    a. numbers and figures
    b. words
    c. animal figures
    d. lines and circles

Selection Test

What the Art May Tell
from *Painters of the Caves*
by PATRICIA LAUBER

COMPREHENSION QUESTIONS

Circle the letter of the best answer to each of the following items. *(50 points)*

1. Cave paintings were not created to decorate shelters because
   a. the caves were believed to be haunted
   b. people were not allowed to decorate
   c. art had not yet been invented
   d. people seldom lived deep in the caves

2. All of the following animals were food to the cave painters **except**
   a. reindeer
   b. birds
   c. lions
   d. bison

3. The shamans are represented in the cave art as
   a. lightning bolts
   b. part animal, part human
   c. horses
   d. the setting sun

4. All of the following are probable reasons why cave paintings were created **except**
   a. they were easy and fun to create
   b. writing did not exist
   c. the paintings told a story
   d. they helped with hunting

5. What was an effect of people raising crops and herd animals?
   a. the forests spread north
   b. animals moved to find plants
   c. people settled in one place
   d. rockfalls blocked cave entrances

VOCABULARY

Using your knowledge of the underlined words, circle the letter of the word or phrase that best completes each statement. *(50 points)*

6. A shaman is someone who is <u>spiritual</u>, or
   a. earthly
   b. unholy
   c. humorous
   d. supernatural

7. When shamans <u>appealed</u> to the spirits, they
   a. defended them
   b. made a request
   c. protected them
   d. told them something

8. To create the paintings on the ceiling, people used <u>scaffolds</u> or
   a. raised platforms
   b. bamboo sticks
   c. long paint brushes
   d. ladders made from animal bones

9. If an image or story makes an <u>impression</u> on you, it
   a. gives you the wrong idea
   b. does not make you feel anything
   c. leaves a scar
   d. has an effect on you

10. During the Ice Age, there were great <u>glaciers</u> or large masses of
    a. ice
    b. frozen earth
    c. hail and frost
    d. snow clouds

(**Selection Test**)

A Bundle of Bog Bodies
from *Bodies from the Bog*
by JAMES M. DEEM

COMPREHENSION QUESTIONS

Circle the letter of the best answer to each of the following items. *(50 points)*

1. During the 1600s, some of the bog bodies were
   a. sent to a museum
   b. dropped into the ocean
   c. examined by experienced scientists
   d. ground up and sold as medicine

2. Scientists are more interested in real, not paper, bog bodies because paper bog bodies
   a. are too fragile to examine
   b. show signs of decay
   c. may have been inaccurately or falsely reported
   d. are not as old

3. The Osterby head belonged to
   a. a Swabian man
   b. an elderly woman
   c. a child
   d. a royal subject

4. Many of the bog bodies were
   a. found buried in mountain cairns
   b. victims of violent crimes
   c. wrapped up like mummies
   d. mostly decayed

5. This selection is supported by
   a. the author's sense of humor
   b. an interview with a bog body expert
   c. the author's opinion
   d. facts and examples

VOCABULARY

Using your knowledge of the underlined word, circle the letter of the word or phrase that best completes each statement. *(50 points)*

6. If a substance is <u>ground</u> into powder, it is
   a. roasted   c. crushed
   b. smothered   d. whipped

7. A <u>grisly</u> discovery was made in one of the bogs. It was
   a. insignificant c. huge
   b. charming   d. horrifying

8. When people <u>deposited</u> bodies in the bog, they _____ them.
   a. removed   c. saved
   b. revived   d. put

9. If a person is <u>mortally</u> wounded, he or she will surely
   a. die
   b. live
   c. become ill
   d. become infected

10. When the curator said he was sending the museum its <u>customary</u> bog body, he meant it was
    a. the first one
    b. the usual bog body
    c. an extraordinary one
    d. inspected by the government

Selection Test

Hammurabi's Babylonia
from *The Babylonians*
by ELAINE LANDAU

COMPREHENSION QUESTIONS

Circle the letter of the best answer to each of the following items. *(50 points)*

1. Agriculture was strong in Babylonia during Hammurabi's reign because he
   a. kept up an irrigation system
   b. gave farmers money
   c. wrote a code of laws
   d. allowed women to own property

2. All of the following items were included among those that Babylonian traders brought home except
   a. gold
   b. woven cloth
   c. precious gems
   d. wood

3. Babylonian women had the right to
   a. ignore the wishes of their fathers
   b. choose their own husbands
   c. vote
   d. own property

4. This selection concludes that Hammurabi's legal code was an important step toward
   a. creating harsh punishments
   b. teaching future Babylonian rulers
   c. creating a just society
   d. obeying the gods

5. Hammurabi's legal code allowed a woman who could prove accusations against her husband
   a. to leave him and keep her dowry
   b. no rights
   c. to marry her husband's brother
   d. to be protected by royal guards

VOCABULARY

Using your knowledge of the underlined word, circle the letter of the word or phrase that best completes each statement. *(50 points)*

6. A Babylonian <u>artisan</u> might do all of the following except
   a. construct weapons or farm equipment
   b. create murals and other decorations
   c. make shoes, belts, and water bags
   d. plant, cultivate, and cut trees

7. When Hammurabi <u>prescribed</u> behavior for slaves, he
   a. authorized what they could do
   b. forbid them to earn wages
   c. offered training
   d. ignored behavior he did not like

8. If a system <u>thrived</u> under your leadership, that system
   a. did poorly   **c.** grew
   b. disappeared   **d.** became law

9. When Hammurabi developed his <u>code</u> for the Babylonians, he created
   a. slavery   **c.** works of art
   b. a set of rules   **d.** irrigation

10. If you make <u>accusations</u>, you are
    a. creating a craft object
    b. praising a person or action
    c. charging someone with doing wrong
    d. creating cuneiforms

(**Selection Test**)

from Writing and Alphabets
from *Alphabetical Order:*
How the Alphabet Began
by TIPHAINE SAMOYAULT

COMPREHENSION QUESTIONS

Circle the letter of the best answer to each of the following items. *(60 points)*

1. In most civilizations, the earliest writing was connected to
   a. schools and clubs
   b. business and government
   c. religion and magic
   d. sports and leisure

2. Instead of using an alphabet, ideograms and pictograms use
   a. pictures and symbols
   b. hand signals and body language
   c. rhythm and rhyme
   d. synonyms and antonyms

3. Forms of writing have been found from as early as 3400 B.C. in
   a. England and Ireland
   b. Germany and Poland
   c. Virginia and Tennessee
   d. Mesopotamia and China

4. The Sumerian writing system was called cuneiform because
   a. the writers used a tool made of pine cones
   b. the marks in the clay were wedge shaped
   c. only the elite of Sumerian society could write
   d. it was created by a woman named Cuneiform

5. The people living in Mesopotamia had to establish trade with other peoples because Mesopotamia
   a. lacked certain raw materials
   b. wanted to conquer new land
   c. feared their goods were inferior
   d. wanted to get to know their neighbors

6. Mesopotamia is part of modern-day
   a. France   c. Egypt
   b. Russia   d. Iraq

VOCABULARY

Using your knowledge of the underlined word, circle the letter of the word or phrase that best completes each statement. *(40 points)*

7. If you made a statement that you wanted to be taken literally, then your meaning would be
   a. the opposite of what you said
   b. impossible to determine
   c. based on exactly what you said
   d. based on your next statement

8. If an ancient priest noticed a distinctive mark on the back of a tortoise, that mark would show
   a. a clear difference from other marks
   b. a striking similarity with other marks
   c. a clear geometric pattern
   d. the age of the tortoise

9. If an event proved to be an inspiration to you, then that event would
   a. leave you too tired to think
   b. cause you to lose hope
   c. cause you to feel very hungry
   d. spark a bright idea or impulse

10. A figure that has a triangular shape has
    a. no beginning and no end
    b. three sides
    c. no regular features
    d. five sides

Selection Test

Enheduana of Sumer
from *Outrageous Women*
of Ancient Times
by VICKI LEÓN

COMPREHENSION QUESTIONS

Circle the letter of the best answer to each of the following items. *(50 points)*

1. In Enheduana's day, books were written on
   a. narrow paper   **c.** temple walls
   b. pointed sticks   **d.** soft clay

2. Enheduana moved to the city of Ur in order to
   a. attend the best college in the land
   b. perform her duties as high priestess
   c. escape her father's tyranny
   d. take advantage of the excellent weather

3. Each spring, Enheduana conducted a ceremony retelling the story of the sacred marriage between
   a. a shepherd and a moon-goddess
   b. a trader and a high priestess
   c. the king and queen of Akkad
   d. a cupbearer and a princess

4. Enheduana served as high priestess until
   a. her father died
   b. the end of her life
   c. her brothers took power
   d. her nephew became king

5. Archaeologists feel that Enheduana was a very popular writer because they found
   a. an old bestseller list that included her name
   b. a copy of her book in nearly every house
   c. more than fifty copies of one of her poems
   d. statements from other writers saying so

VOCABULARY

Using your knowledge of the underlined word, circle the letter of the word or phrase that best completes each statement. *(50 points)*

6. An item that is shaped like a <u>crescent</u> would most resemble
   a. a loaf of bread before it is sliced
   b. a tablet of clay before it has hardened
   c. the moon when it is in a quarter phase
   d. a ziggurat without the top section

7. A <u>sacred</u> book would most likely have something to do with
   a. religion   **c.** school
   b. politics   **d.** business

8. In ancient times, <u>sacrifices</u> to gods usually involved something
   a. brought from a foreign land
   b. precious or important, such as the life of a human or animal
   c. plentiful, such as clay tablets or cooking tools
   d. worthless or useless, such as table scraps or lawn clippings

9. A person who has <u>supreme</u> authority would be
   a. responsible for unimportant things
   b. the least powerful person around
   c. responsible for only one thing
   d. the most powerful person around

10. A person who is <u>composing</u> a piece of writing is
   a. editing the piece
   b. reading the piece
   c. writing the piece
   d. printing the piece

Selection Test

The Patient and Persistent Babylonians
from *Greek and Roman Science*
by DON NARDO

COMPREHENSION QUESTIONS

Circle the letter of the best answer to each of the following items. *(50 points)*

1. The Babylonians apparently chose a numerical system based on the number 60 because
   a. they believed that there were 60 gods
   b. 60 can be easily divided by 2, 3, 4, and 5
   c. they felt there was no need to count higher
   d. each ziggurat had 60 priests and priestesses

2. Today we still see traces of the Babylonian system of counting in the fact that there are 60
   a. seconds in a minute
   b. hours in two and a half days
   c. days in two months
   d. planets in the solar system

3. The Babylonian scholars who studied the skies were
   a. kings
   b. commoners
   c. priests
   d. professors

4. What the Babylonians called a "hairy" or "guest" star we today call a
   a. moon
   b. comet
   c. black hole
   d. supernova

5. Babylonian astronomers named planets after
   a. kings and queens
   b. slaves and servants
   c. priests and scholars
   d. gods and goddesses

VOCABULARY

Using your knowledge of the underlined word, circle the letter of the word or phrase that best completes each statement. *(50 points)*

6. A number that is <u>divisible</u> is capable of being
   a. divided by another number
   b. taken to a higher magnitude
   c. used in a sexagesimal system
   d. multiplied by itself three times

7. If you found <u>remnants</u> of any ancient civilization, you would have found
   a. ziggurats or pyramids
   b. an entire, unchanged culture
   c. traces or fragments
   d. squares or cubes

8. We consider our grandparents to be our <u>predecessors</u> because they are our
   a. relatives or people who live near us
   b. ancestors or people who came before us
   c. teachers or people who instruct us
   d. protectors or people who look after us

9. A person who is responsible for the <u>archives</u> of a school club is in charge of
   a. documents or records used for evidence
   b. costumes or disguises used for plays
   c. uniforms or instruments used for parades
   d. rooms or buildings used for meetings

10. The <u>rudimentary</u> instruments used by Babylonian astronomers were
    a. advanced
    b. powerful
    c. elementary
    d. complicated

Selection Test

from **The Monster Humbaba**
from *Gilgamesh: Man's First Story*
by BERNARDA BRYSON

COMPREHENSION QUESTIONS

Circle the letter of the best answer to each of the following items. *(50 points)*

1. Enkidu interprets Gilgamesh's first dream as meaning that
   a. they should go back home
   b. Humbaba will eat them
   c. Enkidu will injure his hand
   d. they will defeat Humbaba

2. When Enkidu tries to open the gate, he is
   a. thrown backward with great force
   b. pulled up the mountain by Humbaba
   c. informed that he was at the wrong gate
   d. told that he must answer three questions

3. Gilgamesh and Enkidu can tell they are getting closer to Humbaba because they
   a. see hundreds of bodies piled in mounds
   b. hear his heartbeat and smell smoke
   c. see his head above the trees
   d. hear him bellowing like a bull

4. As they approach the monster, Gilgamesh shows his daring by
   a. cutting down a tree
   b. singing a war song
   c. loudly ringing a bell
   d. rolling loose stones

5. Humbaba tries to trick Gilgamesh by
   a. pointing up and saying, "Look"
   b. pretending that he is dead
   c. groveling and wailing for help
   d. setting fire to the cedar forest

VOCABULARY

Using your knowledge of the underlined word, circle the letter of the word or phrase that best completes each statement. *(50 points)*

6. When Enkidu's hand was <u>paralyzed</u>, he could not
   a. stop it from shaking
   b. move it or feel it
   c. remember how to raise it
   d. take his glove off

7. If you wanted to <u>flail</u> something, you would
   a. throw it or toss it in the air
   b. pet it or treat it very kindly
   c. move it or beat it wildly about
   d. protect it or keep it in safety

8. If something is <u>poised</u>, that thing is
   a. balanced   c. deadly
   b. rolling   d. boring

9. Someone who <u>ignited</u> a tree would have
   a. carved initials in it
   b. watered it
   c. set fire to it
   d. planted it

10. A sound that <u>reverberated</u> would have
    a. caused trees to fall down
    b. taken on a life of its own
    c. been heard only by animals
    d. echoed back or resounded

(*Selection Test*)

from Education:
The Sumarian School
from *The Sumerians: Their History, Culture, and Character*
by SAMUEL NOAH KRAMER

COMPREHENSION QUESTIONS

Circle the letter of the best answer to each of the following items. *(60 points)*

1. The father suspects that his son has been
   a. idling about in the public square
   b. doing math with his monitor
   c. writing graffiti on walls
   d. working far too hard at school

2. After the son finishes his assignment, the father wants him to
   a. relax and read
   b. return to him
   c. talk back to the monitor
   d. take a walk

3. The father believes that the monitor will like his son if his son
   a. takes the monitor some cookies
   b. spends time in the public square
   c. tells the monitor a funny joke
   d. shows that he fears the monitor

VOCABULARY

Using your knowledge of the underlined word, circle the letter of the word or phrase that best completes each statement. *(40 points)*

4. When the father tells his son to recite his assignment, he is telling his son to
   a. explain why his school assignment is so important
   b. relax and not worry so much about his school work
   c. answer questions orally or to read aloud publicly
   d. find a homework assignment that had been lost

5. When the son reports to his monitor, he will be reporting to a person who
   a. appoints
   b. instructs
   c. protects
   d. slithers

Name _____ Class _____ Date _____

COMPREHENSION QUESTIONS

Circle the letter of the best answer to each of the following items. *(50 points)*

1. The step pyramids were built as a
  a. tribute to the sun god
  b. symbol of peace
  c. war monument
  d. stairway to heaven

2. All of the following tools were used by the ancient Egyptians to build pyramids **except** the
  a. lever   **c.** compass
  b. inclined plane   **d.** wedge

3. To level the construction site, the builders used
  a. a plumb bob
  b. water-filled trenches
  c. bulldozers
  d. an inclined plane

4. Treasures were often buried with a pharaoh because the Egyptians believed that the ruler
  a. would need them in the afterlife
  b. did not want his successor to have them
  c. was often greedy
  d. wanted to prove how powerful he was

5. To move the large stones to the upper levels of the pyramids, the workers used
  a. a wooden hoist
  b. ladders placed inside the chambers
  c. a catapult
  d. ramps of mud and sand

VOCABULARY

Using your knowledge of the underlined word, circle the letter of the word or phrase that best completes each statement. *(50 points)*

6. An ancient Egyptian <u>surveyor</u> would
  a. polish the pharaoh's jewelry
  b. paint the inside of the pyramids
  c. check each layer of stonework
  d. design the pyramid for the pharaoh

7. To make underground chambers for a pyramid, the chambers must be <u>excavated</u>, or
  a. studied
  b. dug out
  c. filled in
  d. flooded

8. Before building, the Egyptians had to decide on a <u>site</u>, which was a
  a. location   **c.** vision
  b. quotation   **d.** price

9. The pyramids are <u>exposed</u> to the environment, meaning they are
  a. unoccupied   **c.** harmful
  b. protected   **d.** uncovered

10. If you find the <u>remains</u> of a building, you would see its
  a. complete structure
  b. ruins
  c. swimming pool
  d. lawn

Selection Test

COMPREHENSION QUESTIONS

Circle the letter of the best answer to each of the following items. *(100 points)*

1. Inside a pyramid you might expect to find all of the following **except**
   - **a.** a mummy
   - **b.** a sarcophagus
   - **c.** palm trees
   - **d.** treasures

2. The first step in the mummification process was to
   - **a.** take out the body's internal organs
   - **b.** dry out the body
   - **c.** have the priest say prayers
   - **d.** wrap the body with linen

3. The canopic jars were used to hold
   - **a.** the pharaoh's amulets
   - **b.** the body's internal organs
   - **c.** the pharaoh's treasure
   - **d.** special food for the journey in the afterlife

4. When a mummy was ready for burial, it was often placed
   - **a.** on a granite slab
   - **b.** inside a tar-filled canopic jar
   - **c.** in a woven casket
   - **d.** in a nest of two or three human-shaped coffins

5. Why don't mummies smell bad?
   - **a.** They are too old to have an odor
   - **b.** They were filled with sand
   - **c.** They were properly dried and stuffed
   - **d.** They were treated with bitumen

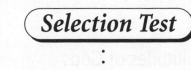

Selection Test

from **The Finding of the Tomb**
. . . . *from The Tomb of Tutankhamen*
by HOWARD CARTER AND A. C. MACE

COMPREHENSION QUESTIONS

Circle the letter of the best answer to each of the following items. *(50 points)*

1. Carter knew that he was not the first to enter King Tut's tomb when he saw
   a. an opened door
   b. an opened coffin
   c. pieces of broken pottery
   d. writing on the tomb's wall

2. Clearing the debris was a slow job because the workers had to
   a. rest frequently due to the heat
   b. sort through it for delicate objects
   c. crawl through narrow tunnels
   d. use outdated tools

3. Carter realized that the tomb was Tutankhamen's when he identified
   a. the seal impressions
   b. King Tut's burial mask
   c. the gold statues
   d. the stairway and doors

4. To create suspense for the reader, Carter provides details about
   a. the people who worked with him
   b. Tutankhamen's life
   c. the weather and the environment
   d. reaching and opening the second doorway

5. Once Carter looked through the second door, he discovered
   a. statues and gold
   b. false doors
   c. that he could not breathe the air
   d. that the tomb was empty

VOCABULARY

Using your knowledge of the underlined word, circle the letter of the word or phrase that best completes each statement. *(50 points)*

6. If someone were <u>plundering</u> a tomb, he or she would be
   a. restoring it   c. drawing it
   b. excavating it   d. robbing it

7. A lot of rubble <u>encumbered</u> part of a doorway, which made the entry
   a. effortless   c. difficult
   b. small   d. comfortable

8. Carter came upon a <u>replica</u> of the first door. This means that, compared to the first door, the second door was
   a. broken   c. smaller
   b. similar   d. older

9. There were other digs in the <u>vicinity</u>, or in the
   a. surrounding area   c. same era
   b. city   d. hillside

10. If you were waiting to hear a <u>verdict</u>, you would be waiting for
    a. instructions   c. a summary
    b. proof   d. a decision

Name _____ Class _____ Date _____

Selection Test

Multitudes of Gods
from *The Ancient Egyptians*
by ELSA MARSTON

COMPREHENSION QUESTIONS

Circle the letter of the best answer to each of the following items. *(50 points)*

1. The most important god who was considered the source of life was
   a. Anubis, the protector of the dead.
   b. Ra, the sun god
   c. Horus, the sky god
   d. Khnum, the potter

2. Many of the Egyptian deities had
   a. homes on Mount Olympus
   b. no special powers
   c. features of a certain animal
   d. a human head and an animal body

3. One reason the Egyptians had so many deities was related to
   a. their many festivals
   b. their respect for multiple roles
   c. the need for local gods
   d. their fear of uncertainty

4. Who cared daily for the gods?
   a. the priests
   b. the public
   c. the pharaohs
   d. the children

5. Which of the following was true about Egyptian deities?
   a. They were completely unlike real persons
   b. Each deity had at least one special role
   c. They lived inside the pyramids
   d. The most important gods were homey, personal deities

VOCABULARY

Using your knowledge of the underlined word, circle the letter of the word or phrase that best completes each statement. *(50 points)*

6. A contradictory statement is one that
   a. is in opposition
   b. can be supported
   c. has many meanings
   d. explains a process

7. The ancient Egyptians believed that their world was filled with chaos, or
   a. trickery   c. direction
   b. symbols   d. disorder

8. A belief in deities is a belief
   a. in complex ideas
   b. in gods and goddesses
   c. that people can live in the afterlife
   d. that nature is all-powerful

9. Pyramids were built during different dynasties, or
   a. environmental conditions
   b. forms of government
   c. periods during which a certain family rules
   d. time zones

10. If a region suffers from a famine,
    a. there is a great food shortage
    b. there has been a flood
    c. a contagious disease threatens the population
    d. winds have destroyed whole villages

Name _____ Class _____ Date _____

Selection Test

The Other Half of History:
Women in Ancient Egypt
by FIONA MACDONALD

COMPREHENSION QUESTIONS

Circle the letter of the best answer to
each of the following items. *(50 points)*

1. Why couldn't a woman be a divine ruler in
   ancient Egypt?
   a. Women were not aggressive enough
   b. Women were not allowed in temples
   c. There were gods that prohibited it
   d. Only a man could be a living god

2. Hatshepsut became a pharaoh because
   a. she seized control during a war
   b. the people voted her in
   c. Thutmose III was too young to rule
   d. the gods appointed her

3. Nefertiti is often shown in carvings as
   a. an equal to the pharaoh
   b. a cruel and ruthless queen
   c. a negotiator
   d. a dull, lifeless queen

4. Cleopatra is known for her involvement with
   a. Rome   c. Ethiopia
   b. Punt   d. Spain

5. All of the following jobs were done by
   women in ancient Egypt **except**
   a. looking after goddesses' statues
   b. reading prayers at religious ceremonies
   c. making offerings
   d. supervising temple estates

VOCABULARY

Using your knowledge of the underlined words, circle the letter of the word or phrase that
best completes each statement. *(50 points)*

6. A priestess <u>supervised</u> servants, meaning that
   she
   a. paid them
   b. controlled their freedom
   c. managed their work
   d. ignored them

7. When Hatshepsut went on an <u>expedition</u>, she
   was
   a. shopping
   b. making a journey
   c. hunting
   d. traveling to a battle

8. If you are appointed <u>regent</u>, your job is to
   a. rule in someone's place
   b. rule with someone
   c. assume complete control
   d. give money to the ruler

9. If you found ways of <u>exercising</u> power, you
   would be
   a. assigning your rights to others
   b. using your authority
   c. in training
   d. learning about your job

10. People hoped for <u>prosperity</u>, or
    a. religious freedom
    b. political tranquillity
    c. peace
    d. good fortune and wealth

(**Selection Test**)

from Kush—The Nubian
Kingdom
from Africa, Egypt, Kush,
Aksum: Northeast Africa
by KENNY MANN

COMPREHENSION QUESTIONS

Circle the letter of the best answer to each of the following items. *(50 points)*

1. What caused a renewed interest in the
   ancient civilizations of Kush?
   a. archaeological digs during the building of
      the Aswan High Dam
   b. the discovery of gold and ebony
   c. the growth of population in the area
   d. a war that broke out between Kush and
      Egypt

2. The ancient Egyptians called Nubia *Ta-Seti*,
   meaning
   a. "land of the ostrich" c. "remote region"
   b. "land of the bow"   d. "boiled meat"

3. One of the reasons Nubia, or Kush, was an
   unknown area is probably because
   a. it did not allow many people to enter
   b. people were afraid of the animals
   c. it was remote
   d. nobody really knew where it was

4. Europeans may not have shown as much
   interest in Nubia as they did in other African
   countries because
   a. Nubia did not have any precious items
   b. the Europeans were biased
   c. the Nubian queen did not welcome them
   d. Nubia did not practice Christianity

5. The Nubians were among which civilization's
   most hated enemies?
   a. Libyan   c. Macedonian
   b. Kushite   d. Egyptian

VOCABULARY

Using your knowledge of the underlined word, circle the letter of the word or phrase that best completes
each statement. *(50 points)*

6. A dire situation is one that is
   a. frightful   c. unusual
   b. nonthreatening   d. ordinary

7. Information about Nubia that has been
   gleaned from other peoples has been
   a. ordered   c. kept secret
   b. gathered   d. burned

8. A location that is inaccessible is one that is
   a. easy to reach   c. risky
   b. off limits   d. unreachable

9. If a person has a bias, it means that he or
   she is
   a. impatient   c. prejudiced
   b. open-minded   d. kind

10. An eminent archaeologist is one who is
    a. dead   c. disloyal
    b. too smart   d. important

Selection Test

from Astronomy and
Timekeeping
from Science in Ancient Egypt
by GERALDINE WOODS

COMPREHENSION QUESTIONS

Circle the letter of the best answer to each of the following items. *(50 points)*

1. Where did the sun god Ra sail his boat during the dark hours?
   a. across the sky
   b. under the earth
   c. behind the moon
   d. over the heavens

2. The ancient Egyptians based their calendar on the
   a. sun
   b. planets
   c. Milky Way
   d. Big Dipper

3. One reason the Egyptians adjusted their calendar was to be able to predict
   a. the date of the new year
   b. the occurrence of a solar eclipse
   c. the changing of the weather
   d. the flooding of the Nile

4. Using Sirius to calculate a year was lucky because
   a. its location is in a constellation shaped like a pyramid
   b. lunar eclipses were confusing people
   c. its cycle is 365 1/4 days long
   d. it is the brightest object in the sky

5. Astronomers decided that a month would have three weeks. To compensate for the lost time, people enjoyed five days of festivals created by the god
   a. Ra
   b. Thoth
   c. Anubis
   d. Min

VOCABULARY

Using your knowledge of the underlined word, circle the letter of the word or phrase that best completes each statement. *(50 points)*

6. The Egyptians were methodical people who
   a. used an orderly system
   b. made many mistakes
   c. allowed chaos to rule
   d. prepared sloppy charts

7. An Egyptian legend claims that a god fashioned or _____ the moon's light into days.
   a. robbed
   b. allocated
   c. preserved
   d. turned

8. A prominent object in the sky is one that is
   a. dim
   b. famous
   c. easily seen
   d. unknown

9. A constellation of stars is a group of stars that
   a. predicts the weather
   b. has been given a definite name
   c. is the brightest object in the sky
   d. only appears a few minutes at dawn

10. Ancient peoples reckoned or _____ time by natural occurrences.
   a. calculated
   b. thought about the gods' influence over
   c. ignored
   d. feared

Selection Test

Deborah
from *Women of the Bible*
by CAROLE ARMSTRONG

COMPREHENSION QUESTIONS

Circle the letter of the best answer to each of the following items. *(50 points)*

1. Deborah stood out among Hebrew judges because she was
   a. never wrong
   b. extremely tall
   c. the only woman
   d. also a leader

2. The palm tree was the tree of life and the symbol of
   a. judges
   b. hope
   c. despair
   d. victory

3. The Israelite leaders went to Deborah hoping that she could
   a. rescue them from years of oppression
   b. arrange peace with the Canaanite army
   c. find a place for the Hebrew army to train
   d. help them purchase nine hundred chariots

4. Deborah summoned Barak and ordered him to gather
   a. a dozen palm trees
   b. fifty-five more judges
   c. nine hundred chariots
   d. ten thousand men

5. With a blow to the head, Jael killed
   a. Barak
   b. Sisera
   c. Deborah
   d. Heber

VOCABULARY

Using your knowledge of the underlined word, circle the letter of the word or phrase that best completes each statement. *(50 points)*

6. When a group is <u>oppressed</u>, they are
   a. cared for and pampered
   b. granted all of their freedoms
   c. treated harshly and unjustly
   d. allowed to operate a newspaper

7. A story that tells of a people's <u>plight</u> gives details about their
   a. system of government by judges
   b. comfortable and secure way of life
   c. rule over another group of people
   d. bad or dangerous state or condition

8. If you offered <u>refuge</u> to someone, you would be offering them
   a. safety or shelter
   b. fruits or vegetables
   c. money or goods
   d. food or drink

9. Jael secretly <u>sympathized</u> with the Israelites, meaning that she
   a. felt they had nobody to blame but themselves
   b. did not understand why they would go to war
   c. hoped they would fail to achieve their goals
   d. shared or understood their feelings or ideas

10. When Jael acted <u>brutally</u> toward the general, she acted in an
    a. emotional, kind, or caring manner
    b. unfeeling, cruel, or direct manner
    c. indirect, sneaky, or secret manner
    d. amusing, funny, or cheerful manner

Name _____ Class _____ Date _____

Selection Test

Judaism
· from *One World, Many Religions*
by MARY POPE OSBORNE

COMPREHENSION QUESTIONS

Circle the letter of the best answer to each of the following items. *(60 points)*

1. Today the ancient land of Ur is known as
   a. the Promised Land
   b. Iraq
   c. Canaan
   d. Egypt

2. Abraham's descendants came to be known as
   a. Israelites   c. Egyptians
   b. Abrahamians   d. Canaanites

3. When Abraham's descendants became too numerous, the ruler of Egypt
   a. allowed them to go home
   b. gave them their own land
   c. forced them into slavery
   d. sent them into the desert

4. God told Moses that he should
   a. make peace with the Egyptian king
   b. send soldiers after the fleeing slaves
   c. remind Abraham about his promise
   d. lead the Israelites back to Canaan

5. With his people trapped at the Red Sea, Moses's prayers to God were answered when
   a. the waters of the Red Sea parted
   b. Pharaoh's army was struck blind
   c. a heavenly bridge led them to safety
   d. God gave him two tablets of stone

6. The most important part of the Torah, the Jewish holy book, is
   a. the story of the Garden of Eden
   b. the history of different families
   c. the Ten Commandments
   d. the Trek Out of Egypt

VOCABULARY

Using your knowledge of the underlined word, circle the letter of the word or phrase that best completes each statement. *(40 points)*

7. The Israelites are considered descendants of Abraham because they
   a. promised to follow Abraham's teachings
   b. can trace their families back to Abraham
   c. believe that Abraham is the one true God
   d. followed Abraham to the Promised Land

8. When a friend says your new clothes are stunning, your friend means the clothes are
   a. striking or remarkable
   b. ordinary or common
   c. difficult or stubborn
   d. shiny or bright

9. The locusts and hailstorms that struck Egypt were plagues because they
   a. hurt the Egyptian economy
   b. were small and easy to ignore
   c. were sent as divine punishment
   d. happened after Moses met Abraham

10. An infestation of locusts would be marked by
    a. destructive swarming
    b. small groups swarming
    c. good swarming
    d. a lack of swarming

Selection Test

The Writings
from *A Treasury of Jewish Literature: From Biblical Times to Today*
by GLORIA GOLDREICH

COMPREHENSION QUESTIONS

Circle the letter of the best answer to each of the following items. *(50 points)*

1. The Psalms are believed to have been written by
   a. Solomon
   b. King David
   c. Michelangelo
   d. Alfred, Lord Tennyson

2. The second section of the Bible, called the Prophets, urges people to
   a. express their disappointment
   b. pose basic ethical questions
   c. live moral and just lives
   d. mold their own destinies

3. The Book of Job questions the
   a. justice of God
   b. purpose of life
   c. need for songs
   d. desire for money

4. The Song of Songs consists of a series of
   a. love poems
   b. songs about prophets
   c. questions about God
   d. statements about life

5. Rabbis have interpreted the Song of Songs as a recitation of God's love for
   a. King David
   b. Passover
   c. the Talmud
   d. Israel

VOCABULARY

Using your knowledge of the underlined word, circle the letter of the word or phrase that best completes each statement. *(50 points)*

6. The Torah legislates how people should live their lives because it contains
   a. poems
   b. questions
   c. songs
   d. laws

7. When your teacher implores you to do something, you are being asked
   a. repeatedly
   b. hopelessly
   c. earnestly
   d. distantly

8. In order to live a just life, a person has to be
   a. upright and virtuous
   b. blessed and grateful
   c. emotional and poetic
   d. free and spontaneous

9. An affirmation is the act of declaring something to be
   a. eternal
   b. ethical
   c. false
   d. true

10. A steering wheel is an integral part of a car because it is
   a. optional
   b. essential
   c. unnecessary
   d. sometimes useful

Name _____ Class _____ Date _____

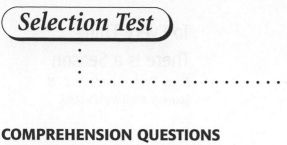

Selection Test

The Mystery of Qumran and the Dead Sea Scrolls
by HERSHEL SHANKS

COMPREHENSION QUESTIONS
Circle the letter of the best answer to each of the following items. *(50 points)*

1. There are doubts about the story of the discovery of the Dead Sea Scrolls because
   a. archaeologists like to argue
   b. only scraps of each scroll could be found and read
   c. other men claimed to be the shepherd who found them
   d. hundreds of scrolls were found in different caves in the area

2. Archaeologists digging in the ancient settlement of Qumran were hoping to discover clues to the mystery of who
   a. killed the shepherd called edh-Dhib
   b. wrote the Dead Sea Scrolls and why
   c. first discovered the Dead Sea Scrolls
   d. should decide what the scrolls mean

3. Few of the scrolls could be read because so many of them were
   a. stored in jars
   b. written in Hebrew
   c. found in tatters
   d. wrapped in linen

4. The Copper Scroll from one of the caves lists places where
   a. treasure was hidden
   b. scrolls were written
   c. Essenes were buried
   d. jars were manufactured

5. One reason scholars believe Qumran was a Jewish settlement is that Jewish names were found on
   a. mailboxes   c. baths
   b. scrolls   d. pottery

VOCABULARY
Using your knowledge of the underlined words, circle the letter of the word or phrase that best completes each statement. *(50 points)*

6. If your dog left your homework in tatters, then your work would be left in
   a. envelopes   c. piles
   b. boxes   d. shreds

7. Interesting things can be distractions from your chores because they
   a. involve similar activities
   b. cause a great deal of stress
   c. draw your attention away
   d. take too long to finish

8. Because they lived communally, the Essenes were used to
   a. fighting over tools
   b. living as a group

   c. cooking the same foods
   d. ignoring people from outside

9. People who live in a fortress are residing in a(n)
   a. stronghold   c. shack
   b. apartment   d. cave

10. A building that is fortified will have been
    a. treated for termites, ants, and other bugs
    b. built near a fort or some other military base
    c. built in an isolated area, such as on a large farm
    d. strengthened against attack with walls or forts

Name _____ Class _____ Date _____

Selection Test

COMPREHENSION QUESTIONS

Circle the letter of the best answer to each of the following items. *(100 points)*

1. All of the following are pairs of opposites
   used by the writer of the selection **except**
   a. mourn and dance
   b. love and hate
   c. right and wrong
   d. peace and war

2. In one of the pairings of opposites, the writer
   says that there is a time to rend and a time to
   a. sew
   b. throw stones
   c. plant
   d. break down

Selection Test

Cities of the Indus Valley
from *Weird and Wacky Science: Lost Cities*
by JOYCE GOLDENSTERN

COMPREHENSION QUESTIONS

Circle the letter of the best answer to each of the following items. *(50 points)*

1. Mohenjo-daro and Harappa prospered greatly from
   a. tourism   **c.** rare minerals
   b. artistic crafts   **d.** agriculture

2. We know the people of the Indus Valley enjoyed their leisure time as evidenced by
   a. colorfully painted sticks
   b. toys and games
   c. a large field in the center of town
   d. comical paintings on the walls

3. All of the following are features found in the cities of Mohenjo-daro and Harappa **except**
   a. streets formed in a grid system
   b. sewer and drainage system
   c. a central park
   d. a large citadel

4. It is believed that decorated seals were used
   a. as writing tablets
   b. as markers for a board game
   c. to entertain children
   d. to mark belongings

5. One theory about the decline of the ancient civilizations is that the people
   a. cut down most of the forests
   b. suffered from an incurable disease
   c. warred with neighboring cities
   d. died from starvation

VOCABULARY

Using your knowledge of the underlined word, circle the letter of the word or phrase that best completes each statement. *(50 points)*

6. A noted archaeologist was shocked by the <u>gruesome</u> scene because it was
   a. amazing
   b. horrifying and repulsive
   c. uncommon
   d. difficult to understand

7. Harappa has a <u>circumference</u> or _____ of about three miles.
   a. underground tunnel
   b. altitude
   c. boundary
   d. drainage duct

8. As of yet, no one has been able to <u>decipher</u> or _____ the seals.
   a. interpret   **c.** photograph
   b. count   **d.** train

9. An <u>anthropologist</u> is someone who studies
   a. the stars   **c.** buildings
   b. human origins   **d.** dirt and soil

10. The <u>ecology</u> of a region is the pattern of relationships between
    a. two similar cities
    b. people and animals
    c. people and their surroundings
    d. people and their trade routes

Selection Test

A Vow to Conquer by Dhamma
from *Calliope*
by JEAN ELLIOTT JOHNSON

COMPREHENSION QUESTIONS

Circle the letter of the best answer to each of the following items. *(50 points)*

1. Ashoka changed his approach to ruling after he
   a. had a vision of a great wheel
   b. received news about an uprising
   c. experienced warfare
   d. was defeated in battle

2. What religion influenced Ashoka's new outlook?
   a. Buddhism   c. Jainism
   b. Brahmanism   d. Islam

3. All of the following are activities supported by Ashoka **except**
   a. building hospitals
   b. growing medicinal herbs
   c. constructing roads
   d. tolerating crimes

4. Ashoka thought that spreading the idea of *dhamma* throughout the empire would
   a. convert everyone to his religion
   b. keep his kingdom unified
   c. prevent foreign attacks
   d. advance his popularity among the people

5. This selection concludes that Ashoka is remembered most for his
   a. barbaric actions
   b. conquering new lands
   c. lack of leadership
   d. moral approach to governing

VOCABULARY

Using your knowledge of the underlined word, circle the letter of the word or phrase that best completes each statement. *(50 points)*

6. An ethical ruler is one that
   a. applies moral standards
   b. is unfit to rule
   c. imposes religion on his people
   d. does not listen to the people

7. When Ashoka asked that people be compassionate toward all living things, he wanted people to
   a. take whatever they needed from the earth
   b. be pacifists
   c. be kind and show sympathy
   d. act more superior than the animals

8. A diverse country is one that
   a. is separated by two opposing political groups

   b. practices one religion
   c. has an emperor for a ruler
   d. is made up of many different people and things

9. If you live in a system based on general religious principles, you must follow
   a. the opinions of a few
   b. rules of conduct
   c. the ideas of one leader
   d. rules of the authorities

10. A society that is prosperous is one that is
    a. isolated
    b. poor
    c. successful
    d. conceited

Selection Test

Siddhartha Gautama: The Buddha
from *Buddhism*
by JOHN SNELLING

COMPREHENSION QUESTIONS

Circle the letter of the best answer to each of the following items. *(50 points)*

1. Siddhartha Gautama was a prince. Why did he become disillusioned living at the palace?
   a. Gautama discovered a world of poverty and illness
   b. Gautama's son would not obey him
   c. Gautama was bored with palace life
   d. Gautama wanted to become a ruler of the people

2. The Buddha first went to seek answers to his questions
   a. in the desert of another kingdom
   b. in a monastery in the mountains
   c. under a lemon tree
   d. in quiet places with famous teachers

3. The Buddha reached enlightenment by
   a. sleeping on a bed of thorns
   b. giving up his life of luxury
   c. looking within
   d. completing special exercises

4. According to legend, the Buddha reached enlightenment after
   a. walking in an enchanted forest
   b. meditating under a bo tree
   c. not eating for three weeks
   d. returning to his home at the palace

5. The teachings of the Buddha are called the
   a. sangha   c. Dharma
   b. nirvana   d. parinirvana

VOCABULARY

Using your knowledge of the underlined word, circle the letter of the word or phrase that best completes each statement. *(50 points)*

6. The Buddha said that compounded or _____ things are only temporary.
   a. simple   c. puzzling
   b. complex   d. luxurious

7. A person who is born into a life of privilege has
   a. responsibilities c. few choices
   b. no rights   d. special favors

8. When the Buddha set out on his quest, he was
   a. looking for knowledge
   b. sitting under a bo tree
   c. hiding from the authorities
   d. teaching classes

9. When the Buddha was reluctant to talk about his discovery, he
   a. was eager to share the news
   b. thought he would be punished
   c. wanted to keep it a secret
   d. was unwilling to discuss it

10. A forsaken person is one who is
    a. cheerful
    b. knowledgeable
    c. abandoned
    d. a prophet

Selection Test

Confucianism and Taoism
from *One World, Many Religions*
by MARY POPE OSBORNE

COMPREHENSION QUESTIONS

Circle the letter of the best answer to each of the following items. *(50 points)*

1. Confucius began teaching the wisdom of the old traditions because he
   a. did not like military life
   b. wanted people to be nicer
   c. was concerned about China's future
   d. thought he could become an important leader

2. All of the following are ideas taught by Confucius **except**
   a. the government should not be selfish
   b. people should respect their leaders
   c. all children should get an education
   d. people should take whatever they want

3. Taoism was founded by
   a. Confucius
   b. Lao-tzu
   c. Tao Te Ching
   d. an unknown woman

4. "The Tao" means
   a. "the way"
   b. "the light"
   c. "Old Master"
   d. "the moon"

5. Which event prevented the Chinese from following their ancient religions?
   a. the death of Confucius
   b. a conflict between the Taoists, the Buddhists, and the Confucians
   c. the war between China and Taiwan
   d. the Chinese Communist takeover

VOCABULARY

Using your knowledge of the underlined word, circle the letter of the word or phrase that best completes each statement. *(50 points)*

6. When the rulers <u>relied</u> on scholars for help, they
   a. offered them money
   b. asked for their input
   c. depended on them
   d. wanted to trick them

7. A source of life that is <u>infinite</u>
   a. cannot be understood
   b. has no limits
   c. has boundaries
   d. will eventually die

8. A <u>courteous</u> person is one who
   a. asks many questions
   b. has parents of nobility
   c. is polite
   d. wanders around the country

9. Confucius was known to be <u>humble</u>, or
   a. modest
   b. nimble
   c. respected
   d. lean

10. If a family were to <u>revere</u> a spiritual leader, they would
    a. support him or her financially
    b. be skeptical of the leader's teachings
    c. create a shrine
    d. honor and respect the leader

Selection Test

from **The Great Wall of China**
from *Walls: Defenses Throughout History*
by JAMES CROSS GIBLIN

COMPREHENSION QUESTIONS

Circle the letter of the best answer to each of the following items. *(50 points)*

1. All of the following facts about the Great Wall of China are true **except**
   a. it is long enough to circle the globe at the equator
   b. it was built within ten years
   c. it extends across northern and central China
   d. it is the longest structure ever built

2. Emperor Shih wanted to link smaller walls into one great wall because
   a. he thought it could be used to transport goods
   b. too many people were leaving the country, and he wanted to control the borders
   c. he wanted to protect his country from northern invaders
   d. its construction would provide jobs for many people

3. The Great Wall was built by all of the following **except**
   a. nomadic tribes   c. women
   b. soldiers   d. prisoners

4. According to the selection, who was one of the attackers who broke through the wall's defenses?
   a. Genghis Khan   c. Adolf Hitler
   b. General Meng   d. Confucius

5. Today, the Great Wall of China is being repaired as
   a. a structure for military defense
   b. an earthquake study center
   c. a historical monument
   d. a commercial center

VOCABULARY

Using your knowledge of the underlined word, circle the letter of the word or phrase that best completes each statement. *(50 points)*

6. Emperor Shih was known as a ruthless ruler because he
   a. built roads   c. had no friends
   b. was pushy   d. was cruel

7. Emperor Shih made the Great Wall his first priority because it was
   a. easy to build
   b. important
   c. in need of repair
   d. something he might forget to do

8. If a project is considered ambitious, it
   a. requires great effort
   b. involves very little time
   c. will be easy to do
   d. requires very little work

9. Shih embarked on or _____ many new programs.
   a. ignored   c. began
   b. cancelled   d. postponed

10. When the Chinese Communists restored the Great Wall, they
    a. took over its management
    b. modernized it to put it in use
    c. prohibited people from using it
    d. brought it back to its former condition

Selection Test

March of the Terra-Cotta Soldiers
from *Archaeology's Dig*
by VICTORIA C. NESNICK

COMPREHENSION QUESTIONS

Circle the letter of the best answer to each of the following items. *(50 points)*

1. The discovery of the terra-cotta soldiers is amazing because
   a. so many little pieces have to be put together
   b. there was a large treasure of gold buried with them
   c. the figurines are so small
   d. there is an entire army of life-sized sculptures

2. The farmers who found the first clay head thought
   a. they had released an evil spirit
   b. the head belonged to an important ruler
   c. they had found an ancient toy
   d. they could keep it a secret for many years

3. Many of the statues were destroyed by
   a. an earthquake   c. ancient warlords
   b. angry peasants   d. the emperor

4. Some scholars believe Qin Shihuangdi had these soldiers built
   a. to decorate the royal palace
   b. as a memorial to his conquests
   c. to celebrate the many cultures in his country
   d. as a reminder that a country's military is its greatest asset

5. What do some scholars expect to find in Shihuangdi's tomb?
   a. precious stone models of palaces
   b. more terra-cotta soldiers, horses, and chariots
   c. an explanation as to why the terra-cotta warriors were built
   d. a miniature replica of the Great Wall

VOCABULARY

Using your knowledge of the underlined word, circle the letter of the word or phrase that best completes each statement. *(50 points)*

6. Archeologists who work on conservation projects try to
   a. relocate the site
   b. collect money for research
   c. protect the find
   d. determine the age of a find

7. Scientists believe that exposure to air will cause some items to disintegrate or
   a. disappear   c. fade
   b. burn   d. crumble

8. Souvenirs are things that people buy
   a. to help museums raise money
   b. as a reminder of the past
   c. to add to a private collection
   d. when they cannot afford the real item

9. If you endure a catastrophe, you experience
   a. a heart attack   c. a disaster
   b. great luck   d. a loud noise

10. Shihuangdi's tomb is massive or
    a. huge   c. dark
    b. falling apart d. underwater

Selection Test

from **The Ancient Olympics**
from *The Olympic Games*
by THEODORE KNIGHT

COMPREHENSION QUESTIONS

Circle the letter of the best answer to each of the following items. *(50 points)*

1. Scholars know that the Olympic festival began early in Greek history because
   a. the earliest games consisted of footraces
   b. someone recorded the victory of Coroebus
   c. the earliest Greek poets wrote of the games
   d. the games declined when Greece declined

2. In order to prevent Œnamaus from catching him, Pelops
   a. kidnapped the daughter of the king
   b. cut the axle on Œnamaus's chariot
   c. used thirteen young men as decoys
   d. ordered that a great feast be held

3. For winning a footrace in the Olympic Festival of 776 B.C., Coroebus was awarded
   a. a wreath of olive branches
   b. a villa in Macedon
   c. a chest of gold coins
   d. a statue of Zeus

4. The Olympic festival went into a decline after
   a. chariot races were ruled illegal
   b. Greeks lost interest in athletics
   c. Greece was conquered by Rome
   d. tribal chiefs negotiated a treaty

5. Nero always won at the Olympic festival because
   a. he was ancient Rome's greatest athlete
   b. he built a great temple in honor of Zeus
   c. better athletes were not permitted to play
   d. people were afraid to defeat an emperor

VOCABULARY

Using your knowledge of the vocabulary word, write in the appropriate blank the letter of the word or phrase that best defines the word. *(50 points)*

_____ 6. anonymous
_____ 7. initiating
_____ 8. barred
_____ 9. confined
_____ 10. negotiate

a. try to reach an agreement
b. not known by name
c. kept out or banned
d. limited
e. freed
f. restricted
g. starting the event

_____ 11. hostilities
_____ 12. spectators
_____ 13. pageants
_____ 14. spectacle
_____ 15. bribery

a. dramatic public display
b. friendly relations
c. colorful shows
d. warfare
e. money given to someone to do something illegal
f. onlookers
g. participants

Selection Test

COMPREHENSION QUESTIONS

Circle the letter of the best answer to each of the following items. *(50 points)*

1. Sparta was the most powerful city-state in ancient Greece because of its
   a. army
   b. legends
   c. oligarchy
   d. government

2. Sparta waged a long and famous feud with
   a. Lycurgus
   b. Greece
   c. Athens
   d. Thebes

3. At the age of seven, Spartan boys were taken from their families to begin
   a. Olympic training
   b. military training
   c. business training
   d. diplomat training

4. Compared with women from other Greek city-states, Spartan women had
   a. no restrictions
   b. the same restrictions
   c. more restrictions
   d. fewer restrictions

5. The slaves owned by Sparta's government were called
   a. equals
   b. helots
   c. trainees
   d. perioeci

VOCABULARY

Using your knowledge of the underlined word, circle the letter of the word or phrase that best completes each statement. *(50 points)*

6. The Spartan boy who stole a pet fox cub used deceit by
   a. answering his questioners with facts
   b. amusing his questioners with stories
   c. misleading his questioners with lies
   d. confusing his questioners with details

7. Sparta dominated other ancient Greek city-states, which means Sparta
   a. controlled or ruled over them
   b. assisted or helped them out
   c. disbanded or broke them up
   d. admired or honored them

8. Spartan trainees were expected to endure pain by
   a. complaining to others
   b. ignoring it quietly
   c. screaming until it stopped
   d. working out a remedy

9. It's a bad idea to leave on a camping trip without provisions because you would lack
   a. advice and driving directions
   b. enthusiasm for the trip
   c. experience and leadership
   d. food and supplies

10. Sparta's government was overbearing because it was
    a. arrogant and domineering
    b. helpful and cooperative
    c. distant and secluded
    d. large and unmanageable

Name _____ Class _____ Date _____

Selection Test

In the Footsteps of Alexander the Great
based on the Maryland Public Television series
by MICHAEL WOOD

COMPREHENSION QUESTIONS

Circle the letter of the best answer to each of the following items. *(50 points)*

1. Alexander had created an empire by the time he was
   a. twenty years old
   b. twenty-five years old
   c. thirty years old
   d. thirty-five years old

2. Alexander's empire stretched from the Balkan Mountains to the
   a. Nile River
   b. Indus River
   c. Qattara Depression
   d. Great Sand Sea

3. The author was reluctant to leave the oasis at Siwa because it was
   a. a feast for the senses
   b. like a lunar landscape

   c. late and he was tired
   d. a dry and barren place

4. The city of Samarkand is described as having
   a. a stretch of long, serrated ridges
   b. many luxurious date palms
   c. unbearable heat and a sense of isolation
   d. great domes and brilliant turquoise tiles

5. Cleitus earned Alexander's loyalty, in part, by
   a. serving as satrap of Bactria
   b. praising Alexander's father
   c. finding the Silk Route
   d. saving Alexander's life

VOCABULARY

Using your knowledge of the underlined word, circle the letter of the word or phrase that best completes the statement. *(50 points)*

6. Alexander's <u>vindictive</u> behavior showed that he desired
   a. recognition   **b.** acceptance
   c. revenge   **d.** wealth

7. Alexander's personality is described as <u>dynamic</u> because he was
   a. strong and energetic
   b. ruthless and cruel
   c. smart and curious
   d. sad and gloomy

8. When you're in a <u>melancholy</u> mood, you feel
   a. happy and festive
   b. sad and gloomy
   c. ordinary and dull
   d. calm and orderly

9. The writer felt <u>vindicated</u> because his belief about Alexander's route was
   a. corrected
   b. wrong
   c. resented
   d. justified

10. A landscape that is <u>eroded</u> would show signs of having been
    a. cultivated and cared for
    b. polluted
    c. worn or eaten away
    d. abandoned and neglected

Selection Test

Science in a Hellenistic World
from *Calliope*
by LOUISE CHIPLEY SLAVICEK

COMPREHENSION QUESTIONS

Circle the letter of the best answer to each of the following items. *(50 points)*

1. Archimedes demonstrated how pulleys and levers work by
   a. publishing the book *Elements*
   b. turning a lever into a pulley
   c. pulling a loaded ship to shore
   d. dunking a crown in water

2. According to tradition, when Archimedes first thought of his "law of buoyancy" he
   a. dashed naked to the king's palace shouting "Eureka!"
   b. demonstrated it by pulling a boat with pulleys
   c. wrote a geometry book used for over 2,000 years
   d. proved that the earth revolves around the sun

3. The Hellenistic astronomer who first questioned the belief that earth was at the center of the universe was
   a. Euclid   b. Hipparchos
   c. Aristarchos   d. Herophilos

4. Herophilos is considered the father of scientific
   a. astronomy   b. anatomy
   c. astrology   d. biology

5. Many scientific advances of the Hellenistic period were put aside or forgotten after the death of
   a. Alexander the Great
   b. Ptolemy I
   c. Erasistratos
   d. Cleopatra VII

VOCABULARY

Using your knowledge of the underlined word, circle the letter of the word or phrase that best completes each statement. *(50 points)*

6. A person who is skilled at maneuvering would be good at
   a. moving things
   b. drawing images
   c. studying plans
   d. dissecting bodies

7. Archimedes' "law of buoyancy" explained why things
   a. sink   b. fly
   c. move   d. float

8. A comprehensive plan of action would have a(n)
   a. narrow scope   b. wide scope
   c. lack of details d. impressive record

9. Scientists who study anatomy are interested in
   a. learning the weight of gold objects
   b. solving problems with mathematics
   c. the structure of the body
   d. the alignment of heavenly bodies

10. An innovative idea is one that is
    a. tried and true
    b. risky and untested
    c. new and different
    d. dull and unusable

(**Selection Test**)

Doing the Impossible
from *Calliope*
by GLENNA DUNNING

COMPREHENSION QUESTIONS

Circle the letter of the best answer to each of the following items. *(50 points)*

1. After taking the city of Saguntum in Spain, Hannibal began preparing to
   a. conquer Spain
   b. return home
   c. attack Rome
   d. tour Gaul

2. Hannibal had to approach Italy by an overland route because Rome
   a. controlled the Mediterranean Sea
   b. was thousands of miles from water
   c. was located in the middle of the Alps
   d. was defenseless against such an attack

3. After marching for four months, Hannibal's army reached
   a. Spain   b. Rome
   c. Gaul   d. the Alps

4. To cross mountains, Hannibal's army had to walk in a long column because
   a. they wanted to look like an army
   b. the passes were steep and narrow
   c. they were worried about attacks
   d. the Gauls persuaded them to do so

5. When the Romans heard that Hannibal's army was at hand, they
   a. panicked and surrendered
   b. destroyed Hannibal's army
   c. found it impossible to believe
   d. pledged allegiance to Carthage

VOCABULARY

Using your knowledge of the underlined word, circle the letter of the word or phrase that best completes each statement. *(50 points)*

6. Hannibal's daring plan <u>translated</u> into a successful crossing of the Alps, which means it
   a. delayed the crossing
   b. required the crossing
   c. prevented the crossing
   d. resulted in the crossing

7. By formally agreeing to be an <u>ally</u>, Saguntum became Rome's
   a. partner   b. enemy
   c. problem   d. disaster

8. Newspapers act as <u>chronicles</u> by preserving
   a. pages of advertisements
   b. examples of opinions
   c. thousands of words
   d. records of events

9. Hannibal's army <u>replenished</u> their supplies when they
   a. restocked
   b. resigned
   c. reduced
   d. repeated

10. When people pledge <u>allegiance</u> to a country, they are promising their
    a. negligence
    b. attention
    c. loyalty
    d. curiosity

Selection Test

from **Stadium of Life and Death**
from *National Geographic World*
by JERRY DUNN

COMPREHENSION QUESTIONS

Circle the letter of the best answer to each of the following items. *(50 points)*

1. The only large machines used to make the Colosseum were
   a. trucks **b.** mixers
   c. hoists **d.** cranes

2. The Colosseum's arena was as long as a modern
   a. football field **b.** tennis court
   c. baseball field **d.** basketball court

3. Seating in the Colosseum was arranged so that slaves sat with
   a. important citizens
   b. poor people
   c. priestesses
   d. foreigners

4. A series of cages beneath the stadium floor held
   a. poor people
   b. wild animals
   c. slave gangs
   d. retired gladiators

5. According to an old saying, when the Colosseum falls
   a. earthquakes will occur
   b. people will starve
   c. Rome will end
   d. Italy will rise

VOCABULARY

Using your knowledge of the underlined word, circle the letter of the word or phrase that best completes each statement. *(50 points)*

6. A majestic structure like the original Colosseum is one that is
   a. dated or old fashioned
   b. crumbling or collapsing
   c. shabby or grungy
   d. impressive or grand

7. Someone who accomplished an amazing feat could be proud of his or her
   a. development **b.** achievement
   c. enjoyment **d.** attachment

8. Unlike the Colosseum, many ancient ruins collapsed long ago when they
   a. were torn down for scrap
   b. passed away or ran out
   c. were rebuilt from scrap
   d. fell down or caved in

9. By designing the Colosseum to handle crowds efficiently, Roman architects avoided
   a. wasting time, energy, money, and materials
   b. having to build a second stadium for slaves
   c. saving time, energy, money, and materials
   d. delays caused by stupidity and foolishness

10. A hill that is sloping would be slanting
    a. left or right
    b. sideways or edgewise
    c. upward or downward
    d. east or west

Selection Test

Who Were the Gladiators?
from *Gladiator*
by RICHARD WATKINS

COMPREHENSION QUESTIONS

Circle the letter of the best answer to each of the following items. *(50 points)*

1. Gladiators who trained and fought in the ring for three years could become
   a. teachers **b.** senators
   c. citizens **d.** emperors

2. Retired gladiators were often lured back into the arena by promises of
   a. slaves **b.** power
   c. money **d.** homes

3. Gladiators were sometimes forced to fight without
   a. weapons **b.** concern
   c. reason **d.** training

4. When the Roman Empire was at its height, more than half of all gladiators were
   a. slaves **b.** volunteers
   c. criminals **d.** noblemen

5. A carving found in Asia Minor shows a gladiatorial battle between two
   a. sesterces **b.** animals
   c. emperors **d.** women

VOCABULARY

Using your knowledge of the underlined word, circle the letter of the word or phrase that best completes each statement. *(50 points)*

6. A war of conquest is one in which the main objective is to
   a. defend territory
   b. prevent conflict
   c. acquire territory
   d. avoid defeat

7. A person who has successfully auctioned a piece of antique furniture has
   a. bought it at the highest bid
   b. sold it to the highest bidder
   c. restored it to mint condition
   d. donated it to a good cause

8. Romans felt that making criminals become gladiators was a deterrent because people thinking about commiting crimes would be
   a. encouraged **b.** misinformed
   c. discouraged **d.** overlooked

9. A teacher who asks you to dispose of your soda can would like for you to
   a. get rid of it
   b. pick it up
   c. share it
   d. save it

10. An exhibition by gladiators would put their skills on
    a. pedestals
    b. notice
    c. platforms
    d. display

Selection Test

The Spread of
Christianity
from *Calliope*
by PAMELA PALMER

COMPREHENSION QUESTIONS

Circle the letter of the best answer to each of the following items. *(50 points)*

1. Early Christians lived and worshipped
   a. in a simple style
   b. in ornate palaces and places of worship
   c. in the New World
   d. with immediate governmental support
      and no opposition

2. As more people joined the new faith,
   members began to be called
   a. "wanderers of the desert"
   b. "friends of faith"
   c. "seekers of the truth"
   d. "people of the way"

3. The preachers of the Gospels were called
   a. sermonizers   b. deacons
   c. evangelists   d. bishops

4. Many early followers were attracted to the
   new faith by miracles performed by
   a. Peter
   b. Paul
   c. Marcion
   d. Corinth

5. In the early years, most Christian services
   were held in
   a. public buildings
   b. private homes
   c. grand churches
   d. simple parks

VOCABULARY

Using your knowledge of the vocabulary word, write in the appropriate blank the letter of the
word or phrase that best defines the word. *(50 points)*

_____ 6. imminent

_____ 7. decreed

_____ 8. authoritative

_____ 9. commemorated

_____ 10. envious

a. official

b. distant

c. marked or celebrated
   the memory of

d. established by
   command

e. proud of

f. about to happen

g. jealous

_____ 11. invalid

_____ 12. diversity

_____ 13. converts

_____ 14. precedent

_____ 15. heritage

a. variety

b. beliefs or traditions
   handed down from
   the past

c. current trends

d. items with great
   similarities

e. people who change
   religions

f. very sick person

g. example to be
   followed

Selection Test

· *from* **The Buried City of Pompeii**
by SHELLEY TANAKA

COMPREHENSION QUESTIONS

Circle the letter of the best answer to each of the following items. *(50 points)*

1. Before Vesuvius erupted, Pompeii had been experiencing
   a. falling pumice **b.** tidal waves
   c. drenching rain **d.** earth tremors

2. After the column of pumice and ash collapsed, the volcano spewed
   a. more pumice and ash
   b. extremely hot rock and gas
   c. a thick cloud of smoke
   d. flaming pieces of wood

3. Within three hours after an avalanche reached the city walls, Pompeii was completely
   a. buried
   b. evacuated
   c. washed to out to sea
   d. untouched by disaster

4. When people started digging up the ruins of Pompeii in the mid-1700s, the work at first was
   a. quick and easy
   b. neat and organized
   c. slow and treacherous
   d. sloppy and disorganized

5. When Giuseppe Fiorelli was put in charge of the excavation of Pompeii, he recorded each new find and made
   a. major renovations
   b. lots of money from selling artifacts to museums
   c. detailed maps
   d. scale models

VOCABULARY

Using your knowledge of the underlined word, circle the letter of the word or phrase that best completes each statement. *(50 points)*

6. When the <u>summit</u> of Vesuvius cracked open, the cracks appeared at the volcano's
   a. sheer cliffs
   b. highest point
   c. lower foothills
   d. northern banks

7. People who <u>suffocated</u> in the explosion of of Vesuvius breathed in the hot ash and were
   a. smothered **b.** revived
   c. rescued **d.** mummified

8. When people began excavating Pompeii in in <u>earnest</u>, their efforts became
   a. sincere **b.** relaxed
   c. deceitful **d.** indifferent

9. Being an <u>archaeologist</u> involves all of the following **except**
   a. scientific training
   b. examining artifacts
   c. digging up remains
   d. studying volcanoes

10. The House of Menander was undergoing <u>renovations</u> because it was in need of
    a. dusting
    b. workers
    c. repairs
    d. owners

Content-Area Reading Strategies

for the
Language Arts Classroom

by DR. JUDITH IRVIN
Florida State University

While teaching social studies in middle and high school, I worked primarily with students who struggled with reading and writing. In my desperate attempt to help them learn the content of history, geography, world cultures, economics, and so forth, I did what many good teachers did—I avoided the textbook. I engaged the students in inquiry, conducted simulations, showed videos, created maps and charts, and led lively discussions and debates. Oh, I trotted the textbook out occasionally to use the pictures, diagrams, and primary source material, but it was simply too difficult (or too much trouble) to ask students to read it.

When I did ask students to read, I used the only approach I knew—round-robin reading. This familiar classroom practice of having different students read paragraphs worked about as well as it did when I was in school. The students counted the paragraphs to see which one would be assigned to them and then agonized until their turns were over. No one really concentrated on what was being read. The strong readers were bored, and the struggling readers were embarrassed. I modified this approach by having students volunteer or call on the next reader. I even employed what is now called jump-in-reading, in which volunteers just start reading when another stops. These modifications created slightly more interest in the material, but they didn't stimulate any thought or motivation to learn. So, in desperation, I simply gave up using the textbooks.

How I Learned to Teach Reading

Shortly after I shelved my textbooks, our principal made the announcement, "Every teacher is a teacher of reading." I learned that I was supposed to set aside my beloved history and geography to teach "finding the main idea" and "locating information" through skills worksheets. In my class, this generated even less enthusiasm than round-robin reading.

I became resentful. I nodded dutifully at in-service sessions and talked about how important it was that students read and write better. Then I shut my door and went back to my way of teaching social studies because I was annoyed at being asked not to teach what was important to me and to my students.

After a few more years, I began my Ph.D. studies in social studies education at Indiana University. During this time, I began taking courses in reading education. To my amazement, I discovered that I had been using very effective learning strategies through the social studies methods I had learned and applied in my classroom. But I fell short of helping students apply those concepts when reading their textbooks.

I finished my doctorate in reading education and wrote a dissertation that incorporated both social studies theory and reading theory. In all fairness to my former principal, the field of reading education was redefined during the period between his mandate and my doctoral studies and has continued to evolve over the past two decades.

The Study of Reading

The research in reading falls into four categories:

- the text
- the context for learning
- the learner
- the learning strategies

These four factors can be conveniently separated for the purposes of discussion, but of course they are intricately linked and occur simultaneously. The figure below shows how these influencing factors interact with each other.

The Text: Narrative to Expository Good readers have expectations from text. When I curl up with a romance novel, I rarely bring a highlighter. Being residents of Florida, my husband and I read our homeowners' insurance policy very carefully after a hurricane. This is not the same way I read poetry or a menu. Good readers are flexible with a variety of text; poor readers read everything pretty much the same way.

Elementary students read primarily narrative text. Likewise, teachers teach children how to read a story by thinking about the setting or characters or by answering comprehension questions. Yet when elementary teachers embark on a social studies lesson, they generally jump straight to the content. They spend no time at all on how to read the textbook. When students enter middle school,

the demands for reading informational or expository text are much greater. Textbooks filled with new concepts replace stories. Charts and diagrams replace pictures. The vocabulary is more difficult and often essential in understanding the text.

Who in middle and high schools helps students read and write expository text? When I ask this question of a school faculty, the language arts teachers point to the social studies and science teachers because they are the ones with these types of textbooks. The social studies and science teachers point to language arts teachers because they "do" words. Even when students attend a reading class, what is usually taught is more narrative and on a lower reading level. What happens when students enter a social studies class and no one has helped them understand how to read the textbook?

Teachers often comment that students do not read anything outside of school. In reality, students read all kinds of text. They read e-mail, notes, magazines, TV listings, cereal boxes, video game instructions, T-shirts, movie posters, signs, song lyrics, and much more. We can connect to our students' real-world literacy by creating links from what they read outside of school to what we want them to read in school. We can connect song lyrics to poetry, movies to short stories, Internet

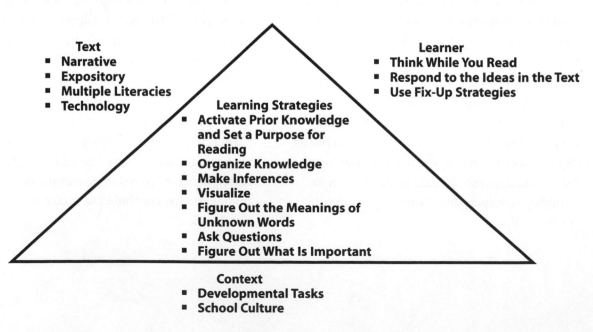

Text
- **Narrative**
- **Expository**
- **Multiple Literacies**
- **Technology**

Learner
- **Think While You Read**
- **Respond to the Ideas in the Text**
- **Use Fix-Up Strategies**

Learning Strategies
- **Activate Prior Knowledge and Set a Purpose for Reading**
- **Organize Knowledge**
- **Make Inferences**
- **Visualize**
- **Figure Out the Meanings of Unknown Words**
- **Ask Questions**
- **Figure Out What Is Important**

Context
- **Developmental Tasks**
- **School Culture**

sites about rock stars to biographies, video game instructions to expository text. Unless we recognize and provide links to the kinds of reading and writing that adolescents encounter in the "real world," they may never value what we are trying to teach them.

The Context for Learning Middle and high school students are immersed in life. The developmental tasks of becoming autonomous, forming a positive self-concept, learning social skills, progressing academically, and engaging in abstract thinking are all very important. To facilitate these developmental tasks, educators can create positive climates that reward effort as well as ability, provide a relevant curriculum, and motivate students to learn. We teachers have to ask ourselves, "What is worth knowing for adolescents in today's society?" and "How do we present this knowledge so that it makes sense to the lives and experiences of our students?"

The Learner Our students come to us knowing a lot of "stuff." This prior knowledge includes all that they have experienced, including their values, beliefs, and culture. You can think of this accumulated prior knowledge as a file cabinet. We all have multiple file folders, skinny or thick, on a variety of topics. For example, I have a big, thick file folder on soccer. My husband is a soccer coach; my daughter and son play soccer; and I played on a recreational team. On the other hand, I have a skinny file folder on football. I rarely attend a game and do not know much about the players.

Sometimes our job as teachers is to hand students a folder and have them label it and put things in it (building background information). Sometimes our job is to have students retrieve folders and read through them (activating prior knowledge). Sometimes our job is to help students organize their folders, placing labels on different parts so they can use this information in a new context (organizing knowledge). A good guiding principle is that students cannot learn anything new unless they are able to connect it to something they already know. To become strong readers, students must engage with the text in various ways.

- **Think While You Read** Many students see reading as something to get through, rather than something to absorb, integrate, synthesize, and extend. Their eyes glance over the words, but they may not learn or remember the information because they have not thought about it.

- **Respond to the Ideas in the Text** When students are engaged in reading, they respond to the ideas in some way. They ask themselves questions, organize the ideas in a map, and connect the ideas with what they already know.

- **Use Fix-Up Strategies** Strong readers keep track of whether things make sense to them and do something to "fix up" their comprehension if things do not make sense. They might use the glossary, re-read, read ahead, think about the topic, or ask someone.

- **Activate Prior Knowledge and Set a Purpose for Reading** Before reading, good readers activate what they know about a topic by looking at the table of contents, glossary, titles, captions, section headings, and/or graphics. They make connections from the text to their experience and prior knowledge. They may skim the structure of the text for main ideas and think about what they will be expected to do with the reading.

- **Organize Knowledge** During and after reading, strong readers summarize the major ideas. They may skim the text and re-read portions to take notes or to create a concept map or an outline. This organization and reorganization of knowledge helps students understand, remember, and use the major concepts presented in the text.

- **Make Inferences** Strong readers make inferences throughout their reading. That is, they connect what is in their heads with what is on the page. If they see a building with an onion-shaped dome, they might infer that the setting is in Russia. Accurate inference making depends on the background knowledge of the reader.

- **Visualize** Proficient readers visualize the information presented in text. Nonproficient readers, on the other hand, do not seem to be able to create pictures in their minds. Having students sketch images or create concept maps, diagrams, charts, or other visual representations of the information helps them create these visual images.

- **Figure Out the Meanings of Unknown Words**
As students read increasingly complex text, they encounter words they do not know. Previewing text for key vocabulary and using context and structural analysis can help students increase their understanding and their vocabularies.

- **Ask Questions** Before and during reading, strong readers ask themselves questions such as, "What do I know about this topic?" or "What is the meaning of a concept in bold print?" These questions indicate that students are thinking about the reading and connecting the ideas in the text to their prior knowledge.

- **Figure Out What Is Important** One of the most common question types on standardized tests is "finding the main idea." To comprehend text, readers must identify, remember, and summarize the major ideas presented in the text. Figuring out what is important in the text should be tied to the purpose for reading. Taking notes from text, constructing a concept map, or creating an outline all involve identifying what is important in the text.

You can talk to students about how effective and efficient learning takes place. If talking about effective reading behaviors becomes a natural part of classroom instruction, students can add these ideas to their repertoires and become stronger, more flexible, and more proficient readers.

The Learning Strategies Veteran teachers have heard the terms *skills* and *strategies* thrown around for many years. Skills must be automatically and consistently applied and require fairly low levels of thinking. Skills take practice. This fact became abundantly clear to me the first time I was in the car with my sixteen-year-old son, who had just gotten his driver's license. Making a left-hand turn in traffic takes a high level of

driving skill and, initially, a lot of concentration. Checking both mirrors, gauging the distances of oncoming cars, and signaling the turn became automatic after practice. My son can now negotiate the same turn while carrying on a conversation and eating a candy bar.

While driving gets easier with practice, we all need a plan when navigating unfamiliar territory. We consult a map, ask for directions, and formulate a strategy for getting to our destination. A strategy is an overall plan requiring higher levels of reasoning. It is flexible in application and involves awareness and reflection.

Proficient reading takes both the execution of skills and a strategy for fulfilling the purpose for reading. With some practice, taking notes becomes a fairly automatic process of identifying important points and recording them in a way that can be used later. But it takes a strategy to put the pieces together to write a report. Before reading, strong readers use strategies to connect with what they know about the topic, while reading to maintain concentration and reflect on ideas in the text, and after reading to organize major points to fulfill the purpose for reading. The learning strategies in this book are designed to engage students in the behaviors of strong reading until these behaviors become part of the readers' repertoire.

Helping Struggling Readers Become Strong Readers

Struggling readers can do the same thing as strong readers, but they need more help, more support, and more scaffolding. For example, my husband purchased a boat that sits very high in the water, which is wonderful when you are in the boat looking down. After snorkeling one day, I learned the downside of a high-riding boat. When it came time to get back in the boat, the platform and the one step were too high. I wanted two more steps—the scaffolding I needed to start climbing into the boat. Struggling readers have a similar dilemma. They often have difficulty getting started, and then they easily give up.

To avoid this, introduce each strategy with fairly simple reading so that students learn the steps of the strategy and do not have to face the additional challenge of difficult text. As you select an appropriate strategy, consider the students' prior knowledge about the topic, the type of text, and the purpose for reading. You will find that some strategies lend themselves better to the study of world cultures, and others to the study of history or economics. You will also find that you prefer some strategies over others. My purpose is to provide you with options to use in any teaching and learning context. It is my fervent hope that you find that these strategies enhance your instruction by engaging students more actively in learning.

Good Luck and Best Wishes,
Dr. Judith Irvin

Read More About It

Irvin, J. L. *Reading and the Middle School Student: Strategies to Enhance Literacy* (2nd edition). Boston: Allyn and Bacon (1998).

Irvin, J. L., Buehl, D., and Klemp, R. *Reading and the High School Student: Strategies to Enhance Literacy.* Boston: Allyn and Bacon (2002).

Irvin, J. L., Lunstrum, J. P., Lynch-Brown, C., and Shepard, M. F. *Enhancing Social Studies Instruction through Reading and Writing Strategies.* Washington, D.C.: National Council for the Social Studies (1995).

STRATEGY 1: PREVIEWING TEXT

When facing a textbook reading assignment, most students just plow in and try to finish it as quickly as possible. They may leaf through the chapter or passage to see how long it is, taking note of how many pages they can skip because of pictures or graphs. Proficient readers, on the other hand, take a moment to consider the following things *before* they begin a textbook reading assignment:

Purpose of the reading
Important ideas
Connection to prior knowledge

This strategy of previewing text is therefore known as PIC. You can use the PIC strategy to help your students develop good reading habits by encouraging them to spend just a few moments organizing their thinking and setting their goals before beginning a reading assignment. In addition, this process leads students to speculate about the main idea of the passage before they start reading. After reading, they may change what they thought the main idea was or confirm that their prediction was correct.

How Can the Strategy Help My Students?

The PIC strategy can get your students into the all-important habits of setting a purpose for their reading, identifying the most important ideas, and connecting with what they already know. Often when students read, they do not think about what is really important to remember. Previewing reading assignments helps students focus on the most important information and facilitates storing that information in long-term memory. If students take a few moments to go through the steps described below, they will better understand and remember the material they read.

Getting Started

Here are the steps to the PIC strategy:

Step 1: Purpose for Reading. Make sure students know what they will be doing with the information after reading. (That is, what is the assignment or purpose for reading? What will they do with the information?) Have them peruse the structure of the assignment, noting special features such as summaries or guiding questions. Ask students to use the table of contents and glossary of the book to locate information. To establish a purpose for reading, students can ask the following questions.

- What am I going to do with this information when I finish reading?
- How does this text fit in with the material before or after it?

Step 2: Important Ideas. Students should flip through the assignment, noting any headings that indicate the major points in the reading. They should try to understand how this passage fits within the larger chapter, unit, or book. Students should also be familiar with any key vocabulary in boldface type or italics. These words are probably the most important concepts in the text. To identify important ideas, students can ask the following questions.

- Is there anything in the table of contents, index, or glossary that can help me understand the "big ideas"?
- What are the key vocabulary terms I should understand?

Step 3: Connect to What You Know. Students need to think about what they know about the topic before they start reading. Encourage them to wonder about the topic, asking themselves, "What would I like to find out?" Finally, students should identify questions they want answered about the topic. They can organize their ideas with a chart like the KWQ Chart below.

Using the Strategy in Your Classroom

After students have read the text, they should go back to their KWQ charts to see if their questions were answered and to make sure they understand the key vocabulary. Feel free to vary the strategy as students become accustomed to previewing their assignments. You may wish to move from having students complete KWQ organizers to having them address just the purpose for reading, important information about the topic, and connecting-to-prior-knowledge questions in a

quick discussion or pre-reading assignment. You can also add an after-reading component by asking students to discuss, in small groups or as a class, the questions they still want answered. (**See Strategy 7, Graphic Organizers 6 and 7, KWL and KWLS Charts.**) They may have some questions that were not answered in the text. These questions can be the basis of further research or projects.

Extending the Strategy

Books use diagrams, charts, maps, and pictures to help the reader understand the content. As students become more familiar with previewing, you may wish to direct their attention to these graphic features, asking them in what ways these items will extend or support their learning.

The PIC strategy is simply a guide to help students preview the text before reading and focus on the most important points. It can be used in conjunction with other assignments or modified to serve as an aid for studying for a test or writing a report. For example, before students read you can ask them to sketch out a graphic organizer or a concept map (**See Strategies 3 and 4**) to fill in after they read. They can then use this organizer as a writing or study guide. (**See Graphic Organizer 3, Cluster Diagram.**)

Some Final Thoughts

The purpose for previewing text is to get students to recognize the text's main idea, which could be a theme, something important to students, or the first sentence in a paragraph. However, helping students identify the main idea of a text passage is often a difficult challenge. David Moore (1986)

What I *Know* About the Topic	What I *Wonder* About the Topic	Questions I Would Like to Have Answered

suggested that you engage students in stating what the text is about in one or two words and then add two or three other words to go with it. This usually comes closer to the author's intended main idea.

When students first use the PIC strategy, the process will seem very time-consuming. But as they become more familiar with the format and steps, they will move through the strategy more quickly. Feel free to modify the strategy to suit the needs of your students.

Read More About It

Alvermann, D. E. "Graphic Organizers: Cueing Devices for Comprehending and Remembering Main Ideas." In *Teaching Main Idea Comprehension*, J. F. Baumann. Newark, DE: International Reading Association. 1986.

Avery, P. G., Baker, J., and Gross, S. H. "Mapping Learning at the Secondary Level." *The Clearing House* 70 (5) 1997: 279–85.

Heimlich, E., and Pittleman, S. D. *Semantic Mapping: Classroom Applications.* Newark, DE: International Reading Association. 1986.

Romance, N. R., and Vitale, M. R. "Concept Mapping as a Tool for Learning: Broadening the Framework for Student-Centered Instruction." *College Teaching* 47 (2) 1999: 74–79.

STRATEGY 2: UNDERSTANDING TEXT

When you come home at the end of the day and flip through the mail, you probably don't read each item the same way. You would read a letter from a friend differently than you would read a notice from a lawyer you do not know. The items *look* different, use different vocabularies, and have different structures. Strong readers know how to adjust their reading depending on the text and their purpose for reading.

A textbook contains different forms of text. Students must interpret pictures, diagrams, figures, and charts. They read narrative accounts, diaries, and documents that support the major concepts. Then, there is the text itself. Expository or informational text is generally structured in one of the following five forms.

- cause and effect
- comparison and contrast
- description
- problem and solution
- sequence or chronological order

Particular content lends itself more or less to one structure or another. For example, while history is generally conveyed in a sequence or chronological order, geography may be best learned in a descriptive format. In addition, one or more forms may be used within a passage. The more that students can detect the structure of text, the better they can prepare themselves to think in a way that is consistent with that structure.

Signal or transition words usually indicate the structure of the text. Proficient readers intuitively notice the words that indicate the type of thinking required while reading. Signal words tell readers what is coming up. When you see *for example* or *for instance*, you know that examples will follow. On the next page is a chart with some of the most common signal or transition words.

An important reading strategy based on these words is called "Double S: Signal Words That Indicate Structure." This strategy is designed to help students recognize and use signal words to detect the structure of the text.

How Can the Strategy Help My Students?

Good readers are flexible thinkers. Signal or transition words such as *different from, the same as,* or *compared with* indicate that the authors are presenting information that will compare and contrast at least two ideas. This comparison-and-contrast structure is read differently from one in which ideas are presented in sequence or chronological order. Signal or transition words indicate what the structure of text might be. When students notice these words in the text, especially before reading, they tend to get ready to think in a certain way. Struggling readers need to have these words pointed out to them and to be instructed on the function of these words while reading or writing. In time, they should be able to use signal words and move to more complex forms of text.

When students are learning to write expository text and must demonstrate that skill on a task such as producing a sample for a standardized test, these signal or transition words can help them express their points more clearly. As students recognize and use transition words and different text structures, they will (1) comprehend text more effectively, (2) produce more coherent expository writing, and (3) think more clearly and flexibly.

Getting Started

Here are the steps in the Understanding Text strategy.

Step 1: Survey the Text. Have students flip through the text and list all the different types of items they will be reading, such as documents, charts, diagrams, maps, short stories, or expository text. Usually, the expository writing in textbooks explains or informs the reader. But primary source material, such as a diary, may be read differently. The primary source probably supports one or more of the major points presented in the text.

Step 2: Identify the Signal Words. Have students list transition words in the text or allow students to attach self-adhesive notes to the text page to help them locate the transition words.

Step 3: Identify the Structure of the Text. Using their list of transition words, students, individually or in small groups, should identify the main structure of the text: cause and effect, comparison and contrast, description, problem and solution, sequence or chronological order. They should ask themselves, "What kind of thinking will be necessary to understand the information in the text?" and "How would I best display the information after reading?"

Step 4: Predict the Main Idea of the Passage. Using what they know about the signal words and the structure of the text, students should write a sentence stating what they think the main idea of this passage will be.

SIGNAL WORDS

Cause and Effect	Comparison and Contrast	Description	Problem and Solution	Sequence or Chronological Order
because	different from	for instance	the problem is	not long after
since	same as	for example	the question is	next
consequently	similar to	such as	a solution is	then
this led to ... so	as opposed to	to illustrate	one answer is	initially
if ... then	instead of	in addition		before
nevertheless	although	most importantly		after
accordingly	however	another		finally
because of	compared with	furthermore		preceding
as a result of	as well as	first, second ...		following
in order to	either ... or			on (date)
may be due to	but			over the years
for this reason	on the other hand			today
	unless			when

Step 5: Read the Text.

Step 6: Revisit the Main-Idea Prediction. After reading, students should go back to their prediction of the main idea of the passage. They should then display the information on a graphic organizer appropriate to the text structure. (**Graphic Organizer 2, Cause and Effect; Graphic Organizer 11, Comparison and Contrast; Graphic Organizer 3, Description; Graphic Organizer 9, Problem and Solution; or Graphic Organizer 10, Sequence or Chronological Order.**) Then students may write a summary or in some other way organize what they have read.

Using the Strategy in Your Classroom

We know that good readers use signal or transition words to help guide their understanding and their thinking. Struggling readers do not. So teachers can help struggling readers to recognize and use signal words through the Double S strategy. This does not mean asking students to memorize lists of words. Some teachers find it effective to write signal words on posters around the room or to give students a page to put in their notebooks. Students should also add their own signal words to such lists as they find them in the text. In time, they will use these words intuitively, and they will not need to go through the steps of identifying signal words before reading.

Discussing the structure of text is a little more difficult. The best way for students to "see" the structure is through graphic organizers (presented in Strategy 3). The more that students have these conversations about text, the more proficient they will become at recognizing and using text structure to guide their thinking.

For additional help in identifying and discussing text structures, refer to the Text Structure Reference Chart on pages 172–173. In addition to listing and defining the five main expository text structures discussed here, the chart lists the most common signal words associated with each text structure and provides a sampling of questions that students can use to help them recognize the structures and further analyze them.

Extending the Strategy

After students practice locating signal words and identifying text structure, you can link this strategy with Strategy 3: Using Graphic Organizers. The Double S strategy may also be linked to the PIC technique discussed in Strategy 1.

Traditionally, reading and writing have been taught separately. But practice with the Double S strategy also can help students write more effective expository pieces. Writing expository text is a major component of most state assessments.

Some Final Thoughts

Unfortunately, not all texts are written in a format that has an identifiable structure. Similarly, there may be no signal words in the text. The text may also change structure within the passage. These more complex structures demand increasingly sophisticated reading ability. However, the Double S strategy can get students started on the road to becoming independent learners.

Read More About It

Britton, B. K., Woodward, A., and Binkley, M., Eds. *Learning from Textbooks: Theory and Practice*. Hillsdale, NJ: Lawrence Erlbaum Associates. 1993.

Garner, R., and Alexander, P. A., Eds. *Beliefs About Text and Instruction with Text*. Hillsdale, NJ: Lawrence Erlbaum Associates. 1994.

Harvey, S. *Nonfiction Matters*. York, ME: Stenhouse Publishers. 1998.

McMackin, M. C. "Using Narrative Picture Books to Build Awareness of Expository Text Structure." *Reading Horizons* 39 (1) 1998: 7–20.

Quiocho, A. "The Quest to Comprehend Expository Text: Applied Classroom Research." *Journal of Adolescent and Adult Literacy* 40 (6) 1997: 450–54.

TEXT STRUCTURE REFERENCE CHART

Structure or Pattern	Signal Words		Questions for Patterns
Description, Simple Listing, Enumeration Information about a topic is presented through description, listing characteristics, features, and examples.	*to begin with* *characteristics are* *most important* *the following* *in many ways* *for example* *such as* *to illustrate* *furthermore*	*also* *in fact* *finally* *as well* *for instance* *while* *in addition* *another*	What is the main topic? What did the author say about (topic)? How did the author present these ideas? What ideas (or facts) are discussed? Can you think of other ideas or facts about . . . ?
Sequence or Chronological Information is presented in sequence, usually in numerical or chronological order.	*first, second, third* *next* *then* *finally* *after* *until* *before* *first/lst*	*on (date)* *at (time)* *not long after* *now* *as before* *when* *initially* *lastly* *preceding* *following*	What was the first important idea discussed? When did it occur? What is the sequence of events? Why did the author tell about this process in this order? What would be included on a time line of the events? What is the chronological order of the steps?
Comparison and Contrast Information is presented by showing likenesses (comparison) and differences (contrast).	*different from* *in contrast* *alike* *same as* *on the other hand* *however* *but* *as well as* *not only . . . but* *in a like manner* *difference between* *instead of* *compared with*	*either . . . or* *while* *although* *unless* *similar to* *yet* *nevertheless* *also* *likewise* *as opposed to* *after all* *and yet* *as well as*	Why do you think the author wrote about this topic by showing likenesses and differences? What is being compared here? How were they alike? How were they different? What do they have in common? Can you think of other ways these (topics) are alike or different?

Structure or Pattern ▶	Signal Words ▶		Questions for Patterns ▶
Cause and Effect Facts, events, or concepts (effects) come into being because of other facts, events, or concepts (causes).	*reasons why* *if . . . then* *as a result of* *therefore* *because (of)* *thus* *on account of* *due to* *may be due to* *effects of*	*since* *consequently* *this led to* *so that* *nevertheless* *accordingly* *for this reason* *then, so* *in order to*	Can you tell me the cause of _____? What was the effect of _____? How should causes and effects be arranged on a chart? Can you think of any other causes that might produce these effects? Are there any other effects that can result from this cause? Can you think of similar causes and effects?
Problem and Solution or Question and Answer Information is stated as a problem and one or more solutions are presented. A question is asked and one or more answers are presented.	*a problem is* *a dilemma is* *a puzzle is* *solved* *question . . .* *answer* *a solution* *the best estimate* *one may conclude*	*why* *when* *where* *how* *what* *who* *it could be that* *how many*	What were the problems discussed here? Are there solutions to this problem? What are they? What caused the problem? How was it solved? Can you think of any similar problems? How were they solved? How would you solve this problem?

STRATEGY 3: USING GRAPHIC ORGANIZERS

Graphic organizers are made up of lines, arrows, boxes, and circles that show the relationships between and among ideas. They are sometimes called webs, semantic maps, graphic representations, or clusters. These graphic organizers can help students organize their thinking and their knowledge. While textbooks contain many types of text, the largest portion of text is expository or informational. Expository text has five major structures:

- cause and effect
- comparison and contrast
- description
- problem and solution
- sequence or chronological order

In this strategy, four types of text structure will be presented. Description will be presented in Strategy 4 because this type of text is best displayed with a concept map. The four types of text structure with accompanying graphic organizers are shown below and on the following pages.

Cause and Effect: Cause-and-effect patterns show the relationship between results and the ideas or events that made the results occur. (**See Graphic Organizer 2, Cause-and-Effect Chart.**)

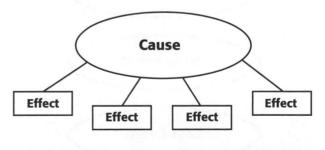

Problem and Solution: Problem-solution patterns identify at least one problem, offer one or more solutions to the problem, and explain or predict outcomes of the solutions. (**See Graphic Organizer 9, Problem and Solution Chart.**)

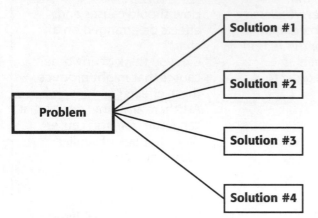

Comparison and Contrast: Comparison and contrast, or Venn, diagrams point out similarities and differences between two concepts or ideas. (**See Graphic Organizer 11, Venn Diagram.**)

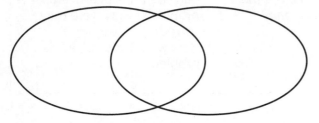

Sequence or Chronological Order: Sequence or chronological-order diagrams show events or ideas in the order in which they happened. (**See Graphic Organizer 10, Sequence or Chronological Order Chart.**)

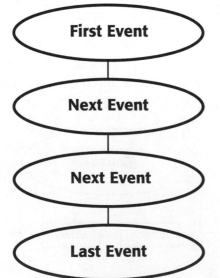

How Can the Strategy Help My Students?

The way that ideas are presented in a textbook dictates the type of thinking that is necessary to understand and remember those ideas. Graphic organizers help students visualize the connections between and among ideas. They also help students organize knowledge so they can use it later to study for a test or write a report. The act of organizing information engages students in learning and helps them make connections to what they already know. In addition, discussing which graphic organizer might best display the information helps students "see" and use the structure of text to understand and remember more effectively.

Getting Started

Any single piece of text can be displayed in more than one way, depending on the purpose for reading and the reader's prior knowledge of the topic. Below are the basic steps in one approach to using graphic organizers.

Step 1: Students preview the material to be read.

Step 2: Students hypothesize which of the four graphic organizers would be best to display the information and their understanding of the material. Their discussion should include the purpose for their reading, and they should note any signal or transition words that may indicate the type of thinking required for the reading and the best way to display the information. Be sure to tell students that the organizers can be modified to meet their needs. For example, the cause-and-effect graphic organizer has room for four effects, but the text may only state one or two.

Step 3: Students read the text silently, taking notes.

Step 4: Students work in cooperative groups to create a graphic representation of their understanding of the text.

Step 5: Students present the finished product to others in the class.

Using the Strategy in Your Classroom

Previewing the text is essential for students to get an idea of the text's "layout." It helps students get ready to think and organize their ideas in a particular way. If students have not had any previous experience using graphic organizers, you may wish to introduce them to the students a little at a time. Here are some tips for helping students become more proficient users of graphic organizers.

- Begin the explanation of graphic organizers with simple text that has an obvious structure.
- Present one graphic organizer at a time.
- Then, move into having students compare and contrast representations.
- Help students use signal or transition words to determine the structure of a text. These are words such as *for instance, similar to, different from,* and *because* that indicate how ideas are related in a text.
- Then, have students use two, then three, then four types of organizers.

As students become more accustomed to discussing and using graphic organizers, they will be able to adapt them to both their purpose for reading and the type of text they are reading. Eventually, students should be able to generate graphic organizers on their own and use them in their note taking.

Extending the Strategy

If students are using webbing in other classes, be sure to explain that using graphic organizers is much the same process as creating webs. This would also be a good time to talk to students about the differences in narrative and expository text. Occasionally, pieces of narrative text are inserted in textbooks to elaborate on a point. Students can be shown the different functions of each type of text—graphic organizers are the perfect vehicle for achieving this goal.

Graphic organizers can also be used as a stimulus for writing expository essays. Students learning to compose essays in cause-and-effect, comparison-and-contrast, problem-and-solution,

or sequence or chronological-order patterns should capture their ideas in a graphic organizer before they begin writing.

Previewing the text is essential in deciding which graphic organizer is most appropriate. Therefore, you may wish to connect this strategy with Strategies 1 and 2.

Some Final Thoughts

Unfortunately, not all texts are neatly packaged into the tidy structures I have presented so far. Sometimes text does not follow a definite structure, and sometimes it changes from one structure to another in the same chapter. When this happens, it is wise to discuss the author's purpose for the text and help students construct their own way of organizing the ideas presented.

Read More About It

Dye, G. A. "Graphic Organizers to the Rescue! Helping Students Link—and Remember—Information." *Teaching Exceptional Children* 32 (3) 2000, 72–76.

Irwin-DeVitis, L., and Pease, D. "Using Graphic Organizers for Learning and Assessment in Middle Level Classrooms." *Middle School Journal* 26 (5) 1995: 57–64.

Robinson, D. H. "Graphic Organizers as Aids to Text Learning." *Reading Research and Instruction* 37 (2) 1998: 85–105.

STRATEGY 4: CONSTRUCTING CONCEPT MAPS

As you saw in Strategy 3, graphic organizers can help students visualize and make sense of expository text. The type of graphic organizer we will focus on now is the concept map. A concept map, sometimes called a semantic map or a cluster diagram, allows students to zero in on the most important points of the text. The map is made up of lines, boxes, circles, and arrows. It can be as simple or as complex as students make it and as the text requires.

How Can the Strategy Help My Students?

Struggling readers often get bogged down in the first three paragraphs of an expository text because they are having difficulty with comprehension. Consequently, they miss the most important points in the passage and never really figure out what the text is about. The concept map is designed to help students focus on and organize the most noteworthy points in the text so they can use them later for a discussion, a writing assignment, or a test. When students preview a reading passage and then work through a reading assignment, they can arrange and rearrange important concepts as needed.

Getting Started

Previewing helps students see the structure of the passage. With a description-type structure, students may notice signal or transition words such as *for instance, for example, such as, in addition*, or *furthermore*. These signal words indicate that the text is describing or explaining important concepts. The following steps may be helpful in having students complete a concept map:

Step 1: Preview the Passage. Previewing can help students determine which kind of structure might best display the ideas in the text.

Step 2: Sketch a Concept Map. Looking at the boldfaced type, headings, and general structure of the text, students should sketch out a map to display the ideas in the passage.

Step 3: Read the Passage.

Step 4: Construct a Map. Using boxes, lines, arrows, bubbles, circles, or any other figure, students can display the ideas in the text in a concept map.

Using the Strategy in Your Classroom

When first introducing the concept map to students, you may wish to create most of the map yourself and have students complete it after they have used a prereading strategy and have read the text. The mapping strategy is most effective, however, if students create their own concept maps. They can embed definitions and examples within the maps to help remind them of the meaning of particular concepts. As students create their own maps, they should consider the content of headings, the signaling power of boldface type, and the organization of the text to help them choose the most important points.

Concept maps work best with text that explains one or more ideas and provides supporting examples. A concept map may be displayed hierarchically, as in the example below, or in a more free-form style, as in the example on page 177.

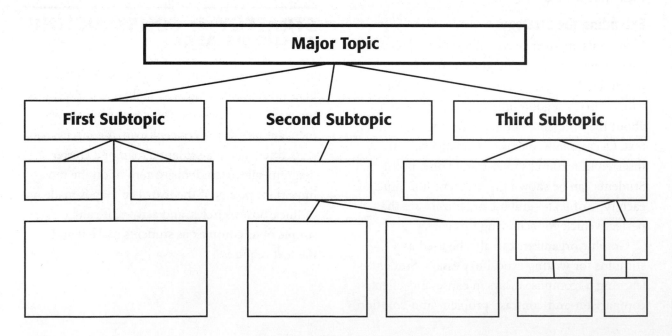

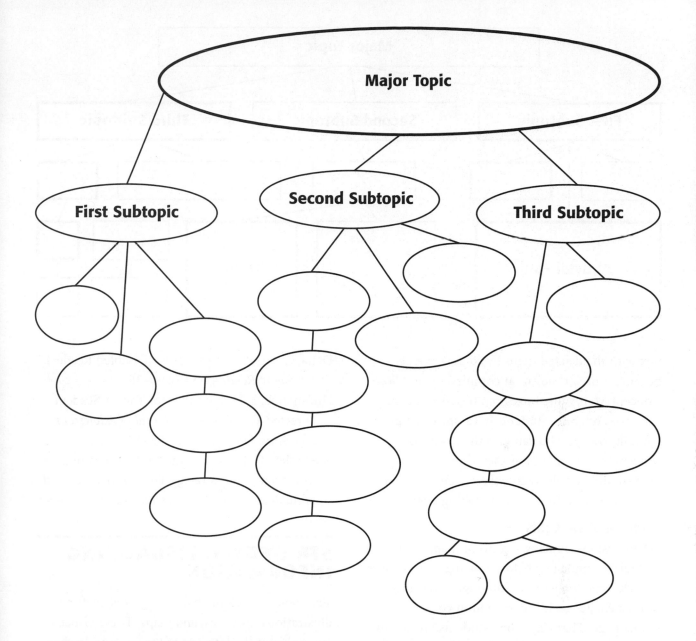

Any combination and organization of circles, bubbles, squares, triangles, lines, or arrows can be used to construct a concept map. Previewing helps students see the overall picture. Sketching gives students an idea of how the key concepts can best be displayed. Constructing the final map helps students understand how the concepts relate to one another. Some teachers suggest sketching the ideas via self-adhesive notes and then constructing the final concept map when students are happy with the display. If some students are more comfortable having a structure to work with, offer them cluster diagrams (**See Graphic Organizer 3**),

and ask them to fill in as many levels as they need and to add boxes if appropriate.

Extending the Strategy

Struggling readers may need more help to begin a task such as creating a concept map. A Cloze Concept Map may support such readers. After students complete a pre-reading strategy on the topic at hand, you can give them an almost-completed map. Some of the boxes should be left blank and have bold lines around them, as shown in the example on the following page.

If you think students may have difficulty even with this task, you may wish to provide a word

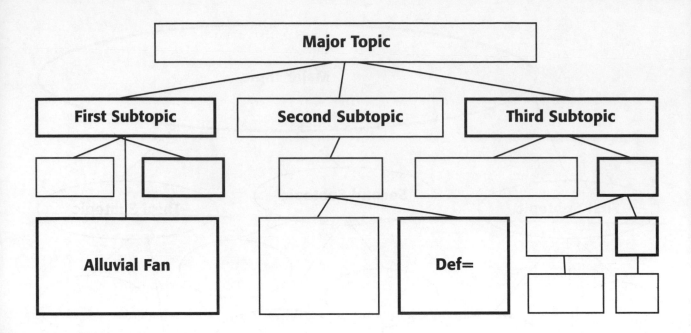

Major Topic

First Subtopic	Second Subtopic	Third Subtopic

| | | | | |

| **Alluvial Fan** | | **Def=** | | |

box with the deleted items listed. As students become more proficient at completing this Cloze Concept Map, more boxes can be left blank. As time goes on, once students have finished a pre-reading strategy, you can give them a blank concept map to fill out as they read. Eventually, they should be able to construct their own maps after previewing the text and making a sketch.

Some Final Thoughts

When first introducing a concept map, use a short and fairly simple text before moving on to a more complex and longer one. Although it is sometimes a challenge, it is best to limit concept maps to one page. That way, when students prepare to study for a test or use the information in writing, the text's most important ideas are displayed in a handy and easy-to-use format.

Read More About It

Chen, H. S., and Graves, M. F. "Previewing Challenging Reading Selections for ESL Students." *Journal of Adolescent and Adult Literacy* 41 (7) 1998: 570–71.

Cunningham, J. W., and Moore, D. W. "The Confused World of Main Idea." In *Teaching Main Idea Comprehension*, J. Baumann. Newark, DE: International Reading Association. 1986.

Dana, C. "Strategy Families for Disabled Readers." *Journal of Reading* 33 (5): 30–35.

Huffman, L. E. "What's in It for You? A Student-Directed Text Preview." *Journal of Adolescent and Adult Literacy* 40 (1): 56–57.

Salemblier, G. B. "SCAN and RUN: A Reading Comprehension Strategy That Works." *Journal of Adolescent and Adult Literacy* 42 (5): 386–94.

STRATEGY 5: VISUALIZING INFORMATION

Textbooks are full of charts, diagrams, pictures, illustrations, cartoons, and maps. These visual aids enhance the learning of the content. In their rush to complete an assignment, students often skip over the visual information that may actually improve their comprehension.

The Information Age has certainly bombarded students today with visual images. Some say that the beautiful picture books, the television, the Internet, CD–ROMs, and so forth may have taken away a student's need (and perhaps ability) to visualize. Others may argue that youth today think in visual images. Whatever the case, proficient readers visualize as they read—struggling readers generally do not.

How Can the Strategy Help My Students?

Visual information displayed in a textbook can be flipped over and ignored or studied and incorporated. What students *do* with the visual information is the important ingredient to comprehending text. Rakes, Rakes, and Smith (1995) suggested that a teacher can help students use information on increasingly interactive levels. The teacher can:

- Provide written or oral directions immediately before students "read" the visual information, such as "On this map, you will notice . . ."
- Direct students' attention through study questions to the important accompanying visuals, such as "This chart displays the most common transportation in America during the Industrial Revolution . . ."
- Encourage students to evaluate the graphics in the text and think about how the graphics and text relate to one another. You might ask, "Given the most important point of this passage, is this graphic representative of . . ."
- Ask students to create their own visuals depicting the information represented in the text. When students draw a sketch or picture of the information in the text, they have made a connection between what they know and what they are reading. Illustrations can be used to summarize text, and graphic organizers and concept maps (Strategies 3 and 4) can assist students in integrating new knowledge with existing knowledge.

The more that students are involved in creating visual images, the more engaged they will be with the ideas in the text. Depending on the purpose of the assigned reading, you may wish to direct students to visuals, have them evaluate the visual information presented, and/or have students create their own graphic representations of the ideas presented in the text.

Getting Started

Here are the basic steps to the Visualizing Information strategy:

Step 1: Preview the Text, Noting the Visual Information Presented. This information may be in the form of charts, diagrams, pictures, or illustrations.

Step 2: Ask How the Visual Information Relates to the Text or Why the Author(s) Included This Information. It is important that students create a link between the text and the visual. You may wish to have students use a transparency over the text to draw arrows between the text and the visual.

Step 3: Generate Questions Raised by the Visual Aid. Students should list two to three questions that arise from this visual aid.

Step 4: Read the Text.

Step 5: Go Back and Review Visual Aids in the Text. Students should evaluate whether the visual accurately displays the most important ideas in the text.

Using the Strategy in Your Classroom

This strategy can, of course, be modified to suit the needs of your students and their purpose for reading. Based on Rakes, Rakes, and Smith's levels of interaction presented above, you could:

- simply direct students to notice the visual element
- provide study questions based on the visual element
- have students evaluate how the visual element helps them better understand the text
- have students sketch their own understanding of the topic of the reading

In addition, questions can direct students' understanding of how the visual element fits with information presented before and after it.

Extending the Strategy

Some educators suggest that after reading, students be asked to draw the visual from memory. This works particularly well for diagrams explained in the text. The act of creating a graphic helps students process it better and connect to the information presented in the text. In addition, this activity can certainly be used to assess how well students understood the text.

Student-created graphics can be extended through group work by having students explain their graphic to other students. They benefit from hearing and seeing the various perspectives of other students. Without employing competition such as "whose graphic is the best?", students can be guided to give feedback on other students' graphics. Giving and soliciting feedback helps them process the ideas in the text more deeply and become better consumers of displays of visual information.

Some teachers have used a Visual Reading Guide (Stein, 1978) for many years. This study guide is simply constructed to direct students to preview the visual information in the text before they read, answering some preliminary questions before and after reading.

The graphic organizers and concept maps presented in Strategies 3 and 4 are additional ways of encouraging students to visualize and organize the ideas in the text. (**See Graphic Organizer 2, Cause-and-Effect Chart; Graphic Organizer 9, Problem and Solution Chart; Graphic Organizer 11, Venn Diagram; and Graphic Organizer 3, Cluster Diagram.**) Some computer software allows students to flip between graphic representations and an outline of the material.

Some Final Thoughts

Not all text has strategically placed visual information that is well explained and connected to the text in the caption. If this is the case, then having students evaluate and/or redraw graphics may be useful. Also, because of time constraints, a teacher can not give this type of attention to every visual aid in the text. But when the visual information does help students better understand the ideas in the text, this strategy can be most helpful. Most students—but especially struggling readers—can benefit from learning how to use the visual aids that often accompany texts.

Read More About It

Hyerle, D. *Visual Tools for Constructing Knowledge.* Alexandria, VA: Association for Supervision and Curriculum Development. 1996.

Rakes, G. C., Rakes, T. A., and Smith, L. J. "Using Visuals to Enhance Secondary Students' Reading Comprehension of Expository Text." *Journal of Adolescent and Adult Literacy* 39 (1) 1995: 46–54.

Scevak, J., and Moore, P. "The Strategies Students in Years 5, 7, and 9 Use for Processing Texts and Visual Aids." *The Australian Journal of Language and Literacy* 20 (4) 1997: 280–88.

Stein, H. "The Visual Reading Guide (VRG)." *Social Education* 42 (6) 1978: 534–35.

STRATEGY 6: BUILDING BACKGROUND INFORMATION

Have you ever tried to read a computer manual or some other highly technical book when you lacked the background knowledge really to understand it? It is frustrating to read something on a topic you know little about. Students encounter that feeling often when they attempt to read many textbooks. You can help students build the information they need to be successful before beginning a reading assignment.

One strategy for achieving this goal is the Predicting and Confirming Activity (PACA). Teachers find this strategy a good way to teach their content. The strategy helps build background information before students read about something they know little about so they will have a context for understanding the ideas presented. (**Graphic Organizer 8, PACA.**)

How Can the Strategy Help My Students?

Students often have no personal connection with much of what we hope they learn in classrooms. They have a context for American history and geography, but often struggle with subjects such as world cultures. For students to learn anything new, they must connect it in some way to something they already know. Good teachers help students make the connection between new information and what students already know.

Getting Started

Here are the steps for the Predicting and Confirming Activity. The Predicting and Confirming Activity uses student predictions to set a purpose for reading. Students make these predictions based on an initial set of information provided by the teacher. Given additional information, students can revise their predictions (or hypotheses) and pose them as questions to be answered during reading.

Step 1: Provide Some Initial Information and Pose a General Question. Provide students with a list of words containing the important concepts in the reading as well as ten to fifteen more familiar terms that students will know. Then, ask them questions about the reading. A word list and a question are usually enough to help students make predictions. But if they are not, you can couple the word list with a short overview of the topic.

Step 2: Write Predictions Based on the Initial Information. These predictions can be discussed and written on the chalkboard or written by individual students or groups of students.

Step 3: Provide New Information. This can be in the form of pictures, charts, diagrams, maps, or other visual information from the textbook, a video, or from reading a story.

Step 4: Review Predictions. Students may revise, confirm, or reject their original predictions. Then they turn the predictions into questions for reading. Based on the new information, students discuss—as a class or in small groups—which of their original predictions they want to keep and which they think no longer apply. They may also revise some predictions to be more accurate. They then turn these predictions into questions they want answered during reading.

Step 5: Read the Text.

Step 6: Revisit Predictions and Answer Questions. Students once again look at their predictions and answer the questions they generated earlier. At this point, students go back to their original predictions and see which ones may be revised or confirmed. They may also check to see if their questions were answered. From here, depending on the purpose of the reading, you may wish to ask students to write about their new learning, formulate study questions and answers, or use some graphic representation of their learning.

Using the Strategy in Your Classroom

The Predicting and Confirming Activity is simply a method for building background information before reading. When students read after completing this strategy, they will be able to connect what they are reading and what they now know about the topic. The predictions turned into questions help guide their reading as well.

When constructing the initial word list, it is important to include both words students will know and some they will encounter in the reading. While discussing these words in small groups in order to write their predictions, students may guess at the meanings of unknown words, or someone in the group may know the word.

If students do not know enough about the topic even to begin predicting, then you could start off with a reading or an overview of the topic or have students leaf through the textbook to get some ideas. You could also direct students to write a sentence using two or more words in the list to construct the prediction.

Extending the Strategy

After questions are formulated and predictions are made, you may wish to use a jigsaw design to complete the reading. Groups would be assigned to answer specific questions about the topic— each group forming an expert group. Then one student from each group would share his or her "expert" information with the base group to complete the synthesizing activity.

If students need additional help in processing new information, you could ask them to visualize. They could also organize their newfound knowledge into a graphic organizer or employ a sketch or diagram. Additionally, they could extend and organize their thoughts by writing a summary or report.

Some Final Thoughts

When using a Predicting and Confirming Activity, students risk forming misconceptions by making predictions based on limited information. Revisiting the predictions is an important part of this strategy, because it is your opportunity to correct these misconceptions and expand students' knowledge about the topic. For this reason, some teachers prefer to display the predictions on an overhead or on the chalkboard. A classroom environment in which students are free to guess and be wrong is an essential component to implementing this strategy.

Some pictures in books are rich with information and some are not. You may need to supplement the text with videos, pictures, or stories. The purpose is to build background information where none or little exists so that students can be more successful when they read their textbook. In the process, students may learn that making and confirming predictions is an essential part of effective reading.

Read More About It

Beyer, B. K. *Inquiry in the Social Studies Classroom.* Columbus, OH: Charles E. Merrill Publishing Company. 1971.

Harmon, J. M., Katims, D. S., and Whittington, D. "Helping Middle School Students Learn From Social Studies Texts." *Teaching Exceptional Children* 32 (1) 1999: 70–75.

Nessell, D. "Channeling Knowledge for Reading Expository Text." *Journal of Reading* 32 (3) 1988: 231–35.

Weir, C. "Using Embedded Questions to Jump-Start Metacognition in Middle School Remedial Readers." *Journal of Adolescent and Adult Literacy* 41 (6) 1998: 458–68.

STRATEGY 7: MAKING PREDICTIONS

Making predictions is one of the most important strategies students can use when approaching a new reading assignment. Hilda Taba (1967) was one of the first educators to suggest a method for encouraging even young children to think at higher levels. Her concept-formation model was later adapted as List-Group-Label, a strategy to activate what students know about a topic, build and expand on what they know, and organize that knowledge before they begin reading.

Building on Taba's original work, reading educators later added the "map" step. This strategy can also be used as a diagnostic instrument to find out what students know about a subject before they read and as an organizational tool to facilitate higher level thinking through making predictions. Because the strategy involves the categorization and labeling of words, List-Group-Label-Map also makes an excellent preceding strategy for a vocabulary development lesson.

How Can the Strategy Help My Students?

When students begin reading without activating what they know first, they often miss the connections that would help them store that information in longer-term memory. In addition, many students lack the ability to categorize and classify information. This process of grouping concepts helps students understand the relationships between ideas. Classifying and categorizing concepts before reading helps students connect to what they already know about a topic and better understand the concepts in the text. Creating a concept map before reading gives students the opportunity to "see" the ideas and their relationships while reading.

Getting Started

Here are the steps in the List-Group-Label-Map Strategy.

The List-Group-Label-Map strategy works best when students already know something about a topic. During the initial discussion, teachers may ascertain how much students already know about a topic and correct any misconceptions they may have.

Step 1: Make a Word List. Direct students to an initial piece of information and ask them to list as many words related to the topic as possible. Pictures are the best and easiest stimulus for this activity, although other visual information in the textbook can be used. These words may be associations they come up with from memory if the topic is very familiar. Many teachers also use videos to elicit words. If you conduct the discussion with the entire class, write the word lists in columns on the chalkboard or on an overhead transparency. If the discussion occurs within a small group, a student can record the words.

Step 2: Look for Word Associations. Students group items by indicating which words belong together. Only one student in a group should indicate which words go together. The teacher (or a student in a group) then marks the words with an *X* or *O* or some other symbol. If another student wants to add to the grouping, it is important that the first student be consulted because he or she may be thinking of a different category. Students can use words more than once.

Step 3: Label Word Groups. Then the student who came up with the original groupings goes back and labels each group. These labels represent concepts, and the words are then examples of these concepts.

Step 4: Make a Concept Map. Individually or in small groups, students use the words listed to create concept maps, following the process described in Strategy 4. (**See Graphic Organizer 3, Cluster Diagram.**)

Step 5: Read the Text. During reading, students may note whether the concept map they created was consistent with the ideas presented in the text.

Step 6: Revisit the Concept Map. After reading, students take another look at their concept map and add information from the reading. Encourage students to elaborate on their maps using the

ideas in the text. These expanded maps connect what they knew before reading with what they learned while reading.

Using the Strategy in Your Classroom

Any picture, video, or other information can be used to generate the word list. Pictures that give a lot of information work best and can be used to build the background information necessary to understand the text. Pictures also help students visualize what they read. To get students started, simply ask them what they see in the picture (or remember from the video). Since the next step is to classify and categorize words, encourage students to choose words that describe what they see rather than make interpretations from the picture.

When students group words, it is important that one person state his or her grouping. If more students get involved, the original labels for the groups may be confused or lost. Words can be categorized in endless ways.

Whenever students are engaged in making predictions, they may form misconceptions about the information presented in the text. You can correct these misconceptions while reviewing their concept maps or during the ensuing discussion.

Extending the Strategy

After you have completed the List-Group-Label-Map process, you may wish to try any or all of the following extension activities:

- *Possible Sentences.* Students connect two or more words from the list and write sentences inferring what the text will be about. These sentences can be formulated into a paragraph, and students can compare their predictions.
- *Writing Summaries.* Using the list and the concept map, students can write a summary of the information after reading. A visual display of the ideas and words in a list can help students who have difficulty writing summaries.

- *Comparing and Contrasting.* One approach is to lead students to compare and contrast one piece of information with another and then lead them, through carefully designed questions, to make a generalization using both sets of information. **(See Graphic Organizer 11, Venn Diagram.)**

List-Group-Label-Map can be combined with other strategies such as Understanding Text (Strategy 2). Depending on the needs of your students, how familiar they are with the topic, your instructional objectives, and the purpose for the reading, many of the strategies presented in this book can be used to support one another.

Some Final Thoughts

The List-Group-Label-Map strategy can be used by itself to generate information and inferences about a text before reading it, or it can be used with other strategies to extend students' thinking and help them summarize and make predictions. The strategy is a vehicle for using the wonderful

visual information generally displayed in textbooks to connect readers with text.

Read More About It

Blevins, W. "Strategies for Struggling Readers: Making Predictions." *Instructor* 108 (2) 1990: 49.

Caverly, D. C., Mandeville, T. F., and Nicholson, S. A. "PLAN: A Study-Reading Strategy for Informational Text." *Journal of Adolescent and Adult Literacy* 39 (3) 1995: 190–99.

Foley, C. L. "Prediction: A Valuable Reading Strategy." *Reading Improvement* 30 (3) 1993: 166–70.

Nolan, T. E. "Self-Questioning and Prediction: Combining Metacognitive Strategies." *Journal of Reading* 35 (2) 1991: 132–38.

Stahl, S. A., and Kapinus, B. A. "Possible Sentences: Predicting Word Meanings to Teach Content-Area Vocabulary." *Reading Teacher* 5 (1) 1991: 36–43.

Taba, H. *Teacher's Handbook for Elementary Social Studies.* Reading, MA: Addison-Wesley. 1967.

STRATEGY 8: ACTIVATING AND USING PRIOR KNOWLEDGE

Strong readers know that asking questions and thinking about ideas while reading help them understand and remember text. Students who begin reading a text with no preparation and no thought about the topic often can complete an assignment but do not seem to remember much about what they read. One way to help students clear this hurdle is the KWL strategy, which was developed by Donna Ogle in 1986 and further refined by Carr and Ogle (1987).

KWL stands for What I *K*now, What I *W*ant to Know, and What I *L*earned. The purpose of this strategy is to activate students' prior knowledge:

BEFORE reading by adding background information and helping students monitor their learning

DURING reading by thinking about what they want to know or the questions they want answered about the topic, and

AFTER reading by helping them organize what they know through listing the things they learned about the topic.

The KWL chart looks like this:

▶ What I *Know*	▶ What I *Want to Know*	▶ What I *Learned*

How Can the Strategy Help My Students?

Students do not tend to use their prior knowledge about a topic when they read unless it is "activated." The KWL helps students review what they know about a topic, set a purpose for reading based on what they want to know, and organize what they learned after reading.

For struggling students, extra support can be given by the teacher or other students by helping them study the charts, diagrams, maps, and pictures in the book to make some inferences or guesses about the topic. Nonproficient and second-language learners can gain background information by listening to the discussion of others.

Getting Started

Here are the steps in the KWL strategy. The KWL activity is most successful when students know something about the material but need to build on what they know to comprehend the text. Students can complete the KWL activity individually, in a group, or as part of a class discussion.

Step 1: Fill Out the First Two Columns of the KWL Chart. Students should write down everything they *k*now for sure about the topic. Then they should write down everything they *w*ant to know about the topic in the middle column. There is no set of correct answers, but misconceptions or wrong information can be flagged for further discussion. What they want to know should be phrased as questions.

Step 2: Read, View, and/or Listen to Content about the Topic.

Step 3: Fill Out the Learned Column. Students should work in small groups to elaborate on their answers.

Step 4: Construct a Concept Map. This map represents an integration of what students knew before reading and what they learned.

Step 5: Write a Summary. Using the concept map, students can write a summary of what they learned about the subject. The summary helps students focus on the most important points in the reading.

Using the Strategy in Your Classroom

The KWL strategy works best with topics about which students have some prior knowledge. If they know very little about a topic, students will have trouble filling in the first two columns of the chart. The purpose of the strategy is to *activate* what students know about a topic and, through discussion and further learning, *build background information.* If students are unsure how to identify what they know, they can scan their reading and make questions from subheadings. If the topic is too broad and students know a lot about it, they may get bogged down making a list. Sometimes you will not know how much prior knowledge students have until the brainstorming begins. To solve this problem, you might have your students create a concept map first so they can organize their thoughts about the topic. Then have them summarize the key points in the What I Know column. (**See Graphic Organizer 6, KWL Chart.**)

Another possibility is that when you ask students what they want to know, they will respond "nothing." That's why I like to refer to the middle column as "what you *think* you know." These statements of what they think they know can then be turned into questions they want answered in the reading. (**See Graphic Organizer 7, KWLS Chart.**)

Extending the Strategy

Because KWL is such a popular strategy, teachers have devised numerous variations. One variation, known as WIKA, was developed by Richardson and Morgan (2000). WIKA stands for *What I Know Activity*. Some teachers find that the original format for KWL does not fit into the before-during-after framework, which is more clearly identified in the WIKA.

In this variation, the before-during-after instructional framework is clearly identified above the five columns.

WIKA

Before Reading		During Reading	After Reading	
What I Already Know	What I'd Like to Know	Interesting or Important Concepts from the Reading	What I Know Now	What I'd Still Like to Know

Other teachers have used these variations:

KWHL

What I *Know*	What I *Want* to Know	*How* I Will Find Out	What I *Learned*

Or:

KWLS

What I *Know*	What I *Want* to Know	What I *Learned*	What I *Still* Want to Know

Some Final Thoughts

Feel free to modify the KWL strategy for your topic and the special needs of your students. If your students need more help thinking of what they know about a topic, you can show them a video, bring some pictures to class, have them leaf through their textbook, or read them a story. The first time you use any strategy, pick an easy text and keep the directions clear and simple. As students become more proficient using the strategy, more difficult text and variations may be used.

Some teachers are frustrated using a KWL because it takes longer to get "through" content. Keep in mind, however, that students tend to retain the information longer when they use this strategy. True, it takes some time for students to understand the KWL steps, but the purpose is to get them in the habit of thinking of what they know about a topic before they start reading.

Read More About It

Bryan, J. "K-W-W-L: Questioning the Known." *The Reading Teacher* 51 (1) 1998: 618–20.

Cantrell, J. "K-W-L Learning Journals: A Way to Encourage Reflection." *Journal of Adolescent and Adolescent Literacy* 40 (5) 1997: 392–93.

Carr, E., and Ogle, D. "K-W-L Plus: A Strategy for Comprehension and Summarization." *Journal of Reading* 30 (7) 1987: 626–31.

Heller, M. "How Do You Know What You Know? Metacognitive Modeling in the Content Areas." *Journal of Reading* 29, 1986: 415–22.

Huffman, L. E. "Spotlighting Specifics by Combining Focus Questions with K-W-L." *Journal of Adolescent and Adolescent Literacy* 41 (6) 1998: 470–72.

Ogle, D. "K-W-L: A Teaching Model that Develops Active Reading of Expository Text." *The Reading Teacher* 39 (6) 1986: 564–70.

Richardson, J. S. and Morgan, R. F. *Reading to Learn in the Content Areas*. Belmont, CA: Wadsworth. 2000.

STRATEGY 9: ANTICIPATING INFORMATION

Anticipating what a text is going to be about helps readers connect the text with what they already know. Activating and using prior knowledge is an essential component of comprehending text. A strategy known as the Anticipation Guide was developed by Harold Herber in the early 1970s and has been used and modified over the years. The strategy is particularly well suited to teaching informational or expository content and helping students clarify their opinions and ideas about a topic.

How Can the Strategy Help My Students?

Middle- and high-school students love to debate, discuss, and voice their opinions. The Anticipation Guide uses this natural tendency to connect the ideas in a text with students' experience and knowledge. The Anticipation Guide helps students

- activate knowledge about a topic by voicing an opinion before they read
- focus their attention on the major points during their reading
- provide a structure for discussing the text after they read.

As students state their opinions about a text's topic, they become more engaged and invested in supporting their viewpoint. This discussion alerts them to the important ideas in the text. In addition, students have a structure for discussing these ideas, and teachers can ask additional questions or make comments that expand student thinking.

Getting Started

Here are the steps to the Anticipation Guide strategy.

Anticipation Guides work best with material that prompts students to form an opinion. For example, one teacher started a unit on comparative governments with this statement: "It is fair that some people make more money than others." The impending discussion on either side helped students understand socialist and democratic philosophies before reading about them. The steps of an Anticipation Guide are as follows:

Step 1: Identify the Major Concepts. Before students begin the activity, determine the main ideas of the reading selection, lecture, or film and write several statements that focus on the main points in the text and draw on students' backgrounds. Four to six statements are usually adequate to generate discussion. The statements can be presented in a chart like one below. **(See Graphic Organizer 1, Anticipation Guide.)**

Step 2: Identify Agree/Disagree Statements. Students point out statements with which they agree or disagree, then write *agree* or *disagree* in column A. Rather than analyzing too much or second guessing, students should merely respond to the statements. Students respond individually— either negatively or positively—to each statement and can then compare responses in small groups.

Step 3: Engage in a Prereading Discussion. You may wish to get a hand count of responses to the statements and ask students to justify their responses with reasons or evidence. Then engage students in full discussion of the pros and cons of each statement. You may wish for students to compare answers within a small group before moving to a large group discussion.

Step 4: Read the Text. Students should be directed to look for ideas either that support or contradict the statements they just discussed.

Step 5: Revisit the Statements. Students should look at the statements they chose earlier to see if they have changed their opinions and then write *agree* or *disagree* in column B. The purpose of this strategy is not to engage students in competition to see who is right or wrong, but rather to activate their opinions about issues that are related to the text and to expand their thinking.

Step 6: Engage in a Postreading Discussion. Looking again at the statements, students should compare their before-reading reactions to their after-reading reactions. Ask them to justify their new or continuing beliefs based on the reading.

Using the Strategy in Your Classroom

The challenge in designing an Anticipation Guide is creating statements, rather than questions that may signal students that there is a right or wrong answer. The statements also need to connect what students already know with the major ideas in the text. In a sense, the statements represent the "so what" of the reading; that is, how this selection relates to the lives of the students.

Duffelmeyer (1994) maintained that effective statements

- convey a sense of the major ideas that the student will encounter.
- activate and draw upon the students' prior experience.
- are general rather than specific.
- challenge students' beliefs.

After reading, students may wish to add to the statements or modify them in some way. The statements can be the basis for a writing assignment or an essay answer for a test.

Extending the Strategy

Writing assignments are a natural extension of the Anticipation Guide. Writing a persuasive essay

A	Statements	B
Before Reading Agree/Disagree		**After Reading** Agree/Disagree

is required on many standardized tests. Students could be encouraged to take one or two of the statements, document them with evidence found in the text, and construct a persuasive essay. You may wish to work with an English/language arts teacher on this assignment.

As students get more proficient at using an Anticipation Guide, you can include some distracter statements that have little to do with the content. Critical readers can detect irrelevant comments as not central to the main argument. For students who are not yet ready to read this critically, these statements can be discussed after the reading.

Some Final Thoughts

While exchanging information with their class-mates, it is easy for students to form misconceptions. It is particularly important that you correct these misconceptions during the prereading and postreading discussion. Creating a classroom environment where students are free to make predictions and venture opinions is the key to stimulating discussions. But monitoring those discussions is also an important role of the teacher.

The Anticipation Guide is an excellent method for promoting active reading, directing students' attention to the major points in the text, and helping them to use evidence to modify erroneous beliefs. Using the natural propensity of adolescents to debate and argue engages them in the content by connecting the topic to their lives.

Read More About It

Conley, M. "Promoting Cross-Cultural Understanding Through Content-Area Reading Strategies." *Journal of Reading* 28 (7) 1985: 600–05.

Duffelmeyer, F. A. "Effective Anticipation Guide Statements for Learning from Expository Prose."*Journal of Reading* 37 (6) 1994: 452–57.

Erikson, B., Huber, M., Bea, T., Smith, C., and McKenzie, V. "Increasing Critical Reading in Junior High Classes." *Journal of Reading* 30 (5) 1987: 430–39.

Herber, H. L. *Teaching Reading in Content Areas.* Englewood Cliffs, NJ: Prentice-Hall. 1978.

Merkley, D. J. "Modified Anticipation Guide." *Reading Teacher* 50 (4) 1996–97: 365–68.

STRATEGY 10: TAKING EFFECTIVE NOTES

Identifying the most important ideas in a text and capturing them in the form of notes for study or writing a report can be a formidable task for many students. Any of the prereading strategies suggested in this book can help students focus on the most important points before they read. The INSERT Method (Interactive Notation System for Effective Reading and Thinking) was developed by Vaughn and Estes (1986) to assist students in clarifying their understanding of the text and making decisions while they read. This strategy can help students concentrate on important information and can provide the structure to organize those ideas after reading.

How Can the Strategy Help My Students?

Most students, especially those who struggle with reading assignments, do not understand that comprehending text involves *responding* to it in some way. In fact, some struggling readers do not realize that *thinking* is necessary while reading. Strong readers integrate the information in the text with what they already know. They constantly make decisions or have a running conversation with themselves such as the following:

- This point is important, but this one is a detail.
- This seems like an example used to help me understand the text.
- I already knew that.
- I didn't know that.
- This is in boldfaced type—must be a major concept.
- I don't understand this explanation.
- This map must be here for a reason—probably to illustrate the important ideas.

The INSERT Method prompts students to have these types of conversations while they read. It also provides a structure for students to organize effective notes after they read.

Getting Started

Vaughn and Estes suggested that the INSERT Method helps students think more and better while they read. I adapted this method into the steps below to extend this strategy and help students capture the most important ideas into effective notes.

Step 1: Introduce Students to Symbols in INSERT. An endless set of symbols can be used to help students focus on the text. Which ones you choose depends on the purpose for reading and type of text. Some examples are listed below.

- ✔ Knew this already
- *** Important information
- ++ Supporting detail
- Ex Example of important concept
- ?? Don't understand this

Step 2: Read the Text and Respond Using Symbols. Students are not normally allowed to write in textbooks. But the INSERT Method requires that students respond in writing to the ideas in the text. Some teachers fold a sheet of paper lengthwise into three sections, place the INSERT symbols at the top with a line to indicate the page number, and instruct students to place this sheet alongside the book for notetaking. Other teachers have students record their responses with a felt-tip marker on blank transparency sheets. Still others prefer to have students mark passages in the text using self-adhesive notes with colors corresponding to symbols or with preprinted symbols.

Step 3: Use Symbols to Organize Notes from the Reading. This is a good time to have students compare notes. Students can meet in small groups to share what they thought were the most important points, the details, and/or the examples presented in the text. The discussion helps

students understand how to find the main idea in passages and organize information. They can then organize these main ideas in the form of notes. Depending on the purpose for reading, the notes could be arranged in different ways. The information could be placed in a concept map or used as part of a larger essay.

Using the Strategy in Your Classroom

The INSERT Method engages students in the major points of the text and helps them organize their thinking. Feel free to change the symbols depending on your purpose for having students read a selection. For example, if students are reading a position statement of some sort, you may wish to use the following symbols:

- A Agree with this statement
- D Disagree with this statement
- I Interesting statement

Categorizing the ideas in the text engages students in thinking and making decisions about the text. In time, students will make these distinctions on their own as they comprehend text.

Extending the Strategy

Taking notes from text is an important skill that must be used to write a report or make a presentation. The Cornell, or divided-page, note-taking system is a popular system used in many middle and high schools. In this system the important points are listed on the left side of the paper, and the details are listed on the right. The page might look like the example on the top of page 191. (**See Graphic Organizer 5, Key Points and Details Chart.**) This information can also be translated into a concept map (see Strategy 4) or a graphic organizer (see Strategy 3) to help students see the relationships between ideas.

Some Final Thoughts

The INSERT Method is a simple yet powerful strategy for helping students respond to reading informational or expository textbooks. This strategy is most effective when used with a prereading strategy that activates what students

▶ Key Points	▶ Details

know about a topic before reading or a postreading strategy such as creating a concept map or graphic organizer. The purpose of this strategy is to help students think about and respond to text.

Read More About It

Czarnecki, E., Rosko, D., and Fine, E. "How to Call Up Notetaking Skills." *Teaching Exceptional Children* 30 (6) 1998: 14–19.

Randall, S. N. "Information Charts: A Strategy for Organizing Student Research." *Journal of Adolescent and Adult Literacy* 39 (7) 1996: 536–42.

Rankin, V. "The Thought That Counts: Six Skills That Help Kids Turn Notes into Knowledge." *School Library Journal* 45 (8) 1999: 24–26.

Tomlinson, L. M. "A Coding System for Notemaking in Literature: Preparation for Journal Writing, Class Participation, and Essay Tests." *Journal of Adolescent and Adult Literacy* 40 (6) 1997: 468–76.

Vaughn, J. L., and Estes, T. H. *Reading and Reasoning Beyond the Primary Grades.* Needham Heights, MA: Allyn and Bacon. 1986.

Weisharr, M. K., and Boyle, J. R. "Notetaking Strategies for Students with Disabilities." *The Clearing House* 72 (6) 1999: 392–95.

STRATEGY 11: DEVELOPING VOCABULARY KNOWLEDGE

All readers encounter words they do not know; strong readers have strategies for determining what to do about those words. Proficient readers use any or all of the following strategies when they encounter an unknown word:

- Skip it and read on.
- Reread.
- Think about what they are reading.
- Sound out the word to see if they have heard it before.
- Look at the headings and subheadings of the text.
- Guess at whether the word is a noun or an adjective.
- Associate the parts of the word (prefixes, root words, suffixes) with more familiar words.

In my opinion, teaching students strategies to use when they encounter an unknown word is more useful than teaching them a host of vocabulary words in isolation. If they don't use these words in writing or see them in reading, students tend to forget them after the weekly vocabulary test.

The Contextual Redefinition strategy helps students learn to use context and structural analysis to determine the meanings of unknown words. An important element in this strategy is teacher modeling of the process of determining the meanings of words. This can be done by sharing the associations that come to mind when using structural analysis.

How Can the Strategy Help My Students?

Structural analysis (or morphemic analysis) involves determining the meaning of an unknown word by associating the word's prefixes, root words, or suffixes with meaningful parts of other words. When applied to informational or expository texts, structural analysis can be paired with contextual analysis to create a powerful strategy for determining the meanings of unknown words.

Context present at the sentence level is not always helpful. The larger context of the paragraph or the entire passage should be used.

Questions such as "What is this passage about?" or "What type of word would go there?" help students make good predictions about the approximate meaning of a word. Depending on the word or its function, an approximate meaning is often enough to comprehend the text.

Another helpful question is "How important is this word to understanding the passage?" Strong readers make good decisions about when to simply guess at a word's meaning and when to stop and determine the meaning. Consider the following sentence: "Her mauve skirts fluttered as she fell over the precipice." A proficient reader might guess that *mauve* is a color and move on without determining the exact color. However, the same reader might stop to determine the meaning of *precipice* since it explains what the woman fell over.

Getting Started

Contextual Redefinition is a good strategy for introducing the key vocabulary in an informational or expository selection. The strategy helps students learn and engage deeply with the important concepts of the reading selection, and helps them practice the behaviors and thinking that proficient readers use to figure out unknown words.

Step 1: Identify Unfamiliar Words. Before students begin reading, select the word or words likely to be unfamiliar to them. Words that contain meaningful morphemes for analysis work best, so select words with familiar prefixes, suffixes, and root words that students can associate with other words. Having students guess the meanings of particular morphemes is far better than just telling them the meanings. By guessing, students become actively involved in the reading.

Step 2: Guess Word Meanings. Present the word in isolation and ask students to make guesses about its meaning. The only clues they have at this point are their associations with the prefixes, root words, and suffixes. Some of these guesses will be wrong or even funny. Remember that the

process of using structural analysis is important, not proving someone's guess right or wrong.

Step 3: Refine Guesses. Using the unfamiliar word, write (or borrow from the text) a series of sentences, including more contextual cues in each one. Have students refine their guesses about what the word means as you present each sentence.

Step 4: Verify Meanings. Have students verify the word's meaning in a dictionary or glossary. If students have no idea what a word means, a dictionary or glossary may not be helpful because many words have more than one meaning. Therefore, a dictionary or glossary should be the last place they go, not the first. The purpose of these references is to verify an already good guess about the word's meaning. (**See Graphic Organizer 4, Contextual Redefinition Chart.**)

Using the Strategy in Your Classroom

Most people use a variety of strategies simultaneously to comprehend text. Structural and contextual analysis are two of the most helpful. Another helpful strategy is to examine the syntax of the sentence or the way that the word functions in the sentence. While presenting the sentences with increasingly rich context, make sure to help students see how each sentence gives them the very important clue of syntax.

When using structural analysis to help students associate new words with known words, you should point out that these conventions do not always apply. For example, *-er* at the end of a word usually means "someone who does something," so a painter is one who paints. But is a mother one who moths? Is a father one who faths?

The powerful component of the Contextual Redefinition is the teacher modeling. Struggling readers in particular need to experience successful models of reading behavior and thinking.

Extending the Strategy

Wordbusting, also known as CSSD, is a parallel strategy to Contextual Redefinition. The steps to Wordbusting are as follows:

- *Context.* Use clues from the surrounding words and sentences.
- *Structure.* Look for familiar roots, prefixes, or suffixes.
- *Sound.* Say the word aloud. It may sound like a word you know.
- *Dictionary.* Look up the word.

Some Final Thoughts

Educators are desperate to teach vocabulary because students can use these words to write, speak, and think more clearly. Vocabulary is also a common component of standardized tests. Well-meaning teachers often assign lists of words with instructions to use them in sentences or copy their definitions. When presented in relative isolation from any meaningful content, these words are only slightly learned and rapidly forgotten.

Contextual Redefinition enables students to determine the meanings of unknown words during reading. In addition to learning strategies, students need to practice these strategies by reading narrative and expository text that contains unfamiliar words.

Read More About It

Cunningham, J. W., Cunningham, P. M., and Arthur, S. V. *Middle and Secondary School Reading.* New York: Longman. 1981.

Gifford, A. P. "Broadening Concepts Through Vocabulary Development." *Reading Improvement* 37 (1) 2000: 2–12.

Ittzes, K. Lexical "Guessing in Isolation and Context." *Journal of Reading* 34 (5) 1991: 360–66.

Simpson, P. L. "Three Step Reading Vocabulary Strategy for Today's Content Area Reading Classroom." *Reading Improvement* 33 (2) 1996: 76–80.

Watts, S., and Truscott, D. M. "Using Contextual Analysis to Help Students Become Independent Word Learners." *The NERA Journal* 32 (3) 1996: 13–20.

NOTES

GRAPHIC ORGANIZER *for Content-Area Reading Strategies*

ANTICIPATION GUIDE

A **Before Reading** Agree / Disagree	**Statements**	B **After Reading** Agree / Disagree

GRAPHIC ORGANIZER *for Content-Area Reading Strategies*

2

CAUSE-AND-EFFECT CHART

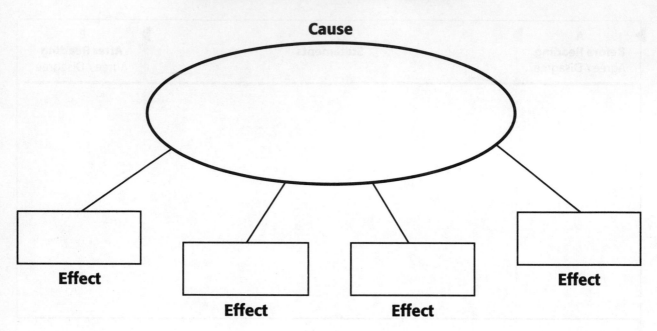

Cause

Effect

Effect

Effect

Effect

GRAPHIC ORGANIZER *for Content-Area Reading Strategies* **3**

CLUSTER DIAGRAM

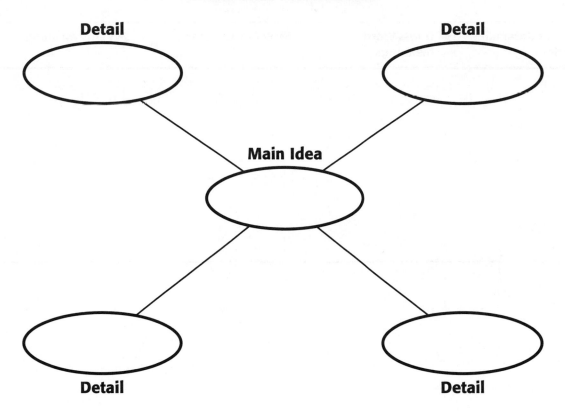

Detail

Detail

Main Idea

Detail

Detail

GRAPHIC ORGANIZER *for Content-Area Reading Strategies*

4

CONTEXTUAL REDEFINITION CHART

▶ Identify Unfamiliar Words	▶ Guess Word Meanings	▶ Refine Guesses	▶ Verify Meanings

Name ______________________ Class ______________ Date ___________

GRAPHIC ORGANIZER *for Content-Area Reading Strategies* 5

KEY POINTS AND DETAILS CHART

Key Points	Details

Name ______________________ Class ______________ Date ____________

GRAPHIC ORGANIZER *for Content-Area Reading Strategies* 6

KWL CHART

What I *Know*	What I *Want* to Know	What I *Learned*

GRAPHIC ORGANIZER *for Content-Area Reading Strategies* ⑦

KWLS CHART

▶What I *Know*	▶What I *Want* to Know	▶What I *Learned*	▶What I *Still* Want to Know

GRAPHIC ORGANIZER *for Content-Area Reading Strategies* 8

PREDICTING AND CONFIRMING ACTIVITY (PACA)

▶ General Information	▶ Prediction	▶ Confirmation

GRAPHIC ORGANIZER *for Content-Area Reading Strategies*

PROBLEM AND SOLUTION CHART

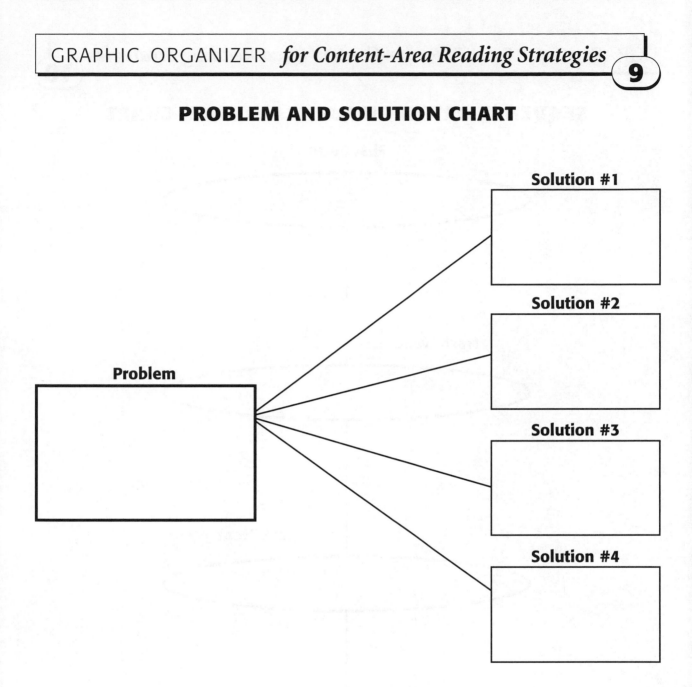

Problem

Solution #1

Solution #2

Solution #3

Solution #4

GRAPHIC ORGANIZER *for Content-Area Reading Strategies* (10)

SEQUENCE OR CHRONOLOGICAL ORDER CHART

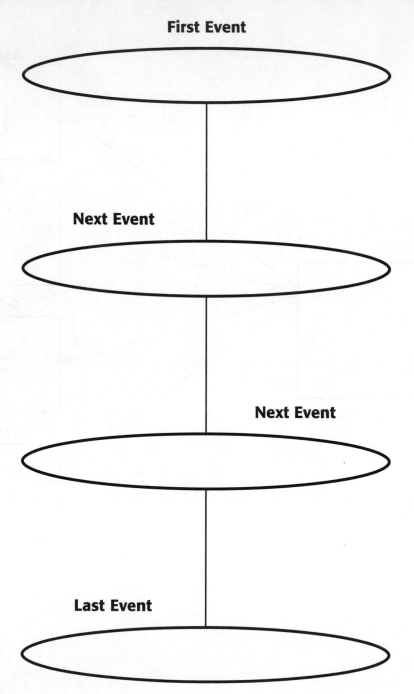

First Event

Next Event

Next Event

Last Event

GRAPHIC ORGANIZER *for Content-Area Reading Strategies* **11**

VENN DIAGRAM

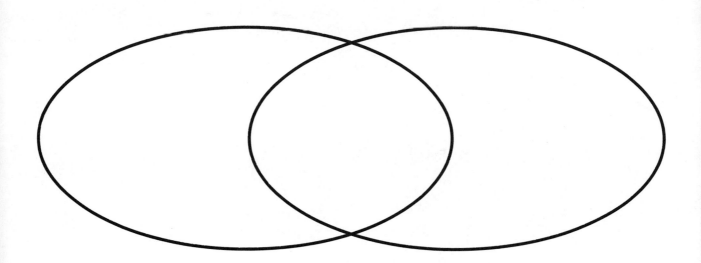